The Plants
that shaped
our
Gardens

The Plants
that shaped
our
Gardens

DAVID STUART

FRANCES LINCOLN

Frances Lincoln Limited
4 Torriano Mews
Torriano Avenue
London NW5 2RZ

British Library Cataloguing-in-Publication data
A catalogue record for this book is available from the British Library.

ISBN 0 7112 1891 9

Printed and bound in Singapore

2 4 6 8 9 7 5 3 1

TITLE PAGE: The tropical American vanilla orchid (*Vanilla planifolia*), painted by Claude Aubriet
(1665–1742). First described in Philip Miller's *Gardener's Dictionary* of 1731, it was grown in the
glasshouse at the Chelsea Physic Garden.

OPPOSITE: The doctor-botanist Philipp von Siebold will have known this enchanting garden in the
Dutch trading post of Deshima at Nagasaki. The scroll was painted by an artist of the Nagasaki
school (1720–1850).

CONTENTS

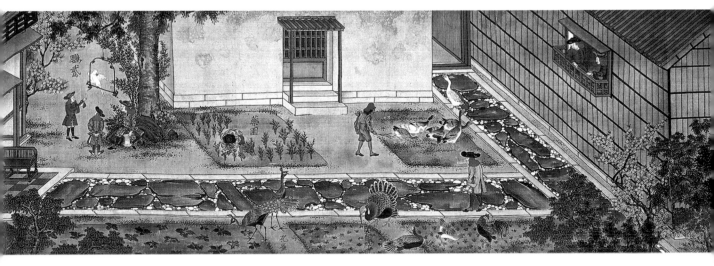

INTRODUCTION

The idea for this book first took root on a spring evening in the garden room of a village house in a remote part of Scotland. It had been a hard winter. The lemon tree, a Meyer's lemon, had lost most of its leaves. Even so, a couple of weeks of warmer weather had brought on a scattering of ivory-green flower buds, and now the first waxen, starry white flowers had opened. Skeins of their glorious perfume wound through other plants coming into bud or leaf. It suddenly seemed so unlikely: brugmansias, clivias and a wonderful epiphyllum whose ancestors must have once flowered in the jungles of Ecuador, had all somehow arrived here, under the chill skies of the north. In this cold, unlikely place were plants from the hot deserts of South Africa, from the coastal beaches of Amazonia, from the forest branches of Brazil and central America, and from the jungle floors of East Asia.

Some of the plants slowly beginning to grow had long histories in the garden. The gaunt twigs of 'sambac' jasmine were perhaps distant cuttings from plants that once used to tumble over balustrades in the 'moonlight' palace gardens of Jahangir and Shah Jahan. The oleanders, with their glossy sheaves of new flower buds, were possibly descended from the first ones brought back to Europe in the mid-sixteenth century by a Frenchman called Pierre Belon. Some were more recent arrivals, such as the tough orchid *Coelogyne cristata* first collected by Joseph Dalton Hooker in northern India in the late 1800s, or the elegant *Begonia burle-marxii* discovered in Brazil only a few decades ago.

None of these plants had arrived in this garden room directly from their place of origin. A few among them had been ardently sought and bought. Most had been given, or found, or arrived in some forgotten way, without any great forethought on their owners' part. But if they had arrived without our determination, they had, in a way, arrived on theirs. All plants are designed to colonize new territories, and some of these had taken that built-in urge to an extreme, using humans – whether our friends, friends of friends many decades ago, or neighbours – as ways of getting here, just as in the past they had used plant collectors and all subsequent gardeners as conduits, as a way of expanding their geographic range.

This interaction of plants and gardeners is crucial to how our gardens have looked over the millennia. All gardens can be seen as possible places for colonization by ambitious plant species, and how our gardens look has been determined by plants that have colonized them – the plants that have managed to exploit gardeners' instinct to collect.

Thus major collectors have been, and are, central to questions of the garden's capacity for change and design. The nineteenth-century Scots gardener James Tweedie, for instance, almost single-handedly caused a garden revolution. His collection of South American verbenas and petunias made possible a new sort of gardening in Europe, using half-hardy bedding plants. The great twentieth-century collector Ernest Henry Wilson introduced lilies and ligularias that proved to be some of the crucial plants that drove the creation of the 'marginal' gardens around the new garden pools, recently created expressly to show off the new hybrid water lilies then pouring out of the garden of their breeder, Latour-Marliac. His introduction of endless splendid plants from China – alpine primulas, rhododendrons, aquatics, new species of maple, old varieties of Chinese fruit trees – are still having immense impact on our gardens. Only slightly less central are the gardeners who delight in crossing new species or the selection of new variants that can be derived from within a species. Enveloping them, and providing the real engine for the garden's change, are all of us gardeners who are only too susceptible to a lovely plant's blandishments. In this respect, garden designers, long subject to adulation and critical scrutiny, are almost marginal.

For almost all gardeners, collecting plants for our gardens is a very minor strand of our interests. Only for some of us does collecting become an overwhelming obsession. All obsessions are dangerous, and their intensity can create astonishing human stories, many of which are told in this book.

Some collectors have been strange and complicated men. Take, for example, the pirate William Dampier, who cheerfully broke off from robbery and murder to take delight in the exotic flowers of whatever landfall he made and became the first European to collect plants from Australia. Born in 1651 in the tiny village of East Coker near Yeovil in Somerset, England, he was orphaned at a young age, became ungovernable and, to everyone's relief, ran away to sea. He prospered in a way that would have been unimaginable in East Coker. At twenty-two, he was under-manager of a Jamaican sugar estate. Bored by this occupation, he soon joined a band of lawless log-cutters in the forests of Yucatan. When he took to the sea next, it was as a fully fledged thug. With other buccaneers, he plundered and murdered his way across the Isthmus of Panama, then headed south down the Colombian coast. By now, he was entranced by plants, and travelled with his vasculum (a vessel for carrying botanical specimens) and plant presses, as well as his glinting weapons.

Dampier became a pirate captain by seizing a Danish ship at Sierra Leone. Using the proceeds of that blood-soaked raid, he navigated an immense journey back across the Atlantic, round Cape Horn, to the calmer coasts of Chile. More blood later, he went northwards to Mexico, then on across the Pacific to China and from there to what is now Australia and he was the first European to explore vast stretches of its north-eastern coast. There cannot have been much to plunder, and perhaps his botanizing infuriated the crew. For whatever reason, he was abandoned on the Nicobar Islands in the Bay of Bengal and his fickle pirates sailed off. He made his way eastwards, with a few plants and a native canoe, across two hundred miles of open sea to Sumatra. From there, he managed to reach London.

Publishing an account of his travels, and being both charming and personable, he was soon lionized. With his experience of the South Seas, he also interested the Admiralty. Somehow unaware of his criminal background, they commissioned him to undertake an official journey to Australia, then called New Holland. This made him more popular still. Samuel Pepys asked him to supper, as did the aristocratic gardener John Evelyn. Both men asked him to bring back Australian flowers for their gardens. In 1699, he sailed off, collecting plants in Java, Timor, New Guinea, Brazil and Australia. After another astonishing trip, his ship, HMS *Roebuck*, foundered on the return voyage and sank 'through perfect age' at Ascension. Much of his collection, and all of Pepys's hoped-for flowers, were lost. There was a darker side to his story too. Once home, Dampier was court-martialled for extreme cruelty to his lieutenant, and stripped of his captaincy. In 1703, he was back in the South Seas, once more a pirate, now with two ships crammed with rogues. He eventually died in London in March 1715. What remained to him of his plant material is still preserved at Oxford University.

Driven and tempestuous men like him have made good collectors; men with weaker wills are often destroyed. By the nineteenth century, plant collecting had become a way of life in its own right. Men went travelling who never really, even in the half-light of the rainforest, or the snow-light of a Himalayan cliff, managed to leave home. One such was Augustus Margary, a young man of considerable promise. As a young British consular official in China, he was detailed to travel over thousands of miles of unmapped territory to see if it was possible to travel up China's great Yangtze River, and connect with the Irrawaddy. The journey was terrible, but he became increasingly fascinated by the plants he encountered. To remind himself of 'home', every evening he treated his native bearers to a concert. Standing erect in front of his tent, he sang songs like 'The Lass of Richmond Hill' and always finished off with a rendition of 'God Save the Queen'. Alas, he also travelled with a beloved dog. Thinking it amusing in an English sort of way, he let the dog be carried in his curtained litter, while he himself walked. In China, the litter was close to being a sacred object, denoting the status not only of its occupant but of the whole travelling party. To put a dog inside it was sacrilegious. Augustus didn't notice the escalating discontent. Almost at the end of his epic journey, his servants could take no more. He was murdered.

Although none of Margary's plants made it to the garden, many collectors like him, making equally terrible journeys, were each responsible for enabling two, sometimes three, thousand species to colonize gardens worldwide. In this book I have selected some of the stories of the many such journeys by plants and collectors. Some are extraordinary tales about particular plants – for example, the romantic story of how the first bougainvilleas reached Europe from South America. Some I have chosen because they are about plants of great beauty or of special consequence in the evolution of our gardens. Likewise, I have chosen the stories of collectors for their significance for particular parts of the garden, rather than for their overall careers. Together these stories show to what extremes the plant-collecting instinct can drive a human being and how through people, over the centuries, individual plants have expanded their geographical dominion.

The foot of the Too-Hing (Two Peaks) in Le Nai province, China; an engraving after
Thomas Allom (1804–72). To be carried in this uncomfortable-looking manner was
a vitally important badge of status in China well into the twentieth century.

TREASURE IN
THE EAST

Constantinople, 1512. Ruthless and immensely energetic, Selim I ousted his father, Bayazit II, from the Topkapi Fortress and became the Ottoman Empire's new sultan. Bayazit, once vastly powerful himself, had become more absorbed with the future of his soul than with the continuance of his empire. Its frontiers were beginning to crumble. He had many other sons, all with equal rights to inherit his endangered state. Selim needed to consolidate his gains at once. He began to have his many brothers, and all their sons, killed. He also knew that his empire might face collapse on his own death if his own sons fought for his throne, so he had all but one of them murdered too. Even as all this violence was swirling through the pavilions and gardens of Constantinople, his formidable military prowess was adding to his vast dominions. Soon he had complete control of every trade route that ran between Europe and the East. Unwittingly, he thereby changed Western gardens for ever.

The very foundations of many European states shook as the wealth of their merchants took the force of the Ottoman Empire's stranglehold on trade with the East. They had to do something at once. They sought sea routes around Africa in order to reach the spices, silks and medicaments that came only from China or India. They were so desperate that they also tried sailing due West from Europe, across the uncharted and dangerous Atlantic, and encountered the Americas. The colossal impact of that discovery was tempered by the great risks of the journey. The overland routes still seemed very much safer, so some European states sent ambassadors to Selim at Constantinople to attempt to negotiate easier trading with and through his empire. Seeing huge

The crown imperial (*Fritillaria imperialis*) from a florilegium drawn by Pieter van Kouwenhoorn, a Dutch artist who flourished in the 1620s. Despite its strong and foxy smell, it became an important cut flower for grand rooms.

commercial advantages, he began to allow them some concessions. Among the merchandise that travelled along these new trade routes there were garden plants. Selim's vast empire thus caused European gardeners to grow new plants not only from Virginia and Mexico, but also species from his own rich lands, and garden variants developed in his own flower-loving culture.

Selim reigned until 1520, when his one surviving son, sumptuously arrayed and jangling with gold, rode in through the great gates of the Topkapi Fortress. Even more extraordinary than his ruthless father, he was a great military commander, a passionate builder of mosques, palaces, bridges and aqueducts. He was also a passionate lover of flowers. With fabulous power and fabulous wealth he was almost at once called Süleyman the Magnificent. European ambassadors were overwhelmed by the riches that they saw in his city. Süleyman's courtiers soon arranged for them to have, as well as greater treasures, lesser ones: bulbs and seeds to send home to their masters and friends. The English ambassador William Harborne posted bulbs home to Lord Salisbury, who in turn handed them on to John Gerard, London herbalist and producer of the great *Herball* of 1597. Of one magnificent new scarlet lily he wrote that it came from 'Constantinople, whither it is brought by the poore peasants to be solde, for the decking up of gardens. From thence it was sent among many other bulbs or rare and daintie flowers, by Master Harborne, Ambassador there, unto my honorable good Lord and master, the Lord Treasurer of England, who bestowed them on me for my garden.' But though Harborne, the first English ambassador to be sent to Turkey, sent a number of plants back to his own country, by far the most important ambassador was Ogier Ghiselin de Busbecq (1522–92). A Flemish aristocrat, he was sent from Vienna by the Emperor Ferdinand I.

De Busbecq was fascinated by both the past, and the gardens, of Turkey. Upon arrival in Constantinople, he began to send back to Vienna marvellous plants like the crown imperial (*Fritillaria imperialis*), and the very first cultivated tulip. He had noticed scarlet fields of it near Adrianople (modern Edirne), where it was grown to supply the huge flower markets of Süleyman's capital city, which still function on their original site. The new tulips were grown in Vienna in 1554, in Antwerp by 1561, and in London by 1580. He sent home other marvels: the horse chestnut tree (*Aesculus hippocastanum*), the first lilac (*Syringa*), mock orange (*Philadelphus*), the Syrian rose (*Hibiscus syriacus*) and the first cultivated forms of *Hyacinthus orientalis*. Gardeners were fascinated.

More importantly, de Busbecq had also unearthed some ancient classical manuscripts, notably a wormy and crumpled copy of Pedanios Dioscorides' *De Materia Medica*. Dioscorides was a Greek citizen of Cilicia who served as a soldier, and probably as a physician, in the Roman army around AD 60. His book carefully described the plants used in contemporary medicine. By the sixteenth century, doctors in northern Europe had only the shadowiest and most corrupted traditions of which plants they should be using. The book de Busbecq saw would allow doctors to start using the real classical plants, which they hoped would give authentic classical cures. It was a transcription made around 512. Perhaps it had reached Constantinople from one of the Arab cities conquered by Selim's expansion of his empire into Syria, Mesopotamia, Arabia and Egypt; perhaps it had merely lain in some imperial library for more than a thousand years. When de Busbecq came across it, it was in the possession of one of Selim's physicians. Even though the manuscript was in very poor condition, de Busbecq urged his master Ferdinand I to acquire it. Its owners clearly knew its importance, and it took seven years of negotiation before it eventually reached Vienna, where it remains. The book was rapidly copied and circulated, but adventurous doctors soon wanted to see the plants for themselves.

Ambassadors, finding the great city so well provided with flower and plant markets, found it easy to collect new things to send to their masters and friends. However, to find the plants of classical apothecaries needed more exploration, and a much more adventurous spirit. One such spirit was the redoubtable Pierre Belon (1517–64). Like all doctors of his time he was necessarily a botanist too. Born at Cérans Foulletourte in France, he studied natural history and medicine with the great European scholar Valérius Cordus, with whom he had

This 1526 woodcut shows Süleyman I (the Magnificent) six years after he became sultan.

travelled in Germany and Bohemia. Once back in France he became apothecary to the Bishop of Le Mans, René du Bellay. However, travelling had got into his soul, and he was soon restless. He got himself attached to a diplomatic expedition to the court of Süleyman, so travelled rather comfortably at the expense of Henri II of France and the Cardinal of Tournon. Sailing from Venice in the spring of 1547, he was robbed by pirates near the coast of Crete. As pirates often preferred not to have the guilt of murder on their heads, he was left alone in an empty boat without food or money. Ever resourceful, he quickly learnt how to sail it, and managed to find safe harbour on the enchanting island. His memoirs noted, for the benefit of other indigents visiting Crete, that 'monasteries give such provisions as they have gratis to all travellers whatsoever, as pickled or dried olives, onions, bisquet, salted fish, sometimes fresh for they often go a-fishing, their vessels or boats being cut without great difficulty of the thick trunks of Plain [*sic*] trees; their nets for want of corks are supported by gourds.' He also described several new species of garden plants, including a white form of oleander (*Nerium oleander* 'Album'), the gorgeous *Paeonia clusii*, and the sticky-leafed and aromatic *Cistus ladanifer*, a source of one of the types of laudanum.

Eventually re-financed, he sailed for Constantinople. There, he explored the druggists' shops in the great dusty covered markets, carrying a copy of *al-Qanun fi at-tibb* ('Canon of Medicine') by the eleventh-century Persian physician Avicenna. The trade in medicines was colossally lucrative, and its tentacles extended to all the great empires of the East. Belon noted that camels loaded with medicinal plants were guarded more carefully than those loaded with even the most sumptuous silks from Persia or China. Once out of Turkey, he revisited Crete, then sailed on to Egypt and then to Jerusalem, Aleppo and Lebanon. Loaded with plants, he set sail for home. Again he was raided by pirates, but they left him with seeds or plants of greater celandine (*Chelidonium majus*), the Christmas rose (*Helleborus niger*), Our Lady's thistle (*Cnicus benedictus*), a new species of mandrake (*Mandragora autumnalis*), an as yet unidentified Egyptian peony which was supposed to cure coughs, and dozens more.

Belon tried to persuade Henri II to help him set up a botanic garden in which to grow some of the new plants, but he had to settle for the garden of his patron René du Bellay at Château de Touvoie, Savigné-l'Evêque. There, holm oak (*Quercus ilex*), cork oak (*Q. suber*), spruce (*Picea*), arbutus, Sicilian sumach (*Rhus coriaria*), the manna ash (*Fraxinus ornus*), *Platanus orientalis* and his white oleander flourished for the first time. He published some marvellous and influential books, including *Histoire naturelle des estranges poissons marins etc.* (1551), *De Arboribus Coniferis* (1553), *La nature et la diversité des poissons, avec leur description et naïfs portraits* (1555), and *Portraits d'oiseaux, animaux, serpents, herbes, hommes et femmes d'Arabie et d'Egypte* (1557) containing a curiously diverse selection of animals and plants. It was his travel memoirs, however, that were most widely read. He died mysteriously, assasinated by thieves in the Bois de Boulogne in April 1564.

Belon's travels were influential enough to be copied. One of his most adventurous followers was Leonhardt Rauwolff, a doctor from the ancient city of Augsburg, north-west of Munich in Germany. His trip was financed by a merchant brother-in-law, who no doubt hoped for some commercial advantage. He set off from Marseilles on 18 May 1573, aboard the *Santa Croce*. In Constantinople he discovered that 'in their gardens, the Turks love to raise all sorts of flowers wherein they take great delight, and use to put them in their turbants so I could see the fine plants that blow, one after another, daily without trouble.' He saw turbans sporting sweet violets in December, followed by tulips, hyacinths and narcisci.

However glorious and civilized the court at Constantinople, travel in remoter regions of Turkey was rough and dangerous. In his memoirs, published in 1582, Rauwolff wrote: 'Yet I cannot but describe to you one more plant for the taking of which I and my two comrades fell into great danger. . . . When I was busy about this tender plant and strove to get it out whole, which took me up the more time because I had no proper tools by me, a Turk, well-armed came galloping upon us to see what we were doing.' After a small bribe, the janissary rode off apparently satisfied. Before Rauwolff could bag the plant the Turk came back at full tilt 'with his cymeter drawn and fetched one blow after the other at me, which I still declined running from one side of the tree to the other, so that they went into the tree and mangled it mightily.' The janissary was armed with a bow too, but the intrepid Rauwolff realized that if the Turk decided to make use of it, he would have to put down the scimitar, making it possible, for a moment, to attack. However, for a few more coins, Rauwolff bought off the Turk, who nevertheless made off with Rauwolff's 'tablebook' of records which had fallen out of his wallet during the scuffle. The plant was a species of *Aristolochia*. He described it thus:

Many of the pinks and carnations taken up by seventeenth-century European enthusiasts
were derived from plants sent from the Middle East in the previous century. These woodcuts
are taken from John Parkinson's *Paradisi in Sole Paradisus Terrestris* (1629).

Highly disciplined and celibate, janissaries were the most fearsome soldiers in the Ottoman Empire.

This is called by the inhabitants Rhafut and also Rumigi; it hath a strong yet unpleasant savour and about four stalks of a whitish colour and so tender towards the root and so small as a pack thread whereon at each side grown seven or eight tender ash coloured leaves distributed like unto those of Osmond Royal, only they have round Ears towards the stalk like unto small Sage. . . . [It has] flowers like Aristolochia *yet a great deal bigger and more brownish colour and hanging on longer stalks. The root striketh very deep and is very like to our Pellitory, of a drying quality and somewhat hot as the bitter taste intimates.* ·

Undeterred by this violent encounter, Rauwolff and a friend, Hans Ulrich Rafft, travelled overland through the grey-brown hills to the Euphrates River. Intending to sail down it to Baghdad, they posed as Oriental merchants, wearing long blue robes buttoned right down to their feet, baggy white cotton trousers, collarless shirts and blue-brimmed white 'turbants' such as Christians usually wore. Their shoes were yellow leather with nailed soles, and over their whole ensemble they wore narrow sleeveless goat-hair tunics, reaching to the knees. Rauwolff found the journey agonizing (all botanists and plant collectors will know the feeling), for their barge would often glide past tempting plants on the river bank, visible but out of reach.

When he got back to Tripoli, some other janissaries arrested him as a spy, but once again a payment got him out of trouble. However, when funds from his brother-in law failed, he had to practise medicine to make enough money to get home with his botanical spoils. He was back in Augsburg by 1575, and the seeds and roots he had managed to transport home formed the basis for the botanical garden he set up there. The herbarium of pressed specimens he assembled can still be seen at the herbarium of the University of Leiden in Holland.

Rauwolff was the first European ever to see coffee being prepared, and he discovered what were to become important garden plants such as *Acanthus spinosus, Lilium bulbiferum* and the ineffable butcher's broom (*Ruscus aculeatus*). In gardens in Aleppo he saw some of the varieties of tulips, hyacinths and anemones that were yet to arrive in Europe, but would create a stir when they did. He also found in the local bazaar the first Indian shot (*Canna indica*) collected by any European. He collected the smokebush (*Cotinus coggygria*), now found in at least half of Europe's gardens. Like Belon, he came across its relative *Rhus coriaria*, which gives the spice sumach, still immensely popular in the Lebanon, but never much taken up in western Europe. His journal became the sixteenth-century equivalent of a best-seller, and it fuelled the desire of gardeners to collect tulips and fritillaries, grow new lilies, and plant *Acanthus* and *Rhus*. Yet more travellers were inspired to go and search these mysterious lands for their mysterious plants.

Richard Hakluyt, nephew of the Elizabethan explorer of the same name, wrote of tulips in 1582: 'Within these four years there have been brought to England from Vienna divers kinds of flowers called tulipas and those and others procured a little before from Constantinople by an excellent man called Carolus Clusius.' This was a Latinization of the name of Charles de l'Ecluse, a prodigious scholar in the fullest Renaissance manner: he had studied law at Louvain, philosophy at Wittenberg, and then travelled to Frankfurt, Strasbourg and Lyons. At the University of Montpellier, he discovered the delights of flora. Already a historian, map-maker, mineralogist, zoologist, philosopher and numismatist, he now turned botanist too. From Spain, he collected 200 new plants. From Turkey, he introduced more fritillaries and tulips, many daffodils, the gorgeously perfumed and silvery flowered orris root (*Iris* 'Florentina'), and brought in new forms of ranunculus and hyacinth. From a friend in India, he even introduced the sumptuous tuberose, though like all European gardeners he found it hard to get it to flower more than once. He got the scarlet runner bean from another in Portugal, who had obtained it direct from Brazil. He couldn't stop collecting. Late in life he told his friends that no matter how cruel life could be, and his had indeed been, botany and gardening were everlasting solaces. Perhaps.

De Busbecq, Belon, Rauwolff, Clusius – these are great names in the history of botany and of gardens. Countless, though now unknown, merchants, navigators, diplomats, sailors, doctors, adventurers, even pilgrims, brought back to their own countries pinches of seed, or a bulb, perhaps even a potted plant. In the Middle East, gardeners collected and selected or bred tulips, hyacinths, narcissi, roses, anemones, apricots. In China they developed peonies, chrysanthemums, plums, peaches, lotuses and more roses. And in the Americas, the natives were exploring the vast local flora, finding plants to eat as various as bitterroot (*Lewisia*) and quamash (*Camassia*). In the luxuriant American sub-tropics, they had selected amaranths with edible seed and gorgeously colourful leaves, dahlias with edible roots and brilliant flowers, tropaeolums with edible leaves, flowers and roots, maize with myriad coloured seeds, endlessly varied squashes with flowers perfumed enough to make a gardener faint, countless beans, potatoes, tomatoes, and several cornucopias' worth of tropical fruits. Everyone, suddenly, wanted to collect a plant – all, like mankind everywhere, subject to the collecting instinct.

It may often seem as if by collecting plants humans are exploiting the planet's flora, but that is an entirely human-centred viewpoint. All plants are desperate for territory. In their struggle to survive, and to expand their range, many have evolved extravagantly beautiful designs. These often attract pollinating insects to their flowers, or encourage animals to distribute their seeds. Mankind has always rummaged through this astonishing abundance in pursuit of things of use or beauty and, imagining himself master, has been brilliantly exploited by huge numbers of plants. Verbenas and petunias from South America have

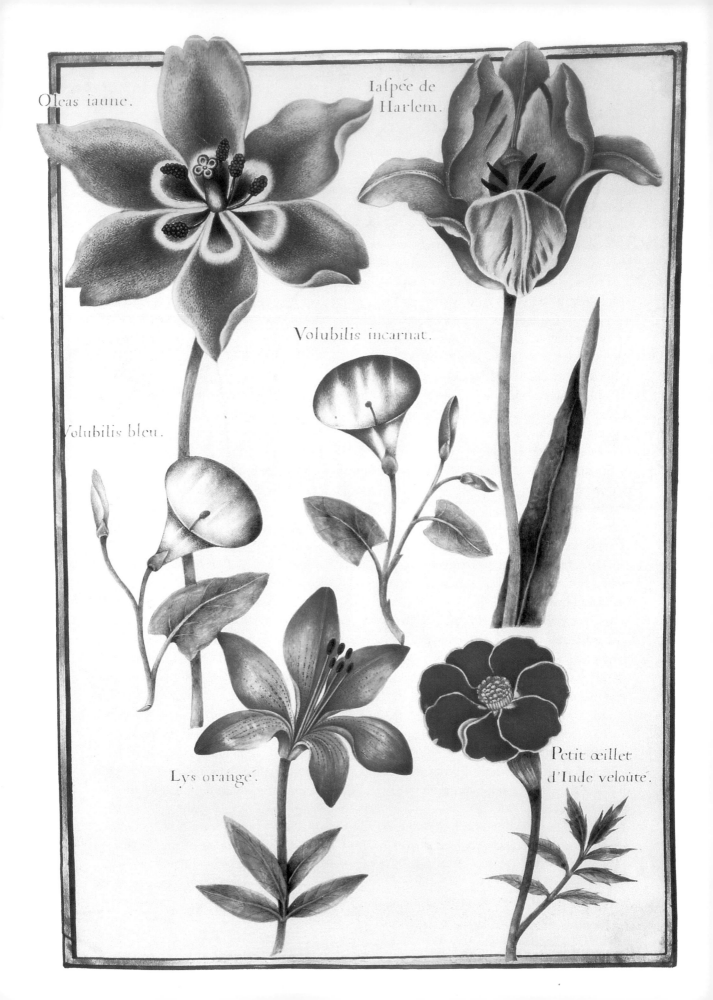

Oleas iaune.

Iaſpée de
Harlem.

Volubilis incarnat.

Volubilis bleu.

Lys orangé.

Petit œillet
d'Inde veloûté.

found themselves niches, along with pelargoniums from South Africa, in bedding gardens almost worldwide from the 1860s onwards. Palms, aspidistras, even some orchids, adapted to life in the deep shade of the jungle floor, have discovered new homes in the drawing rooms of Moscow and New York. Flowers native to the prairies of Oregon or Nevada suddenly have a global range once they reach the herbaceous border. Immense grasses that have evolved to survive the ravaging fires of the pampas of Central America go global as specimens on front lawns or, when fashion demands, as producers of dried-flower stalks to decorate dingy parlours.

The human collecting instinct can also focus on a minute area. Some gardeners fall in love with auriculas or day lilies or tulips or carnations, indeed almost any genus or species that contains a number of variants. They switch on a human craving to have 'all' of something. The need is even more strongly fired if the variants can be crossed to produce new ones that are not found in nature. Species or groups of species then explode, even over a few decades, providing countless new things to feed gardeners' greed, vanity and a sometimes maniacal fascination with increasingly minute differences.

The collecting instinct also changes the way we see our gardens. The oldest garden scheme, vastly ancient and certainly from the dawn of civilization, is made up of four quarters surrounding some sort of symbolic central feature, often a pool, or a sacred tree, or a mount, even a statue of a god or goddess. This 'four-square' garden, anciently a map of the known world, was an immensely stable unit of the garden, and is known incised into pottery shards from 3000 BC, from the great palaces of ancient Mesopotamia, even in the city planning of the ancient capitals of China. In Europe, it was used in many Roman gardens as well as Roman encampments, and survived the fall of that empire in the plans of monastery cloister gardens, and no doubt private gardens too.

By the late fifteenth and early sixteenth centuries, this scheme was becoming increasingly elaborated, and the four squares metamorphosed into elaborate patterns carried out in clipped plants, often evergreens such as box, santolina, phillyrea or sage. Nevertheless, these 'knots' were merely an embroidered overlay upon the ancient garden plan. There were, of course, a few other garden elements: herb gardens of small rectangular beds, easily cultivated, with rows of various flavouring and medicinal plants; kitchen gardens with similar plans; turf seats (descended from the more informal kind of Roman *triclinia*), and orchards too.

But the flora in these gardens was hardly developed from the Roman one, containing a few lilies, vervain, poppies and hyacinths as well as the roses and periwinkles that appear on the walls of the Casa di Livia on Rome's gracious Palatine Hill. Pliny the Younger was delighted with the rosemary hedge and the violets that grew in his garden overlooking the Bay of Ostia. Perhaps he also grew *Hemerocallis fulva* and *H. lilioasphodelus*, once wild in the

This lovely painting by Nicolas Robert (1614–1685) shows two tulips, convolvulus and the gorgeous scarlet and orange *Lilium bulbiferum*. Hard to grow in northern Europe, this lily has never become established there. The French marigold depicted is from North America.

East but long grown in the West. Perhaps he liked the several Italian *Gladiolus* and *Iris* species, and the Roman range of vegetables: onions, garlic, globe artichokes, cabbages, cucumbers, peas, radishes and leeks. Perhaps, like other Romans, he had on the fringes of his garden figs, walnuts, black mulberries, medlars and plums, but nothing more. The only 'new' plants found in medieval gardens were some perhaps brought home by crusaders or their hangers-on, returning from the Middle East: the almost weedy Star of Bethlehem (*Ornithogalum umbellatum*), the Jerusalem flower (*Lychnis chalcedonica*) and a scatter of hepaticas.

The first major wave of new flowers that hit western European gardens in the sixteenth century was therefore quite overwhelming. There was nowhere to put them. The knot garden was too tightly wound to have room for them; other parts of the garden were too utilitarian to show off such treasures. Clearly, the knot garden had to explode wide open to let them in. It did. It rapidly developed into what is now called the parterre. The topiaried plants retreated to the margin of the bed, still giving form to the design of the garden, especially in winter, but leaving central areas of the bed open to allow growing space for the new flowers. The old 'four-square' garden was capable of easy repetition and expansion, with the quarters themselves quartered and variously elaborated. The new scheme made a perfect system in which to display the subtle shapes and colouring of the new Turkish introductions.

The first wave of introductions set the theme for all the subsequent periods of garden design, including our own, being determined by plant introductions. Fashion is secondary. But although astonishing travels in China, Australia, Chile, Peru, western North America and the Indies, described in subsequent chapters, spawned many more introductions, this first wave was perhaps the most exciting of all. Curiously, it is still in progress, even if it is now more like the last swirl of a wave up a shining beach. The late Professor Peter Davis's monumental *Flora of Turkey and the East Aegean Islands*, finished in 1985 and following on from Boissier's *Flora Orientalis* of 1867 and the prodigious eastern travels of the English botanist John Sibthorp, revealed just how many new species had yet to be found in the country. Turkey still offers a wealth of plants; since 1945, over 1,500 new species from there have been described.

Let us return to the closing years of the parterre, at the very end of the seventeenth century, and to France. There, the formal garden, epitomized by André Le Nôtre's immense schemes, beautiful but botanically sterile, had its most grandiose triumphs. A traveller whose discoveries challenged the constraints of the formal garden, forcing it to open up to many new species, was Joseph Pitton de Tournefort. A minor gentleman, immensely clever, vastly educated, and epicurean in his enjoyment of life, he was also a rationalist who could laugh elegantly at the superstitions of some of the natives with whom he came in contact.

He was born on 5 June 1656, at Aix-en-Provence, France. His father intended him for the church, and sent him to a Jesuit college in Aix. However, when his father died, in 1677, Joseph at once turned his attention entirely to botany and medicine. He studied at the Universities of Montpellier and Barcelona, and he had his first experiences of the joys and hazards of plant hunting in the mountains of Dauphine and Savoy in 1678, and in the Pyrenees in 1681. Even that early trip had its adventures, for he was at one point robbed and

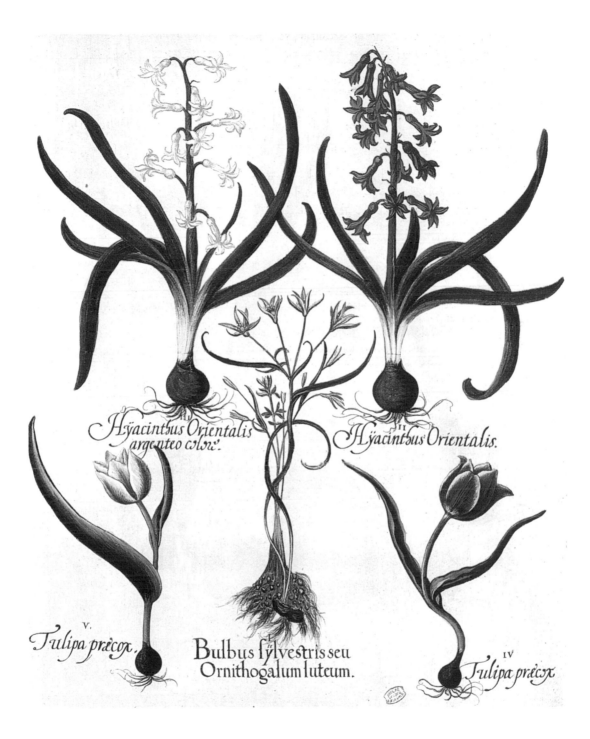

Hyacintʒus Orientalis
argenteo colore.

Hyacintʒus Orientalis.

Bulbus sylvestris seu
Ornithogalum luteum.

Tulipa præcox.

Tulipa præcox.

Hyacinths and tulips pictured in the *Hortus Eystettensis*, a visual directory of every known
shrub and flowering plant, including the latest Oriental imports, commissioned by the
Bishop-Prince of Eichstätt, Germany, in 1613.

Joseph Pitton de Tournefort, Con[seiller] du Roy, pensionnaire de l'Académie Royale des Sciences, Docteur en medecine de la Faculté de Paris, Et professeur en Botanique au Jardin du Roy, &c. ne a Aix en Provce en 1656 mort a Paris en 1708.

Tournefort was destined for the church, but first became a doctor, then an ardent and observant traveller.

stripped by local bandits. They treated him more kindly than they did some of their victims, and considering his distress and the extreme cold gave him back his coat. They hadn't noticed that there was some money tied in a handkerchief, which had slipped inside the coat's lining. Tournefort, clad only in the coat, manage to walk to the nearest town, where he had enough to buy 'a Thrum-Cap, Linen Trowsers and a Pair of Wooden Shoes'.

Like many of the men in this book, he became a doctor. That proved immensely useful, but it was as a botanist that, in 1688, he received an appointment as a professor at the Jardin des Plantes in Paris. Twelve years later he was dispatched by Louis XIV on the same sort of journey as Belon and Rauwolff: 'to discover the Plants of the Ancients, and others, which perhaps escaped their Knowledge'. He was to travel with two friends: a German doctor called Andreas Gundelscheimer, and a young artist called Claude Aubriet (who was soon to give his name to the familiar rock garden plant aubrietia). The artist was essential, Tournefort wrote, for 'It frets a man . . . to see fine Objects, and not be able to take Draughts of them.'

Tournefort's splendid account of the voyage takes the form of a series of letters to the Secretary of State, M. de Pontchartrain. The result is one of the most engaging travel books ever written: *Relation d'un voyage du Levant* (1717), which appeared after his death and was immensely popular, being translated into English (1741) and German (1776). Much of the book must have been recollection, for many of the actual letters that he sent home fell foul of the hazards of travel, their bearers dying of illness or being drowned or assassinated. Tournefort himself faced similar risks, though not only did he survive, but he also collected 1,356 species of plants during this journey: many were new; many are still in our gardens.

He left on the trip on 13 April 1700. After a voyage of nine days from Marseilles, the travellers landed at Khania on Crete, and started out with great expectations to explore near the port. Perhaps he hit a poor season, for although even the immediate vicinity has some interesting plants, Tournefort wrote:

Discontent return'd at every step we took. . . . We ever and anon look'd at one another without opening our mouths, shrugging up our shoulders and sighing as if our very hearts would break, especially as we follow'd those pretty Rivulets, which water the beauteous Plain of Canea, beset with Rushes and

Plants so very common, that we would not have vouchsafed them a look at Paris, we whose Imagination was then full of plants with silver leaves, or cover'd with some rich Down as soft as Velvet, and who fancied that Candia [Iráklion] could produce nothing that was not extraordinary.

They found richer pastures elsewhere, and ended up spending three months exploring the island. Tournefort explored, too, many other islands of the Greek archipelago, encountering some lovely plants and some strange people. On Mykonos, he even had a brush with the living dead. He wrote:

We were present at a very different Scene, and one very barbarous, in the same Island, which happened upon occasion of one of those Corpses, which they fancy come to life again after their interment. The Man . . . was murder'd in the fields, no body knew how, or by whom. Two days after his being bury'd in a Chapel in the Town it was nois'd about that he was seen to walk in the night with great haste. . . . On the tenth day they said one Mass in the Chapel where the Body was laid, in order to drive out the Demon which they imagin'd was got into it. After Mass, they took up the Body, and got everything ready for pulling out its Heart. The Butcher of the Town, an old clumsy Fellow, first opens the Belly instead of the Breast: he groped a long while among the Entrails, but could not find what he look'd for; at last somebody told him he should cut up the Diaphragm. The Heart was pull'd out, to the admiration of all the Spectators. In the mean time, the Corpse stunk so abominably, that they were obliged to burn Frankincense; but this smoke mixing with the Exhalations from the Carcass, increas'd the Stink, and began to muddle the poor Peoples Pericranies. . . . Nothing could be more miserable than the Condition of this Island; all the Inhabitants seem'd frighted out of their senses . . . they knew not now what Saint to call upon, when of a sudden with one Voice, as if they had given each other the hint, they fell to bawling out all through the City, that it was intolerable to wait any longer; that the only way left was to burn the Vroucolacas [vampire] intire; that after so doing, let the Devil lurk in it if he could; that 'twas better to have recourse to this Extremity, than to have the Island totally deserted: And indeed whole Families began to pack up, in order to retire to Syra or Tinos. . . .

Either as a result of this strange episode, or because they just thought the local craft were too flimsy, he and his companions soon got a pirate ship to take them on towards Turkey. He coolly informs Pontchartrain that the boat was 'one of those your lordship has forbidden pickeering from island to island for plunder. I promis'd the Master not to inform against him, and so he convey'd us to Argentiere, the first of August.' This tiny island, where, we are told, 'the Women have no other Employment but making love and Cotton Stockings', was a resort of the pirates, and being 'encumbered with our baggage, and reposing no great Confidence in the People of the Place' they soon moved on. Early in March 1701, they embarked on a Turkish vessel and a few days later arrived in Constantinople. Tournefort was, as many travellers still are, overwhelmed. He found Turkish customs and society immensely strange and fascinating, and couldn't help but describe them to his French audience.

However, Mount Ararat was his destination, and soon he tore himself away from the city. He arranged to join the caravan of the Pasha of Erzurum. To go so far east in European clothes was dangerous, so he and his companions dressed as Armenians, albeit Armenians with Spanish leather boots. Thin Turkish slippers were not much use, he thought, for 'Persons who love to go a-simpling'. Their camping equipment consisted of tents, leather sacks for baggage, baskets, cooking and eating equipment, and a good supply of 'Callicoe Drawers, which serve instead of Bed-clothes in this sort of Roads'. The Pasha was travelling with a wife, mother, daughter, major-domo and other officers. Such were his status and size of retinue, and such was the fear of brigands, that other merchant caravans joined them, so that the eventual company consisted of 300 camels, 600 people, and many sorts of hangers on. In spite of the cleanliness of many of the caravansaries, some important person among the 600 was always ill. Tournefort often used the opportunity to halt the entire caravan, so that he could collect plants while treating the patient. They reached the ancient, spectacularly sited and once beautiful city of Trebizond (modern Trabzon) on 23 May. The rhododendrons were in bloom, and so Tournefort was the first botanist to see and describe the common purple rhododendron (*Rhododendron ponticum*) and the incredibly perfumed yellow azalea (*R. luteum*). Tournefort recalled that it was the honey from the purple species that, in 401 BC, had poisoned an entire army, according to the Greek historian Xenophon. He wrote: 'As beautiful as the Flower is, I did not judge it convenient to present it to the Pasha . . . but as to the flower of the preceding species [the azalea], I thought it so very fine, that I made up great Nosegays of it, to put in his Tent; but was told by his Chiara, that this Flower caus'd Vapours and Dizziness.'

From Trebizond the caravan proceeded by the easiest rather than the shortest route. This suited Tournefort, though 'The Merchants laught heartily to see us mount and remount every moment, only to pick a few Herbs. . . . At the next Lodging we described our Plants while our Meat was in our Mouths, and M. Aubriet drew all he could.'

Turkey is at the junction of three great floristic regions. On 6 or 7 June, they crossed the mountains of the Pontic Range into a new region, and one so rich in flowers that 'we knew not which to fall on first'. After many new plants, and expeditions into Georgia and Armenia, he ends:

The 25th March, in returning from Samos, we went from Scalanova to Ephesus. The next Day we departed to return to Smyrna, and we lay that Day at Tourbale . . . a poor Village, in which we see several old Marbles, which please Strangers, for otherwise the Turks who inhabit it are not very civil. . . . All this Part is is full of Leontopetalon, and Anemonies of a bright shining Fire-Colour. . . .

Maunday-Thursday, the 13th of April, 1702, we set sail with the Wind at South-East, in the Ship call'd the Golden Sun, *commanded by Captain Laurent Guerin of la Cioutad, carrying six pieces of Iron Cannon, and eight Patereroes: It was laden with Silk, Cotton, Goat's Hair, and Wax for Leghorn. The Vessel was of about 6,000 Quintals. After forty Days Sail, in which time we had endured great Storms and contrary Winds, which oblig'd us to take in Refreshements at Malta, we arrived at Leghorn on the 23rd May, and went into the Lazeres. The 27th we came out of the Lazeres, and embark'd on a Felucca, which brought us to Marseilles the 3rd of June, being the Vigil of Pentecost, where we return'd Thanks to God, that he had preserv'd us thro the Course of our Journey.*

Helleborus niger, Orientalis, amplissimo folio, caule praealto, flore viridi, Itineris Tournefort.

Hellebores have been used medicinally and in funeral rites since prehistory. Tournefort added to the number grown in gardens. This is the rare *Helleborus viridis*, painted by the man who accompanied him on his travels, Claude Aubriet.

Tournefort reached Paris amid vast acclaim. The King himself acknowledged the great adventure. Tournefort went on to become one of most influential botanists ever. Among his most important books was the sumptuously illustrated *Eléments de botanique* (1694), which sets out his system of classification. His concept of many genera we still use today, but that we do so is the result of a curious quirk of history related in the next chapter.

In 1708, Tournefort and a professor friend were strolling along a sunlit street in Paris. A passing carriage, speeding, swerved. Both men were hit by the axle tree. The professor was killed at once. Tournefort died a few weeks later.

UNRAVELLING
THE KNOT

Once the parterre had exploded with plants, loosening the bonds of the ancient forms of gardening, huge changes in the way gardens looked and how they were used became inevitable. As trade with and through the East developed, and as settlement in the Americas increased, intense fascination grew among those who stayed at home, whether in Paris, Milan or London, or on their country estates, for objects brought home from these distant lands. Literacy became much more widespread than it had been in previous centuries, so avid collectors could write to friends, relatives, even strangers, who were visiting or who lived in distant places and ask them to send home anything interesting that caught their eye. All over Europe, networks of correspondents began to form, often centred on one or a small number of energetic individuals, reaching across several continents, and quite commonly interconnecting. In cities, clubs and societies began to form, and in gardening these ranged from the modest florists' groups formed to develop perfect forms of tulip or anemone, to extremely high-powered clubs like that held at, and named after, the Temple Bar Coffee House.

At the end of the seventeenth century, the East was still the main source of new plants. But the East wasn't just represented by the spring flowers of Turkey and Persia. It included Russia too. Western gardeners had been familiar with *Iris sibirica* and others since the 1630s, but the Russians themselves were as yet little interested in their own flora. Indeed, its first recorded investigation was made by an English gardener. In 1618, negotiations were in progress between James I and Tsar Mikhail III, who wanted financial and political help in his war against

The gardens of Pieter Bruegel's *Spring*, painted between 1622 and 1635, show some very up-to-date beds being refilled with new flowers for the spring.

27

Mikhail III, Tsar of Russia, here in
Johannn Heinrich Wedekind's painting
of 1728.

Poland. He offered trading concessions in return and, as Russia was an important source of furs and timber, ambassadors were exchanged. Two Russians visited London loaded with sumptuous gifts. In return, King James sent Sir Dudley Digges, of Chilham Castle, Kent, to Russia to meet the Tsar. Digges needed a retinue of supporters, and a gardener called John Tradescant (1570–1638) applied to join the expedition. Tradescant was already well travelled, having been gardener to the Earls of Salisbury at Salisbury House in the Strand, London, and at Hatfield House in Hertfordshire. The gardens at both great houses needed exciting new plants for their parterres and kitchen gardens, and he had already been sent to Europe several times to collect new sorts of vine and rose, and to find black mulberry trees, and *en route* seems to have visited the island of Cos, where he found the eponymous lettuce. In those days he had been a bachelor, but when he married in 1614, he left London and the Earl of Salisbury for his own small property in Kent. However, he clearly enjoyed travelling, and saw the Russian expedition as a way not only of

getting some new species for his latest employer, Sir Edward Wootton, but also of assuaging his own collecting instinct.

As a diplomatic mission, the journey was a waste of time. After six weeks in Russia, Digges heard that the fearsome Poles were already outside the walls of Moscow. The Tsar hardly needed another superfluous ambassador. Digges returned to London. However, Tradescant had set off for Russia earlier, on a stormy six-week voyage aboard the *Diana of Newcastle*. The ship reached the port at Dvina on 14 July 1618, tying up in the Bay of St Nicholas, a trading post first established in 1591. He began collecting almost at once, and returned home with 'many sorts of beryes, on sort lik our strawberyes but of another fation of leaf; I have brought sume of them hom to show with suche variettie of moss and shrubs, all bearing frute, suche as I have never seene the like.' Some of the 'beryes' were *Rubus chamaemorus*, an interesting amber-coloured raspberry. More significantly for the British landscape, he also returned with a cone or two of the common larch (*Larix decidua*), lovely when yellowing in autumn. Nonetheless, Tradescant had had the misfortune to alight on a botanically poor part of that vast country, and he returned home without a huge feeling of success. His career soon became luckier.

By 1625, he was gardener at Oatlands, an estate owned and much used by Charles I, and now vanished beneath London's eastern suburbs. With his much increased income, Tradescant bought himself a house in what was then a village upriver from London, called Lambeth. He also started collecting in a very serious way. The new house had a garden large enough to hold his rapidly increasing collection of plants. Originally called Turret House, his property soon became known as 'The Ark' because Tradescant couldn't stop collecting anything, let alone plants. His treasure trove contained, among trees and shrubs from distant corners of the globe, things as various as birds' nests from China and a pair of gloves belonging to Edward the Confessor.

Many prosperous people were doing much the same thing in assembling a 'cabinet of curiosities', but Tradescant was an indefatigable networker, soon with contacts all over the civilized world. Working for the King at Oatlands gave him access to anyone or any organization he cared to bother. He arranged for the Secretary to the Navy, Edward Nicholas, to ask diplomats like Sir Thomas Roe for plants. Roe had been ambassador to the court of Jahangir, the Mughal

The early 'networker' John Tradescant the Elder in a fine portrait attributed to Emmanuel de Critz (c. 1605–65).

Emperor of Hindustan, between 1615 and 1618, and was an enthusiastic garden builder. Roe had extensive dealings with Constantinople too, still a source of good things.

Tradescant also looked west, and requested the Navy Secretary to ask the Chartered Merchants of the Virginia Company to search for new species to decorate both Oatlands and The Ark. The idea of Virginia obviously fascinated Tradescant. Since 1617 he had been a shareholder in the Virginia Company and, having paid for the transport of twenty-four settlers to the new colony, he had an entitlement to buy 1,200 acres of land there.

That purchase resulted in a flood of plants. Between 1617 and 1634, he added hugely to The Ark's garden, growing all sorts of fine things, from the dazzling annual love-lies-bleeding (*Amaranthus hypochondriacus*), which he called 'The Great Floramour or Purple Flower Gentle', to the enchanting spring-flowering *Dodecatheon meadia* (ineptly named the American cowslip for although it is American it has no relationship to a cowslip). He was the first to grow the still popular *Robinia pseudoacacia*, sometimes called the locust tree, sometimes (wrongly) the acacia. Its fluttering translucent foliage, half engulfing clusters of perfumed pink flowers, can be one of the delights of early summer.

The tree was named after two of his correspondents, Jean and Vespasien Robin, father and son, and both gardeners at the Jardin du Roi in Paris. The Robins were gardeners to

The American cowslip (*Dodecatheon meadia*) illustrated in Mark Catesby's *Natural History of Carolina* (1754).

the kings of France from the 1590s to the 1620s; the Paris garden they established eventually became the Jardin des Plantes. Tradescant's other Paris correspondents were the brothers René and Pierre Morin. Influential nurserymen, they specialized in bulbs and developed new plants, especially double hyacinths and sumptuous anemones for the immense bedding schemes at Versailles and other royal palace gardens.

John Tradescant and his wife had a son, also named John, who has become known as John Tradescant the Younger (1608–62). He too turned out to be a man consumed with a collector's passion for plants. Once old enough, he decided to travel to Virginia himself, perhaps as much to survey his potential acreage as to look at the colony's flora. His three trips to Virginia, in 1637, 1642 and 1654, gave south Lambeth a whole new garden flora. His haul included the bald cypress (*Taxodium ascendens*), the first tulip trees (*Liriodendron tulipifera*), the delightful red maple (*Acer rubrum*) with tufts of scarlet flowers in spring and astonishingly brilliant autumn colours, the American black walnut (*Juglans nigra*), the red mulberry (*Morus rubra*), the shagbark hickory (*Carya ovata*) with its long green pendulous catkins and the amazingly successful Virginia creeper (*Parthenocissus quinquefolia*). He even brought back the poison ivy (*Rhus radicans*), though it seems not to have caught on. Orientals were still reaching the London garden too: Asian persimmon (*Diospyros lotus*), horse chestnut (*Aesculus hippocastanum*), the shrubby and now hardly grown bladder senna (*Colutea arborescens*) and even the mock orange or 'syringa' (*Philadelphus coronarius*), first introduced by de Busbecq and, in following centuries, hybridized with species brought in from North America.

Even as early as the seventeenth century some garden plants met relatives from different continents and crossed. One of the first of these surprises remains immensely influential, and is now found in cities across the globe. It is likely that the London plane (*Platanus* x *acerifolia*) originated in the Tradescants' Ark. Returning from his first trip to Virginia in 1637, the younger Tradescant had material, probably seeds, of the button tree or American sycamore (*Platanus occidentalis*). The Tradescants' garden had had the Turkish Oriental plane

From the time it was first collected by John Tradescant the Younger, the strange tulip tree (*Liriodendron tulipifera*) has intrigued plantsmen. This illustration is from Catesby's *Natural History of Carolina*.

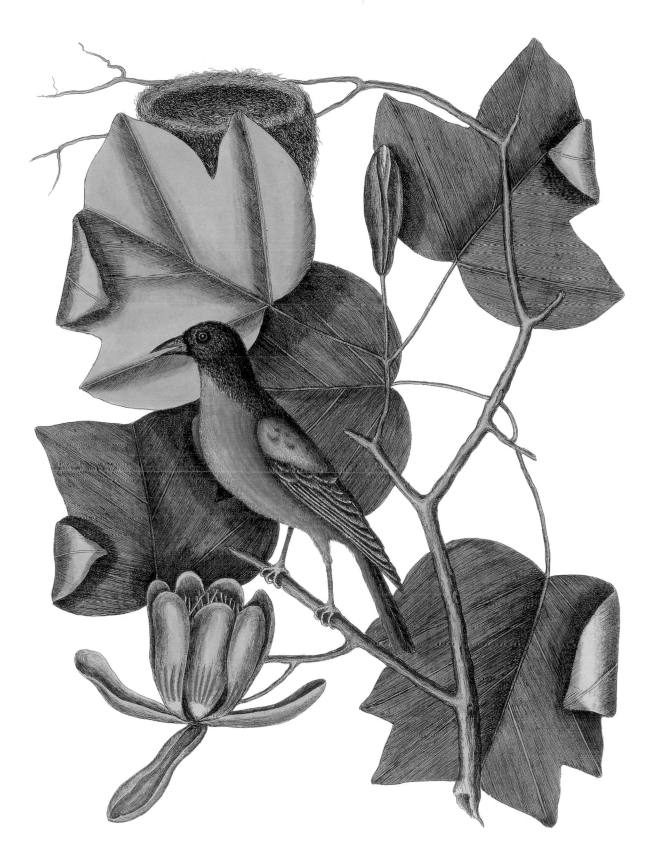

(*Platanus orientalis*) since 1633. Once the American trees flowered, they set seed. Some of the hybridized seedlings looked very vigorous, were fast growing, and were easily propagated by cuttings. The Tradescants probably gave some plants to Jacob Bobart, at the Oxford Botanical Garden. He put one in the garden of Magdalen College. It survives, and is the oldest and largest of all London plane trees. Progeny from the Tradescants' seedlings now thrive in city centres across Europe and North America, and are even grown in China.

Curiously, Tradescant the Younger wasn't a list maker, and seems not to have listed his introductions until the appearance of a lovely book written by a friend of his. John Parkinson's *Paradisi in Sole Paradisus Terrestris* ('A Garden of Pleasant Flowers') appeared in 1629. In it, he assiduously tells the reader which plants he had got from the Tradescants' garden. Once he had a copy, Tradescant the Younger began to list his plants in the few blank pages at the back of the book.

Parkinson was originally apothecary to James I, but Charles I, impressed by *Paradisi in Sole*, made him 'Botanicus Regius Primarius' (the King's first botanist). He was an ardent collector too, and his garden at Long Acre was packed with flowers. He wrote of some of the new anemones that they were 'so dainty, so pleasant and so delightsome flowers that the sight of them doth enforce an earnest longing desire to be a possessoure of some of them at the leaste'. He was at the centre of his own network, and the Tradescants were not his only source of American material. The Dutch were in possession of New Amsterdam until 1667, the French were still in Canada nearly a century later, and Louisiana and Florida remained in French or Spanish hands until the beginning of the nineteenth century, so Parkinson was able to obtain Americans for his London garden from other collectors in Paris, Amsterdam and even Madrid. Some, like the coneflower (*Rudbeckia laciniata*) and *Zephyranthes atamasca*, reached Parkinson via The Ark, having been sent there by Vespasien Robin. *Solidago canadensis*, a good species of golden rod, travelled from Canada to Paris, and thence to London, in only a few seasons.

The Tradescants also sent plants to Fulham Palace. This ancient estate had been the seat of the bishops of London since 704, and was so grand that it was once enclosed by the longest moat in England. The remains of Roman and medieval palaces lie under what is now the east lawn, though of the original thirty-six acres of garden, only thirteen acres remain today. The gardens were already famous in Elizabethan times, when Bishop Grindal introduced the tamarisk and other novelties. The Tradescants' patron was Bishop Compton (1632–1713), a man who had what was at the very least an extreme enthusiasm for growing rare plants. Indeed, towards the end of his life he suffered pangs of conscience about the large amounts of money he had spent on his garden. However much he regretted such frivolity, modern gardeners are in his debt, for many of the rare species he imported from the East, but most especially the West, went on to become influential garden plants.

He was born Henry Compton, the son of Spencer Compton, 2nd Earl of Northampton, at the handsome Elizabethan house of Compton Wynyates in Warwickshire. He had a conventional aristocratic upbringing, and was, in youth, for a while a cornet in the Horse Guards. Turning to the Church, he rose rapidly up the hierarchy, and became Bishop of London in 1675. Developing an interest in the spiritual and intellectual development of

Britain's American colonies, he became Chancellor of the College of William and Mary in Williamsburg, Virginia, and presided over the Church of England in America in the mid- to late 1600s. He was so influential and popular that when the Catholic James II came to the British throne in 1685, the king deemed it impolitic to get rid of him. Compton was eventually suspended from his duties, but allowed to live at Fulham Palace and keep his beloved garden. During his suspension between 1688 and 1689, he set up a wide network of correspondents, and thereby greatly increased his collection. He also had a close friendship with George London, a hugely successful nurseryman and designer who had studied many of André Le Nôtre's designs in France. London was reponsible for the planting of some of the greatest parterres in the country, in the gardens of some of its greatest nobles. London's assistant Stephen Switzer wrote, in his own book *Ichnographia Rustica* (1718), that Compton 'had a thousand species of exotick plantis in his stoves and gardens, in which last place he had endenizoned a great many that have been formerly thought too tender for this cold climate. There were few days in the year, till towards the latter part of his life, but he was actually in his garden, ordering and directing the Removal and Replacing of his Trees and plants.' Many of his trees survived into the late nineteenth century. James II must have ended up wishing Compton had stayed in his garden, for he became instrumental in inviting William of Orange to land on British territory, and later officiated at his coronation.

Compton was not only a networker by letter. He was also a member of the Temple Bar Coffee House Botanists' Club. Temple Bar, like other 'bars', controlled one of the main roads out of London. The botanists met weekly for conversation and no doubt more than coffee at the Rainbow Inn. Alas, there are no surviving records of any of its meetings, except that on Friday 11 May 1691, there were forty members present, and that the membership included eminent men like Compton himself, and George London. Coffee was also served to a number of members of the recently formed Royal Society, including Plukenet, Lister, Doody, Robinson, James Petiver and William Sherard. It also included men who had actually travelled in search of plants like the society doctor Sir Hans Sloane (1660–1753), who became one of the very greatest collectors of the age. His immense collection was eventually given to the state, and went on to form the nucleus of the British Museum.

Let us meet Sloane aboard ship, returning from his duties in Jamaica. It is 1688, and he is accompanying the Duchess of Albemarle, the embalmed body of the Duke, 800 plant specimens and a surprising range of livestock. The Duchess, the Duke, Sloane and all his plants arrived safely in England. Some of the animals did not: an iguana jumped overboard; a crocodile died after plunging into a tub that contained salt water, not fresh; a yellow snake, seven feet long and hungry for the ship's rats, escaped and took possession of the deck-house roof. A few of the passengers complained, and Sloane wrote that 'footmen and other domestics of Her Grace, being afraid to lie down in such company shot my snake'.

Not only was he now personal physician to the Duchess, but he had become romantically attached to a widowed heiress in Jamaica who would eventually become his wife. Sloane, for an unhealthy young man from the obscure village of Killyleagh in County Down, Ireland,

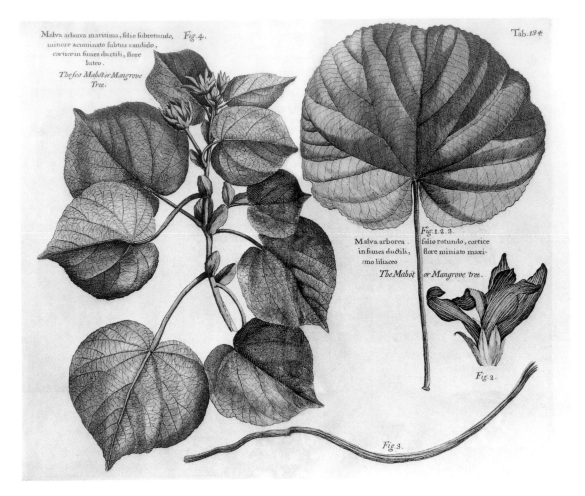

This sumptuous plate from Sir Hans Sloane's *Voyage to the Islands Madera . . . and Jamaica*, published in 1707, shows what disparate plants were thought of as 'mangroves'. Many of his herbarium sheets mounted various plants, and were similarly illustrated.

was doing well. He was born on or around 16 April 1660, one of several sons of Alexander Sloane, tax-collector. When he was sixteen years old, Hans began to suffer from haemoptysis, a condition that caused him to spit blood. He was ill for three years, during which time he began to like flowers – the interest was almost a family trait, for some of his rich relations owned elegant gardens. It may also have been they who spurred his financial and social ambitions. As with so many men in this book, medicine provided the ladder to success. Around 1679, he moved to London to study both it and chemistry. Botany was then a vital component of medicine, and in 1683, he went to France to complete his studies. After Paris, and working with Tournefort at the Jardin du Roi, he finished his studies at the University of Montpellier, with its renowned medical school and its famous botanic garden. As a Protestant, Sloane could not graduate at either Paris or Montpellier, so he moved to the University of Orange, in the south of France, and graduated there on 28 July 1683.

He was already something of a star, and returned to London to work with an extremely successful doctor, Dr Thomas Sydenham. Sloane was soon introduced to some of the most fashionable and wealthy patients in London. Perhaps with their help, he was elected a Fellow of the Royal Society in January 1685, and a Fellow of the Royal College of Physicians two years later. Better still, he became personal physician to the Duke of Albemarle, son of the enriched and ennobled General Monk, who had helped Charles II regain his throne. The young Duke was a rake, and was created Governor of Jamaica to keep him out of mischief. He gave Sloane an initial payment of £300 and agreed a salary of £600 a year. They set sail on 12 September 1687.

The four vessels reached Port Royal on 19 December 1687. After County Down and Montpellier, the tropics had the young botanist astonished. The flora was hardly known in Europe, and he realized he had an enormous opportunity. He at once hired an artist to record the local flora and fauna. He himself recorded his immediate locality with fascinated interest. His duties or his inclination kept him fairly close to Spanish Town (Santiago de la Vega) where his employer lived. Indeed, most of his plant collections came from his own parish of St Catherine and its near neighbours, and most especially from the plantations bountied to officers of Cromwell's army following the capture of the island from the Spanish in 1655. He was a technically excellent collector, for the specimens survived the local, and all subsequent, insect attacks, and still today look remarkably similar to the drawings made from them by his illustrator in 1700–1. He collected some splendidly exotic plants. Jamaica also allowed him a medical practice that was unusually exotic. Though he happily treated rich and poor alike, he perhaps looked askance at one of his patients: the violent pirate (now retired) Sir Henry Morgan. Whether or not he helped Morgan overcome his nightmares, he was unable to help the Duke, who died in 1688, after little more than a year in the tropics. The Duchess decided to return to England with the doctor, his plants and his menagerie, and the body of her late husband.

Back in London, she retained Sloane as her personal physician and, with such illustrious patronage, his clientèle soon once again included the rich and famous. His practice grew by leaps and bounds and in 1695 he established it permanently in Bloomsbury, then the most expensive part of London. That same year he married his rich widow, Mrs Elizabeth Rose (née Langley), and thereafter led a life of domestic quiet, set against an increasingly glittering backdrop. He became an important member of the Royal Society, and put the Chelsea Physic Garden firmly in the hands of the Apothecaries' Society, with Philip Miller in charge, and with the stipulation that it had to present fifty new species of plants to the Royal Society every year. Even in the middle of the eighteenth century, fifty was a modest quantity. By the century's end, fifty new species was hardly anything at all.

Sloane began publishing his accounts of his West Indies trip in 1707, adding to his descriptions and illustrations of plants and animals some fascinating sections on the lives of native Americans, and of the Caribbean and African slaves. He described the music and dance of African Americans and even included pictures of their musical instruments. However great a collector, and however wide-ranging his interests, it isn't clear if he was a talented organizer as well. Certainly, when the great Swedish botanist Linnaeus visited him

The influential gardener and cloth merchant Peter Collinson in an engraving by John Miller.

in Chelsea in 1736, he wrote that 'Sloane's great collection is in complete disorder'. Presumably Linnaeus had no premonition that his own impeccably organized collection, demonstrating his sexual system of plant classification, would end up spending its future only a few miles away from Sloane's, at what is now the Linnean Society on Piccadilly.

Disordered or not, there was no stopping Sloane's collection, or indeed Sloane himself. In 1701, Queen Anne consulted him for the first time, and so his influence spread. His collection began to act as a magnet for others. In 1702, he was bequeathed the vast Charleton Collection. In 1718 he bought the Petiver Collection for £4,000. He was left Sir Arthur Rawdon's immense holdings. These all made Sloane's collection the biggest in the world. Plant specimens made up only a tiny part; Sloane's will lists 'my library of books, drawings, manuscripts, Prints, medals and coins; ancient and modern antiquities, seals and cameos, intaglios and precious stones; agates and jasper, vessels of agate, jasper or crystal; mathematical instruments, drawings and pictures, and all other things'. The final inventory listed 200,000 items.

As the momentum of plant collecting was swinging from East to West, another maniacal collector came on to the stage. This was Peter Collinson (1694–1768). Collinson was an ardent Quaker, which he combined with being a wholesale woollen draper and gentleman's mercer. He had his counting house in Gracechurch Street, London, his enchanting postal address being 'The Red Lion'. He was prosperous enough to own a garden in Peckham and a modest country estate called Ridgeway House at Mill Hill. Quakers, many of whom created successful buisnesses, had problems reconciling personal wealth with their austere religious philosophy. Collinson, who couldn't help but grow anything new he could get his hands on, found this especially hard in his garden, where there should not be 'too great a superfluity of plants and too great nicety of gardens' and that 'all Friends in planting gardens should do it in a lowly mind and keep to plainness and the serviceable part, rather admiring the wonderful hand of Providence, in causing such variety of unnecessary things to grow for the use of man than in seeking to please the curious mind'.

Collinson also suffered from having something of an artist's eye, once comparing tree planting to 'painting with living pencils' in wonderful shades of green. His enthusiasm was not restricted to trees; he received seeds of other plants from Jesuits in China such as the priest Pierre Nicholas le Cheron d'Incarville and Père Jean-Denis Attiret. A Dr Mounsey sent him a hornbeam from Persia. In 1756, a Russian ironmine owner sent him a lily 'as near to black as any flower' that Collinson had seen – perhaps the small but sinister *Fritillaria camschatcensis*. Collinson was the first to succeed in growing the Iceland poppy (*Papaver nudicaule*), which he got from Siberia in 1730 and more in 1759. He grew the first *Delphinium grandiflorum* (of which we will hear more in Chapter Five), sent to him by Dr Johann Ammann, the founder in 1736 of the Botanic Garden of the Imperial Academy at St Petersburg. Collinson sent plants from his own garden out into the world too, notably tulips, carnations, auriculas, crown imperials, blue and white hyacinths, altheas, China asters and Guernsey lilies to John Custis (whose daughter-in-law, Martha Dandridge Custis, married George Washington). He sent books to Benjamin Franklin for his Library Company of Pennsylvania, a sort of book club that grew out of Franklin's 'Junto' group.

The Iceland poppy (*Papaver nudicaule*) reached London from Siberia in the 1720s.

As he imported cloth from around the world, Collinson was in a perfect position to ask his foreign agents to get him plants for his Peckham garden. He also advised some of his grander clients on what to plant in their gardens, whether they wanted new plants or not. Gradually, by hundreds of letters, he began to create an interest, even a fashion, in new American plants. By 1733, he was getting more and more excited about them. He wrote to his Pennsylvania friend Dr Chew, asking for the name of a potential collector. Chew suggested a farming acquaintance called John Bartram. It was an immensely influential piece of networking. Collinson and Bartram soon struck up a close working relationship. Their correspondence lasted for more than thirty-six years until Collinson's death in 1768.

Expeditions were often, and sometimes still are, financed by groups of subscribers who, in exchange for financial support, received a suitable proportion of the resultant spoils. Collinson assembled groups of subscribers, often from his clients and associates. As soon as shipments of seeds from Bartram arrived in England, Collinson would divide and distribute the collections to the various gardens. He himself began to germinate some new Americans in 1734 and 1735; he soon had the first skunk cabbage (*Lysichiton americanus*) ever seen in Europe, arisaemas (called Indian turnip by the American settlers) and more. A handsome ladies' slipper orchid (*Cypripedium* spp.) from American woodlands first flowered in Europe in Collinson's garden in 1738. New recruits to his subscriber groups poured in. The collections continued to arrive for the next three decades, and then, as now, the distribution made endless problems. Some subscribers felt they had not had enough material for their outlay, or not the things they had hoped for. In 1766, Collinson wrote that no sooner would the seed distribution be complete and sent off, than he would receive requests from the subscribers begging, for instance, 'Pray Sir how and in what manner must I sow them, pray be so good, Sir, as to give mee some directions, for my Gardener is a very Ignorant Fellow.'

Yet, for all these new plants pouring into Europe from the Americas, from the Indies, from the Far East, from Russia and southern Africa, gardening among the upper classes had been taking a very strange turn. For millennia, all gardeners had collected plants, and wealthy ones merely had more of the rarest to demonstrate their means. In France during the later part of the seventeenth century, the old formal garden had developed fast into gigantic schemes, sometimes quite literally stretching to the horizon.

The increasing botanical diversity of the age was certainly admired, but was generally restricted to great botanic gardens or to the wilderness areas of a few private ones. Some bulbs, especially hyacinths and tulips, had been taken up enthusiastically as parterre flowers, and huge planting schemes using splendid varieties of them were created for use at Versailles. However, the huge sense of 'state' in French formal gardens, of course especially in those for the court and its greatest courtiers, often designed by Le Nôtre, was worked out using stone, water, grass and an extremely limited number of hedging and tree species, most of them well known to the Romans. (The horse chestnut was the only tree to break the classical barrier.) Indeed, the simplicity of the garden materials gives gigantic gardens like Vaux-le-Vicomte much of their tremendous impact. Nevertheless, in them, order is created at the expense of chaos. Their serene unity is created at the expense of living diversity; their tremendous formality replaces any expression of Nature. The idea of emulating ancient Rome captivated the English rich too, and for much of the later seventeenth century, many wealthy gardeners had essentially followed the grand French style.

However, early in the eighteenth century, William Kent and his patron Lord Burlington, both members of the aesthetes' circles of the capital, but not especially interested in new plants, began a move away from the stupendous rigidities of gardens across the Channel. They wanted something of a landscape around the great new houses then being built, much influenced by the sixteenth-century villas designed by Italian architect Andrea Palladio. The landscapes they wanted were derived not from the real landscapes of Suffolk or Surrey, but from the dreamtime paintings of Claude Lorrain, who frequently depicted views of a never-never land comprising ruinous Roman buildings, picturesque farm houses, meadows, forests and lakes, all fading into a slumbrous blue distance.

Though not a pursuit of plants, their quest was certainly a pursuit of Nature, a concept now rendered far more attractive than it had ever been by the increasing knowledge of its riches over the rest of the planet. The idea of grandeur developed in France, and its simplicity of means, was taken over in England to make landscape. Lawns, clumps of trees, lakes, bridges and temples (fakes if need be), populated by herds of deer or cattle kept off the lawns by a sunken and invisible fence, made a scene every bit as artificial, and every bit as expensive to build, as anything by Le Nôtre. This landscape theme was taken up by a young man nicknamed 'Capability' Brown. He had an immense talent for making sculptural landscapes of great beauty and corresponding expense. The landscape garden became a

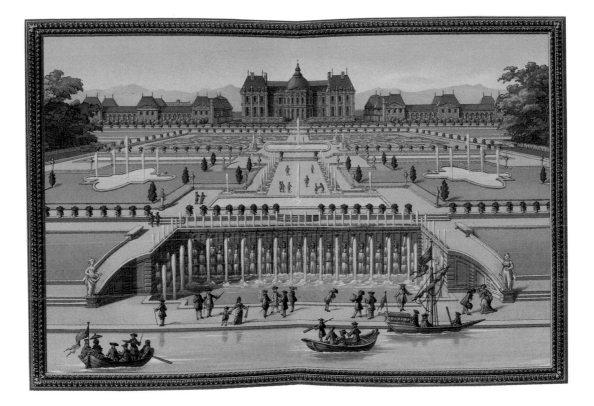

André Le Nôtre designed these gardens at Vaux le Vicomte in the mid-1600s. In them, magnificence was expressed in terms of space and astonishing architecture, but the range of plants was small by today's standards.

fashion amongst those who could afford it, and great formal gardens were swept away to make room for 'Nature', at least a nature unspoilt by anything untoward and unplanned.

Neither the canals and *pattes d'oie* of great French gardens, nor the lakes and temples of English landscape ones were capable of compression into a couple of acres. In the past, almost any garden could have a tiny knot or a parterre in the latest fashion, complete with at least a few fine flowers. Now, the middling ranks of gardeners had become disenfranchised from fashionable 'garden taste' in a way that had never really happened before. Nevertheless, they didn't stop gardening in a huff, even though, sadly, their gardens are rather little documented. It is likely that their gardens were crammed with interesting plants, for nurseries flourished, and garden books, especially ones about the new plants, sold edition after edition

There were also marvellous illustrated florilegiums popularizing the new flowers. The most famous book of all was written by Philip Miller, Hans Sloane's appointee at the Chelsea Physic Garden. Miller, like Sloane, was at the centre of a huge network of correspondents and collectors, and participated in the syndicates formed from 1736 onwards to finance the introduction of new plants from America. He was also often among the first cultivators of new plants reaching Europe, and he had enormous success in keeping them going. The first edition of his great *Gardener's Dictionary* appeared in 1731, with subsequent editions in 1733, 1737, 1743, 1747, 1752, 1756–9 and 1768. A Dutch translation appeared in 1745, a German one in 1750, 1758, 1769 and 1776; even French gardeners had one between 1785 and 1790. The thick folio work, full of engravings, was so expensive that only grand gardeners could afford it. Realizing that there was a far larger market for the book, Miller wrote abridged editions, with only a few of the most utilitarian engravings but essentially the same text. The first 'abridgement' appeared in 1733, and was followed by others in 1741, 1748, 1754, 1763 and 1771.

The book was an extraordinary success. Large numbers of gardeners really wanted to know what new things they could grow, and how they should be grown. One such was Robert James, Lord Petre, who was planning a fabulous garden at Thorndon Hall, Brentwood, Essex, and wanted everything new he could lay his hands on. Intoxicated, he requested lots of forest seed from John Bartram in Pennsylvania, and organized presents and payment. Bartram was entirely happy with this, and even proposed that he be given an annual allowance to cover travel, clothing and provisions. Petre agreed to ten guineas. Miller himself stated in 1754 that 'there are many Persons of Distinction in England, who are pleased to honour the Art of Gardening, by making it a considerable Part of their Amusement; and who have been greatly assisting in the introducing of large Numbers of new Plants, Shrubs and Trees, into the English gardens'.

Miller's book is still of immense botanical importance. When Linnaeus came to London in 1734 to visit Sloane, he naturally went to see Miller too. The men took an instant liking to one another, but Miller, absolutely his own man, was not convinced by Linnaeus's classification of plants, and only began to use his 'binomial' system of Latin plant names in 1768. Miller was also not convinced by Linnaeus's groupings of plants into genera. He thought that Joseph Pitton de Tournefort was a much better taxonomist than Linnaeus, and often used his concept of plant genera in his *Dictionary* rather than the larger and more inclusive genera set up by Linnaeus. As modern taxonomy refuses to acknowledge any genera that predate Linnaeus' *Species Plantarum* of 1753, Tournefort's genera are considered invalid. However, for certain genera, many modern botanists follow Miller, and therefore Tournefort, far more closely than they follow Linnaeus, and have to consult Miller's post-1753 *Gardener's Dictionary* on a weekly or monthly basis.

The great green formal gardens of the French magnates and the great green landscape gardens of English bankers and aristocrats were much closer to each other, in spite of their theoretical differences, than anything that had gone before. While flattering the sense of power of their owners, they denied the riches of Nature. They denied, too, the collecting instinct of most of mankind. Neither Nature nor instinct could be held in check for very long.

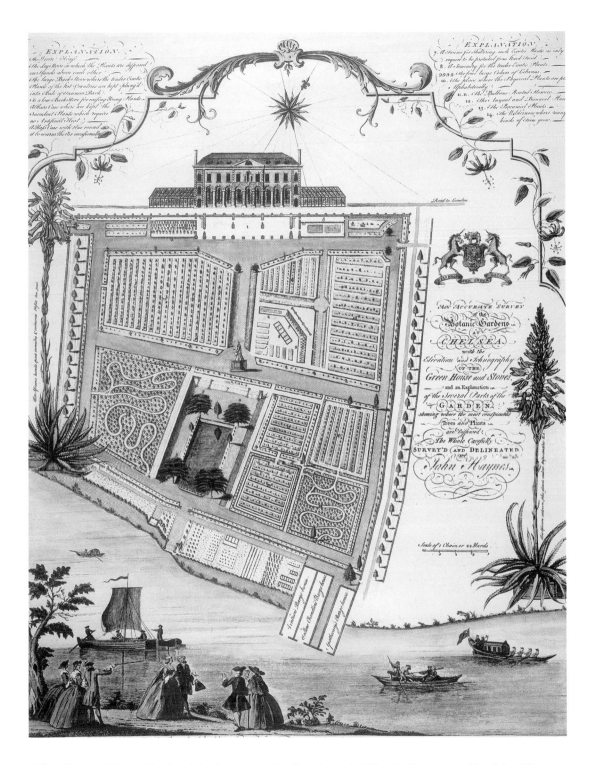

The Chelsea Physic Garden (also known as the 'Apothecaries' Garden'), engraved by John Haynes in 1751. The garden was founded in 1673 as an international botanic garden, and operates on the same site to this day.

THE
AMERICAN
GARDEN

For its first human inhabitants, the American continent was Eden. Food, from the fish in the rivers to the mammoth and buffalo on the plains, was always to hand. The continent's prodigious flora encompassed edible plants that ranged from bitterroot and quamash bulbs to the seed kernels of gigantic conifers. Even the hazards of rattlesnakes, black bears, zigadenus lilies and other poisonous flowers hardly made the Americas less of a garden.

While the civilizations of Central America built sumptuous gardens long before Cortez stumbled into them, the 'American garden' of the late eighteenth century was a short-lived, but very important, garden element in Europe. A few examples still exist, but the style evolved so rapidly that they were seldom created after 1850. Nevertheless, we are still busily building the sort of gardens into which they changed. Their story vividly illustrates how garden design is driven by the collecting instinct.

The sculptural, architectural style of garden design that has become almost entirely associated with Le Nôtre – with its allées and rides, bosquets and topiary – was copied throughout Europe and Russia, and even made inroads into Middle Eastern gardening. It was eventually displaced by the 'landscape movement' evolving in England from the 1720s. However, as we have seen, it too was designed to show the wealth

The Oregon Trail, romanticized here by Albert Bierstadt (1830–1902) shows the rugged terrain explored first by trappers, then by plant collectors like Thomas Nuttall and David Douglas. Here, settlers are moving west.

of the owner, rather than the riches and grandeur of Nature, and it used an extremely limited flora.

While these two styles engrossed estate owners and their less grand imitators, Nature herself was busy subverting them. As European settlers spread out across America, American plants began to reach Europe in increasing numbers. Some were potential food crops, or could be smoked, or used as dyes or as medicines. Many more were none of these things. They were just beautiful, and were sent over simply to service collectors' instincts. Many early collectors were drawn from the middle classes, and had modest gardens. They had no space to plant avenues that stretched to the horizon or to dredge new lakes. Turning their backs on the grand fashions of the time, they collected brand new plants instead of statues and architectural fragments dug from the mud of ancient Rome.

By the early eighteenth century, Nature's subversion began in earnest. The plants sent to Europe from America began to include some magnificent trees and some even more magnificent shrubs. Soon even great landowners took notice and wanted to have at least the trees somewhere about them. Many of the new American species looked 'exotic', and didn't fit at all well into the expensively designed 'landscapes' by William Kent or Capability Brown, filled with native trees. Though some great gardens had arboreta, like that at Dawyck on the Scottish borders, it seemed to many owners that the new trees, shrubs and woodland flowers should all be put into a separate area in the garden devoted to new plants from America. One overriding reason for this was their cultivation; a lot of the new plants had been collected from river banks or swampy ground, and needed to be given the same growing conditions in Europe.

Predictably, such areas became known as 'the American garden'. They were soon fascinating and fashionable places to be. Huge numbers were planted throughout Europe and Russia. The enthusiasm eventually became so extreme that overcollection in the wild led to the extinction of a number of American species, like the Franklin tree (*Franklinia alatamaha*), which is now only found in gardens.

The first intimations of what was to come were the plants collected by the Reverend John Banister (1650–92). He arrived in Virginia in 1678 and, within two years, had prepared a catalogue which provided the first printed survey of American plants. He illustrated the rarer species, and sent drawings and seeds back to the English naturalist John Ray and others. Into a garden culture obsessed with either ancient Rome, or with tulips, auriculas, myrtles and oranges, he let loose some extraordinary finds. One of his first was *Magnolia virginiana*. No gardener in western Europe had even seen a magnolia before. This one, in America called the swamp bay, has huge glossy leaves and beautifully shaped flowers, creamy white and heavily scented, and gardeners swooned. The spice bush (*Lindera benzoin*) followed. Its greenish yellow flowers smell delicious and the bush has leaves that glow buttery yellow in autumn. Even better was the sweet gum (*Liquidambar styraciflua*), which makes an autumn show in scarlet, crimson and orange. No one had seen such colours. The list continued: *Cornus amomum*, a new species of dogwood with blue fruits; the honey tree (*Gleditsia triacanthos*), the fringe tree (*Chionanthus virginicus*) with tassels of scented flowers and dark blue egg-shaped fruit; *Rhododendron viscosum*, one of the first to be grown, with gorgeously perfumed pinkish flowers. So it went on: box elder (*Acer negundo*), dwarf sumach (*Rhus copallina*), devil's walking stick (*Aralia spinosa*), Canadian moonseed (*Menispermum canadense*), red oak (*Quercus rubra*), hop hornbeam (*Ostrya virginiana*), balsam fir (*Abies balsamea*), cotton gum (*Nyssa aquatica*) – gardeners' heads span.

Banister was born into a rustic family at Twigworth, Gloucestershire, in 1650. Even with a modest start, it was soon clear that he was an exceptional and ambitious child, and from an early age he was fascinated by plants. While he was a scholar at Oxford University, not surprisingly, he became a close friend of Jacob Bobart the Younger, then in charge of the Oxford Botanic Garden. This was not the only way he was influenced by Oxford. Close proximity to the wealthier students at the university gave him great social ambitions and he determined to get himself an estate. America seemed the place where this could most easily be accomplished.

He arrived in Virginia during a politically unsettled time, as the concerns of local farmers

The Franklin tree (*Franklinia alatamaha*) by William Bartram (1739–1822). Its last sighting in the wild was in 1803.

clashed with the royal colonial regime. Nevertheless, he was almost immediately entranced by the place: by its sometimes warlike natives and by their extraordinary crop plants. He got on with the single-minded settlers who only wanted to grow huge crops of tobacco and make money as quickly as possible – Banister wanted that too; but he couldn't ignore the Indians' watermelons, brilliantly coloured maizes, countless sorts of potato, musk melons, pumpkins and *Phaseolus* beans (recently introduced to European gardens, but as decoratives not edibles). He even began to collect the numerous varieties of tobacco grown by the Indians, creating an early precursor of the seed banks currently being set up in the modern United States, as part of the great heritage of native Americans.

The first loads of seeds that he sent to Britain, particularly those to Bishop Compton, caused a sensation. He was asked for more, and for drawings of mature plants, cuttings, living plants, herbarium specimens, anything he could send. The Temple Bar Botanists' Club sent him funds, and its member eagerly awaited each Virginia ship to berth at London's docks. Nurserymen such as George London requested, and got, countless packets of seeds. Banister soon had American patrons too, notably among the fabulously landed Byrd family, owners of huge tracts of Virginia. They eventually got hold of his library of botanical books, now part of the Byrd Libary, Westover.

Banister was energetic and astute, and his desire for land was soon abundantly realized. He eventually assembled an estate of nearly two thousand acres, manned by thirty-five

The sweet gum (*Liquidambar styraciflua*) in *Traité des arbres et arbustes* by Henri-Louis Duhamel du Monceau (1700–82).

slaves, mostly captured native Americans, but at least two of whom were recently shipped in from Africa. The Fates seemed to be smiling – until he went on a collecting trip with some friends. Exploring some ancient trading trails, he went off into the vegetation looking for plants. As frequently happens, his movements were mistaken for those of a wild animal. One of the party, Jacob Colson, fired, and Banister fell. Let's hope he fell among a patch of his favourite, and lovely, balm (*Monarda punctata*). The story was hushed up, and relatives and London friends were never given the real details. John Ray thought he had fallen whilst rock climbing, looking for plants.

But these first ripples of excitement were as nothing compared to what was to come – next through the work of Mark Catesby. He became famous in America for drawing the sketch from which Linnaeus named the bald eagle, emblem of the United States, but he came originally from Castle Hedingham in Essex, England. He seems to have first become interested in botany and ornithology through meeting Banister's friend John Ray, who lived near by. He later wrote that he developed a 'passionate desire of viewing . . . the Animal and Vegetable Productions in their Native Countries; which are Strangers to England'.

He soon got the opportunity. His father, a prosperous magistrate, died when Mark was aged twenty-three, leaving him free of the need to work. However, he was an energetic and resourceful young man. A life of genteel ease in the provinces did not attract him. His sister Elizabeth and her husband, a doctor, were already well established in Williamsburgh, Virginia, and he decided to visit them. Arriving in April 1712, he stayed for seven years. Through him once more Bishop Compton, John Ray and other enthusiasts had easy access to American plants. Soon their gardens had *Ceanothus americanus*, the enchanting *Porteranthus* (formerly *Gillenia*) *trifoliata*, among others.

When Catesby got back to Britain, in the summer of 1719, he found that he was much in demand. A group of grandees raised funds so that he could return to America to find yet more handsome plants. These sponsors included Sir Hans Sloane, the immensely wealthy Duke of Chandos (for whom Handel wrote his 'Chandos Anthems'), William Sherard and the King's doctor Dr Richard Mead. Catesby was to be given a post as attendant to the Governor of Carolina, with Charleston (then Charles Town) as his base. In his book *The Natural History of Carolina, Georgia, Florida and the Bahama Islands* (1730–47), he wrote:

With this intention, I set out again from England, in the year 1722, directly for Carolina; which country, tho' inhabited by English above an age past, and a country inferior to none in fertility, and abounding in variety of the blessings of nature; yet its productions being very little known except what barely related to commerce, such as rice, pitch and tar; was thought the most proper place to search and describe the productions of Nature: Accordingly I arrived in Carolina 23rd of May 1722, after a pleasant tho' not a short passage. In our voyage we were frequently entertain'd with diversions not uncommon in crossing the Atlantick Ocean, as catching of sharks, striking of porpoises, dolphins, bonetoes, albacores, and other fish; which three last we regaled on when fortune favored us in catching them; and even the flesh of sharks and porpoises would digest well with the sailors, when long fed on salt meats.

It was to be an extraordinary period in his life, and was to have an immense impact on European and American gardens. South Carolina was still not far removed from its virgin state, and much less explored and cultivated than the Viriginia he already knew. He was there for four years, exploring Georgia too, sending home animal as well as plant specimens, seeds and even plants in tubs of soil. At that time, the Indians were not hostile, and often helped his expeditions. He was quite as fascinated by them as they were by him. Much of his time was idyllic, and only occasionally hazardous. He wrote:

I was much delighted to see nature differ in these upper parts, and to find here abundance of things not to be seen in the lower parts of the country; this encouraged me to take several journeys with the Indians higher up the rivers, towards the mountains, which afforded not only a succession of new vegetable appearances, but most delightful prospects imaginable, besides the diversion of hunting buffello's, bears, panthers, and other wild beasts. In these excursions I employ'd an Indian to carry my box, in which, besides paper and materials for painting, I put dry'd specimens of plants, seeds, &c. as I gathered them. To the hospitality and assistance of these friendly Indians, I am much indebted, for I not only subsisted on what they shot, but their first care was to erect a bark hut, at the approach of rain to keep me and my cargo from wet.

Early one morning he discovered that he had spent the night sharing his bed with a rattlesnake, which slithered out only when dawn came. His travels set the scene for an early aspect of the American garden. Much of the time he collected by river margins or on flat swampy regions close to the coast. European gardeners, trying to make their new rarities happy, built wet, peaty places for them to grow in. This was a complete break with all past gardening, when drainage had always been the first aspect to consider when gardening on new ground.

His haul set European gardeners in a spin. The Carolina spice bush, or Carolina allspice (*Calycanthus floridus*), was an immediate hit. It flowered prodigiously in late spring and early summer, entrancing owners with a smell of pineapples, and fruits that were then the acme of luxury. Catesby liked the plant too, writing: 'The bark is very aromatic, and as odoriferous as cinnamon. These Trees grow in the remote and hilly parts of Carolina, but nowhere amongst the Inhabitants.' Later colonists used the bark as a substitute for

The aromatic Carolina allspice
(*Calycanthus floridus*), introduced by Mark
Catesby in 1726.

cinnamon, but the whole plant smells pleasantly of camphor.

He also sent home, and popularized in contemporary Virginia and Carolina gardens, the Indian bean or common catalpa (*Catalpa bignonioides*). He announced, proudly, that it was not known to any gardener 'till I brought the seeds from the remoter parts of the country'. He went on: 'And tho' the inhabitants are little curious in gardening, the uncommon beauty of this Tree has induc'd them to propagate it; and 'tis become ornament to many of their gardens.' He had found it in the fields of local Cherokee, whose name for it was catalpa. He had also found autumn-flowering *Wisteria frutescens* with its perfumed racemes of lilac-purple blossoms, the weird *Callicarpa americana* with tight clusters of berries the colour of crystallized violets and *Stewartia malacodendron* with its purple-eyed flowers. In the 1830 catalogue of Conrad Loddiges and Sons, London, this was named 'Stuartia' after Lord Bute, a Stuart.

Eventually Catesby's time in Carolina drew to a close. He spent part of 1725 and 1726 collecting in the easy warmth of the Bahamas, where he became fascinated by the beautiful fish of the warm sub-tropical waters. Once back in greyer and chillier London, he set about popularizing the plants he had found. He went into the selling business, in association with a Fulham nurseryman called Christopher Gray. Needing more stock, Catesby began requesting additional seeds and plants from friends he had made in Carolina, as well as his long-suffering Williamsburgh sister, whom he relentlessly pestered for material. Realizing that he needed to do some marketing as well, he decided to publish his notes, illustrated with prints taken from his own workmanlike watercolours. Getting plates made was even then an expensive business, and he didn't have enough of his father's money left to risk the outlay. So, resourceful as ever, he taught himself how to engrave, and turned his drawings into handsome engravings. The black-and-white prints looked fine, but needed colour to sell. He found that he could employ colourists cheaply, and supervised the painting of the first edition of printed plates. The results, extremely desirable, appeared in batches as *The Natural History of Carolina, Georgia, Florida and the Bahama Islands* between 1730 and 1747. They were a hit, and its pages are still much sought after.

The work eventually comprised two large folio volumes, with 220 of Catesby's own vivid engravings, all hand-coloured and complemented by descriptions in Latin and observations in English and in French. The plates are lovely, combining plants and creatures in a naive way that gives them great charm. The same year that Catesby completed his massive undertaking, he also married Elizabeth Rowland, a widow with a grown daughter. He died just two years later in 1749, leaving two children and almost no money. His unfortunate widow was forced to sell the plates and the remaining copies of his book as her sole inheritance. Nevertheless, thanks to Catesby, the American garden was truly under way.

Any emerging fashion, such as the one for American plants, whets entrepreneurs' appetites. In London, nurseries began to specialize. Auction rooms began to sell off consignments of new arrivals. This frenzy reached its highest pitch a few decades later, fuelled by some extraordinary collectors.

There were, of course, many botanists and plant collectors working in the United States in the mid-1700s: men such as John Clayton, Alexander Garden (after whom *Gardenia* was named, although it is not an American plant), John Mitchell and the splendidly named Cadwallader Colden. However, John Bartram

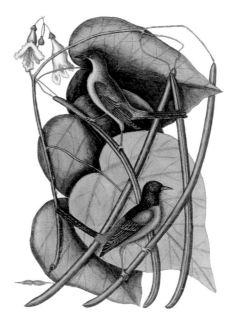

Another of Catesby's 1726 introductions, the catalpa (*Catalpa bignonioides*) thrived in London gardens.

(1699–1777), a modest farmer, was by far the most energetic, and ultimately by far the most influential. Indeed, he founded something of a plant dynasty, and his son is gradually coming to be seen as even more influential in the story of American natural history.

The Bartrams, an English Quaker family, came from the bleak hills of Derbyshire in northern England. John's grandfather followed the colonialist William Penn to the New World, and started farming as soon as he arrived there in the early 1680s. John's father, William, prospered too. John was his second son. John's mother died when he was two, but his father soon remarried. He set out in 1709, with his new wife, to start a farm in North Carolina. His first two sons were left behind in Pennsylvania in the care of their grandmother. This was fortunate for them. Shortly, Indians raided the North Carolina property, killing and scalping John's father, and taking his stepmother and her two children into captivity. Though she and her children were later ransomed, she seems to have disappeared from John Bartram's life. The young John and the original Bartram farm continued to be looked after by his tough and tyrannical grandmother, and he grew up a most unlikely explorer. He was timid and fearful, often in poor health, and terrified of thunderstorms, an unhelpful fear he retained as an adult. Set free on his grandmother's death, he inherited a well-run farm of several hundred acres. He soon showed that he was a good and imaginative farmer. He advocated the drainage of local marshes. He advocated copying the local use of oyster shells as crop fertilizers, used red clover as a ley and wanted the young state to replant its already vanishing woodlands to replenish timber. Indeed, he was an early 'green'. He also took an interest in child rearing, especially with regard to their diet and control. For the latter, he advocated the use of love, not fear.

Before long, he had become a man of consequence in the local community, and counted as friends many of the leading citizens of Philadelphia, including Benjamin Franklin. It was an exciting time. Bartram even played a part in founding the American Philosophical Society in 1743, an organization that still exists, and is still based in its original handsome eighteenth-century house. The Society was soon to have a considerable effect on the American garden in Europe when it helped finance the collector André Michaux to explore vast areas of North America.

It was the American flora that eventually placed John Bartram at the centre of the scientific world. 'I had always since ten years old, a great inclination to plants, and knew all that I once observed by sight, though not their proper names, having no person nor books to instruct me,' he wrote to Peter Collinson in 1764. Bartram's son William believed that his father's interest in plants derived from his recourse to the use of Indian herbal medicines to treat neighbours who were too poor to go to even the cheapest Philadelphia doctors. However, few botanists or plant collectors have any real knowledge of quite why they are fascinated by plants. Bartram began his botanical travels, in the central and southern regions of North America, to get over a great sadness: his first wife's death from an unidentified epidemic in 1727. Once home again, in the following year, he bought a small house and 107 acres of land in Kingsessing on the bank of the Schuylkill River, about three miles from Philadelphia. He remarried and began a major expansion of the house. In a five-acre plot of ground between his new house and the river, Bartram began to make a botanical garden with his newly collected plants. It was soon famous, and often called the first in America, although in fact the city already had a few others. His, certainly, is the only one to survive to the present day.

Eighteenth-century networking gave Bartram the break he needed. Among his friends in Pennsylvania was a Joseph Breintnall. This gentleman had had the clever idea that, instead of pressing plant leaves for herbarium specimens, he would use the fresh material as a printing block to make 'plant impressions'. These allowed several impressions of a leaf to be created before the distortions made by pressing it as a herbarium specimen. It was a 'craft' idea already popular among middle-class ladies. Bartram had been finding Breintnall interesting plants to print, and Breintnall had sent a copy of his prints to the insatiable Peter Collinson in London. Collinson was entranced, and at once latched on to Bartram. Bartram was soon deluged with letters, many enclosing European garden plants and European gardening books, as well as advice, encouragement and money, all sent by Collinson in the hope of receiving new American plants.

Whenever he could take time from his farming duties, Bartram went into the wild, collecting plants for his new English patron and himself. He would ride, head down like most botanists, through America's virgin territories, often in places still unvisited by any white man. Sometimes he travelled alone. Sometimes he used a little-documented sort of folk as guides and translators: white men and women who had been captured by Indians and who had enthusiastically embraced their way of life.

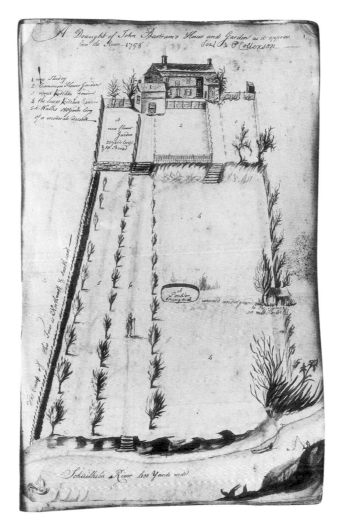

This plan of John Bartram's house and garden in Pennsylvania, drawn by William Bartram in 1758, shows the modest plots where he grew American species, as well as plants sent to him from Europe by Philip Miller and Peter Collinson.

Word of Bartram's collecting spread in Europe, and Collinson, always the entrepreneur, was soon acting as Bartram's agent. Influential patrons poured in, including Philip Miller from the Chelsea Physic Garden and Sir Hans Sloane. There were grandees too, among them three earls and four dukes, even Queen Ulrica of Sweden. Linnaeus himself called Bartram 'the greatest natural botanist in the world'. It was an amazing state of affairs for a modest Pennsylvania farmer. Through Collinson's persistent lobbying of the Duke of Northumberland and others, Bartram's scientific labours received official recognition when he was appointed botanist to George III in 1765. The post's stipend of fifty pounds enabled Bartram to make a long-hoped-for collecting expedition 'to the Floridas', which had come under British dominion in 1763. Accompanied by his son William, he travelled through what is now North and South Carolina, Georgia and Florida. Ultimately, he was responsible for the introduction of between 150 and 200 new American plant species into Europe.

Not all the plants he sent to Europe were of his own discovery. The witch alder was first discovered in the Carolinas by Alexander Garden but Bartram introduced it into European gardens. Bartram suggested that this plant should be named *Gardenia*. It ended up being named *Fothergilla*, after Collinson's associate John Fothergill. Similarly, the gorgeous *Celtis occidentalis* had been first introduced by John Tradescant the Younger in the previous century, but had never established itself in Britain. Plants from Bartram did, and they caused great excitement.

James Logan, a wealthy Pennsylvanian, felt that Collinson was exploiting Bartram. Bartram only managed to scratch a living from the land and really needed proper patronage. He failed to find that himself, but Linnaeus had asked Logan to study pollen in American plants, and as Logan was too busy, he hoped that Bartram would help out. There was a squabble, for Collinson was concerned that this would draw Bartram's attention away from collecting new garden plants. He needn't have worried. Bartram was a collector not a scientist. In any case, the Bartram–Collinson network was soon to be disrupted by the War of Independence. By its end, in 1781, the whole group were either dead or too old for collecting. John Bartram had died in 1777, apparently killed by worrying about the fate of his garden as the English troops approached. In the event, nothing happened to it.

Both the American and the French Revolutions, as well as the huge political and social changes that they enabled, had a tremendous impact on the garden. Not only did they augment the development of the American garden in Europe, but they had a profound effect on how Americans viewed their own gardens, and their own flora.

Another of the plant collectors who fuelled European frenzy for American plants, and who became embroiled in both upheavals, was the Frenchman André Michaux. He was born at Satory, near Versailles, in 1746. Like Bartram, his father was a farmer, a tenant on the King's estates. The young Michaux at first followed in his father's footsteps. Like Bartram, he was plainly a talented and energetic young man, and, via various strokes of good fortune, eventually began to study botany under the eminent botanist Bernard de Jussieu. Well set on a good career, at twenty-three he married Cecile Claye. Then, just as with Bartram, something terrible happened: his beloved wife of eleven months died soon after the birth of their son. He chose to travel as soon as his son was old enough to understand his father's decision. Working by now at the Jardin du Roi in Paris, he set out under its auspices in February 1782. He was going to Persia. As with all his later travels, there seems to have been some element of politics and espionage. This time he was officially part of the entourage of Jean François Rousseau, recently appointed consul at Teheran.

It was a hazardous journey, crossing the stormy Mediterranean Sea in winter, journeying by camel caravan across whistling deserts and facing brushes with brigands and hostile tribes. Michaux soon left his nominal boss to attend to his own affairs. Setting a pattern that was to last through his life, he travelled alone, still sometimes a risky business in the Middle East. Captured by local Bedouins, he was robbed of his horse and his clothing, and left naked in the desert. Half dead, he was rescued by the English consul at Basra. In poor shape after the incident, he nursed himself back to health, and passed the time compiling the first

French–Persian dictionary. Later, he cured the Shah of an illness that no court physicians could cure. He explored the ancient garden traditions of Persia and sent back reports to Paris that were filled with excitement. He had found his vocation.

He spent the next three years in the Middle East, finding new bulbs, new daphnes and oleanders, and collecting some of the ancient garden roses of Shiraz. He sent back local sorts of camellia, mimosa, pomegranates and olives. Among the hundreds of wild plants he brought back with him to France in 1785 was a new genus of perennials, now named *Michauxia* as a tribute to him. Still restless, he was unable to settle anywhere. Then, a remarkable opportunity arose. The French navy was desperate for timber. As elsewhere in Europe, the forests of France had been decimated by the immense need for wood during the long naval war with England. France had built fleet after fleet and was running out of building materials. Looking to America to supply species that might more swiftly replenish French forests, the government cast around for a suitable collector. Michaux was introduced to Thomas Jefferson, the Secretary of State, who was then in Paris.

Michaux was employed to visit America as a plant prospector. His first duty was to find new American trees and to send home wood samples of new species to be tested for strength, durability and utility. He was also to look for American species and varieties that would enrich French orchards, fields and gardens and to import French plants to America; it was thought that American gardeners might favour France over England if they liked French plants. Thus botany merged with political ends; he was to travel as a diplomat as well as a botanist. Ironically, although he was sent out by order of the King of France, France would espouse American ideals sooner and more violently than anyone could have foreseen, and Michaux would become Citoyen Michaux, working for an even newer republic. Together with his young son François, Michaux reached New York on 13 November 1785, only a year after the new Congress had ratified the peace treaty with England. They travelled at once to Philadelphia and presented letters of introduction to William Bartram. Exciting things like new liquidambars, tulip trees and American oaks were soon dispatched to the Jardin du Roi.

Wanting to experiment with sending young plants, rather than seeds, home to France Michaux realized that he needed nursery ground in which to rear them. Though the new Republic forbade foreigners from owning American soil, a special act was passed in 1786 by the New Jersey legislature to allow Michaux to buy about ten acres in Bergen (now Hudson) County, New Jersey. Clearly, the diplomatic aspect of Michaux's appointment was working as well as the horticultural one. The only stipulation was that the land be used solely for the purposes of a botanical garden. Today it is part of the Hoboken Cemetery.

Michaux didn't take long, though, to realize how rich the American flora was further south. The climate there was so different that he needed another garden for his young plants. This time the garden he purchased, in 1786, was almost the size of a farm, containing more than a hundred acres of land near Charleston, South Carolina. There was one difficulty. Few French ships docked at Charleston harbour, and so plants bound for France had to be shipped to New York first. Transit times were longer, and plant survival was inevitably reduced.

The new southern garden was also to store plants from France; American gardens could soon boast mimosas, silk trees (*Albizia julibrissin*), the crape myrtle (*Lagerstroemia indica*), the tea plant and other camellias. Some of his introductions still survive, among them an ancient camellia tree, still growing at the beautiful plantation Middleton Place, and now gradually being propagated.

However, these introductions were as nothing to the flow in the other direction. He found new magnolias in the Carolina Piedmont and Tennessee. A species he named *Magnolia macrophylla* created a sensation in France. (Empress Josephine was among the first to have this new glory in her garden.) He found new oaks, maples and rhododendrons. During his eleven years in America, he shipped upwards of 60,000 living trees and thousands of seed collections, first to the Royal Nurseries, and, after the fall of the Bastille, to the National Nurseries.

The political turmoil in France handicapped Michaux in America. To help offset his difficult financial state, members of the American Philosophical Society promised him backing in 1793. He had to agree to mount a western expedition that would take him across the Mississippi River, across the vast state of Louisiana, and to the headwaters of rivers on the far side of the Rockies that flowed to the Pacific. America was wanting to explore its own vast flora. As Secretary of State, Thomas Jefferson drew up the proposals and subscription lists. The list of subscribers included George Washington, Alexander Hamilton, John Adams, James Madison and Jefferson himself, as well many other less famous men. By this time, Michaux was clearly an ardent republican. On 30 August 1794, on the slopes of Grandfather Mountain, North Carolina, he jubilantly recorded in his diary: 'Reached the summit of the highest mountain in North America. . . . I sang the Marseillaise and shouted, "Long live America and the Republic of France! Long live liberty!"' Sometimes he took his enthusiasm to extremes: while nearly starving on one of his wilderness expeditions, he refused a meal from a frontier settler, a royalist, who insulted the new French Republic. Michaux wrote in his diary that he preferred to go hungry another night and to sleep on his deerskin than in the bed of a fanatical opponent.

Although he failed to make it over the Rockies, he eventually travelled over much of the continent, often making friends with Indians, especially the Cherokee, whom he liked and admired, and whose language he learnt. Travelling was hard. On rivers, his skiffs and birch bark canoes were often swamped and overturned. Horses died, got lost or were stolen. He was often ill with fevers and mysterious infections; often he nearly starved. His son was partially blinded in a gun accident, and was sent back to France. His journals hardly mention any of this, often merely noting 'Gathered seed', 'Prepared seed for shipping' or 'Shipped eleven hundred and sixty-eight seeds and plants'.

He sent home a huge haul of rhododendrons, azaleas, magnolias, many great American trees, asters, lilies, bignonias, twenty-seven species of maple, balsam poplars, agaves, oconee bells (*Shortia galacifolia*), the yellow wood or virgilia (*Cladrastis lutea*), mountain stewartia (*Stewartia ovata*). In Europe, the gorgeous riches of America seemed inexhaustible.

Such was the fashion for the 'American garden' now, that there was a huge market for almost anything green from America. Ironically, Michaux was sometimes dogged by it. He wrote on one trip that he was being shadowed by a Scotsman called John Fraser. 'Since Mr Fraser took his last passage to England, Myself and my Son have promised for him at the Time approved of 4,000 plants of the Rhododendron chiefly of the Scarlet flowering Species and blue and red, and white & red speckled flowering Species . . . 1000 Magnolias & other plants.' Fraser was collecting for the London market, following Michaux around America so that he would not miss anything special.

Michaux returned to France in 1796, but it was a difficult homecoming. The ocean passage had gone easily, and the ship was in sight of the Belgian coastline, when the breeze turned to wind, and the wind to gale. They were in the middle of a terrible storm. His boat, the *Ophir*, soon foundered and broke up. Michaux was swept away and nearly drowned. Unconscious, he was pulled ashore, tied to a floating spar. Boxes of plant specimens were salvaged too. Journals, and every single living plant, were lost. Undaunted, in a day or two, he began drying his collection, and was soon on the road to Paris.

André Michaux (above) rose from 'simple farmer to a name among learned men' according to the Marquis de Lafayette.

Once there, he found that the vast majority of the living plants he had shipped to France over the past eleven years had perished during the revolution and its aftermath. Although he was a revolutionary hero, there was no salary to pay him. Among these disappointments, he was at least reunited with his now fully grown son. François had trained as a physician but shared his father's passion for botany, which was one day to take him to America too.

Though André rejoined the staff of the newly named Jardin des Plantes, and began working on, and publishing, his herbarium collections, he didn't settle. A monograph of the oaks of North America and the vast and important *Flora Boreali-Americana* (1803) did not bring in enough money to keep him. Travelling light had caught his soul. He wanted new countries, new continents if possible. Australia beckoned.

He soon found the opportunity to join an exploring expedition to the South Seas sponsored by the French government under the command of one Captain Nicolas Baudin. François was detailed to oversee the publication of his manuscripts and Michaux left France for the last time in 1800. Things at once began to go wrong. Baudin proved to be at least half mad, and led a ship almost constantly on the verge of mutiny. Michaux was unable to bear it, and left the expedition when it dropped anchor off Madagascar. The island has a unique flora, and Michaux was fascinated. He planned extensive collections and another nursery garden, and built himself a primitive shack. Then, in November 1802, he died, perhaps of malaria, perhaps not. Mysteriously, neither his notes nor his plant specimens were ever found.

The man who had kept crossing Michaux's path, carefully watching what he found, was John Fraser (1750–1811). He was born in Scotland, but moved to London as a young man. Starting life as a mercer, plants caught him, and he switched businesses in the 1780s to become a nurseryman, with a shop in Sloane Square, Chelsea. He was also smitten with an urge to travel and collect. Proposing a journey to Newfoundland, he was astonished to find funding from the Chelsea Physic Garden and the Linnean Society. Still surprised, he found himself in northern North America between 1780 and 1784. At that time the region was still British, but he soon realized that the flora was far richer further south. By 1785, he deemed it possible for a Scotsman to travel in the still anti-British republic, and headed south in the same year that Michaux sailed to America from France.

Fraser had developed a new technique for transporting young plants, packing them with wet moss. Michaux should have copied him, for almost all of Fraser's stock survived the return to England in 1788. He sold the plants off very profitably, and was back in the south-eastern United States on three other trips between 1788 and 1796. By then Russia was also gripped by the American garden fashion, so he took stock to St Petersburg, where he sold the whole lot to the Empress Catherine for an impressive sum. She died the next year, but the new Tsar and Tsarina, Paul I and Maria, appointed him their botanical collector. Fraser returned to America with a royal commission from the Tsar. By now, he was accompanied by his son, also named John. Together they tramped or rode across the wetlands of Carolina, finding dangers and new plants. Disguised as Americans, they even explored mountainous Cuba, then Spanish. Although their ruse was discovered, the Spanish governor allowed them to travel freely explaining, 'My country, it is true, is at war with England, but not so with the pursuits of these travellers.'

The elder John Fraser's collecting activities were curtailed when he suffered broken ribs and other injuries in an accident with his horse early in 1810. He died the following year. His son formed another nursery, devoted to the American flora, in Kent. He called it 'The Hermitage'. Father and son are commemorated in the Fraser fir (*Abies fraseri*) and Fraser magnolia (*Magnolia fraseri*). Their most important legacy, however, was the introduction of a plant that would allow the American garden to evolve into something much more colourful, and more suitable for small gardens. Michaux had been the first to find it, but had not managed to get it back to Europe. In flower it was extraordinary, with trusses of bell-shaped flowers five to six inches across, each flower with five petals joined together at the base, olive green spots on their inner surfaces. When in full fig, the bushes were an almost solid sheet of intense rosy red. First called the mountain rosebay, botanists named it *Rhododendron catawbiense*. By 1809, every gardener in the country wanted it. More surprisingly, it turned out to cross happily with other rhododendrons growing in the American garden. There were soon hundreds of new varieties, referred to as catawbiense hybrids. They were extremely hardy, and for that reason were called ironclads. Flower colours ranged from creamy white and pink through crimson to deep, bluish purple. Though the form and flower colour and shape of the ironclads were rather limited, they brought some showy glitter to the gloomy depths of most American gardens. The enthusiasm for them was vast, and inspired gardeners to slip into their American gardens the occasional rhododendron from other lands.

These rhododendrons were introduced by Joseph Dalton Hooker, whom we will meet properly in Chapter Seven. His contribution to the development of the American garden started with the third of his four Indian trips. He arrived at Calcutta in January 1848, too early in the season to think of going into the mountains. Instead, he joined a Geological Survey group going off to Sulkun, south of the River Ganges. There he hired some elephants, whom he trained to pick flowers for him, and in some style travelled to Mirzapur on the Ganges. He reached Darjeeling in April. He liked the place, so often wrapped in what he called a 'dear, delightful, double-distilled Greenock fog'. Even so, he was there longer than he wanted, as his aim was to go into the Himalayan kingdom of Sikkim, then under British control, but he was held up by political difficulties. However, he soon found that the local region had some astonishing *Rhododendron* species.

Once he got to Sikkim, he began to send home drawings and descriptions of his finds, to be published as *Rhododendrons of the Sikkim-Himalaya* (1849). It was a revelation of the glories of the genus, and included species such as *Rhododendron campylocarpum*, *R. ciliatum*, the glorious *R. cinnabarinum*, *R. falconeri*, *R. griffithianum*, *R. maddenii* and *R. thomsonii*. The gardening world fell in love with them, and planted them in their American gardens, where, in suitably wet conditions, they thrived. As soon as they began to flower, hybridizers, finding that American and Indian rhododendrons crossed with great abandon, got to work. By the end of the 1850s, there were huge numbers of astonishing new hybrids.

These hybrids coincided with an equally huge economic boom. Gardeners with wallets stuffed with new money and heads stuffed with romantic ideas culled from Walter Scott's novels bought themselves Scottish or Cornish estates. The high rainfall, frequent mist and mild air of these oceanic regions was hopelessly unsuited to the gaudy splendour of the popular 'bedding garden', all pelargoniums and verbenas (see Chapter Four). But it perfectly suited tree species from Columbia and Oregon. It also perfectly suited the new rhododendron cultivars pouring forth from nurseries such as Waterer's and Hillier's. The American garden evolved swiftly into the magnate's garden, a mix of evergreens shading a brilliant riot of 'rhodos', a sort of garden still widely admired and sometimes even still copied. The magnate's garden, many examples of which are still in existence, all garishly colourful, became one of the standard modes of gardening for the rest of the century. Surprisingly, no designer emerged to tell the magnates how to plant them. There are still huge acreages of terrifying colour clashes as hundreds of gaudy rhododendrons compete to dazzle the onlooker.

Seeing that the Frasers were making money out of America, other men tried to copy them. Some had terrible times. John Lyon, another Scot, collected, though he didn't discover, the handsome Franklin tree, which became hugely popular in European gardens, though not British ones. Indeed, he may have seen the species' last natural stand. In a journal entry for 1 June 1803, after a five-day trip into the backwoods of Savannah, Georgia, where he found

A sketch from Joseph Dalton Hooker's *Himalayan Journals* (1854), showing his famous rhododendrons in the wild.

some Franklin trees, he wrote: 'It is sufficiently remarkable that this plant has never been found growing naturally in any other part of the United States as far as I can learn, and here there is not more then 6 or 8 full grown trees of it which does not spread over more than half an acre of ground, the seed has most probably been brought there originally from a great distance by a Bird of passage.' He may then have proceeded to dig them up. Certainly, he brought vast amounts of greenery over from America for auction in London. The Scottish gardening writer John Claudius Loudon reported in 1838 that:

He brought an extensive collection to England; the plants composing which were partly disposed of by private account, but were chiefly sold by auction in a garden at Parsons' Green, Fulham. The catalogue of these plants fills 34 closely printed pages, it enumerates 550 lots, and the sale occupied four days. Several of the lots were composed of large quantities of one-year-old seedlings in pots; and ten lots at the end of the sale consisted of fifty different sorts of seeds each. This, it is believed, was by far the greatest collection of American trees and shrubs ever brought to England at one time, by one individual.

Poor Carolina was getting stripped bare.

Though Lyon made money from his collecting, it wasn't easy. On one trip, he was bitten by a mad dog. Alone, he had himself to sear the three punctures in his leg with a burning-hot iron. Sometimes his horse went astray and he was forced to travel on foot. Many times he lost his way. Finally, in 1814, he came down with a fever in the North Carolina mountains and died.

However passionate these collectors were about America and its plants, they were all rooted in the world of human affections and relationships. They accepted the difficulties of travelling as necessities to be endured in the pursuit of that passion. The strangest story of all and, in terms of the plants that resulted from it, the most extraordinary, belonged to another sort of man, someone angry and affectionless who welcomed every punishment that an untamed continent could provide.

In 1799, a grim, humourless and violent stonemason in the village of Scone, in Perthshire, had a second son born to him. The child, christened David, was soon willing to take on his ogre-like Goliath of a father. David's mother, frightened for his safety, packed him off to the village school at the age of three to keep him out of harm's way. The young David Douglas's hatred of authority was already set; he was intensely disruptive and expelled a few years later. At his next school, regular thrashings with tawse did little to affect his resistance. However, he developed a consuming passion for natural history at that time. He left school when ten years old, and went as apprenticed gardener's boy to Lord Mansfield's garden at Scone Palace. Almost as soon as he had completed his training, he began to prosper. In 1818 he moved to Sir Robert Preston's estate at Valleyfield on the Firth of Forth. Preston, sensing the promise of the young man, gave him free access to his library. In 1820, he obtained a job at the new Glasgow Botanic Garden, and went to the thrilling botany lectures being given by Joseph Dalton Hooker's charismatic father, William Jackson Hooker, who was its Regius Keeper. He prospered there too and was plainly on the move.

Rhododendron thomsonii, the parent of many important hybrids, as depicted in Hooker's *Himalayan Journals*.

The passion for American plants was then at its height. When Joseph Sabine, the secretary of the Horticultural Society of London, was looking for a collector in 1823, Hooker senior, who seems to have been a perceptive and kindly mentor, suggested David Douglas. The young man sailed for London, spent a bare three months working in the Society's gardens at Chiswick, then set out on his first mission to America on 6 June.

This trip set a pattern of hardship. The voyage from Liverpool to New York took fifty-nine days. By the second week, all fresh water was rationed. Tobacco was so scarce that the crew used it twice: chewing it first time around, then drying it in the sun to make it smokable. Douglas was relieved to arrive in New York on 3 August. The aim of this first trip was to look for kitchen garden plants, so he spent much time at gardens and nurseries around New York and Philadelphia, making only one journey into the real backwoods.

He returned to England early in January 1824. Through the generosity of American nurserymen, he had with him a wide selection of new apple, pear, plum, peach, and grape varieties that had been developed in America. That kept the Horticultural Society happy. He also had plants of the Oregon grape (then *Berberis*, now *Mahonia aquifolium*) grown from seeds gathered by Meriwether Lewis and William Clark (see Chapter Eight). These created a sensation, and every gardener with even the smallest American garden had to have some.

The Horticultural Society realized that the dour young man really would make a plant collector, and it decided that he could be sent out again in its service. He was soon at sea once more, this time sailing towards great public acclaim. On 26 July 1824, he set out for

David Douglas made a vast contribution to European gardens. His finds included *Ribes sanguineum* and *Mahonia aquifolium*.

the Pacific coast of North America, not by going overland from New York, but sailing via the wild Cape Horn. The pioneering travellers Lewis and Clark had just finished exploring beyond the Rockies and found botanical riches. The Society was determined to tap those riches. The Pacific north-west clearly supported coniferous forests of a complexity and magnificence only made possible by the mild winters and colossal rainfall. This cool rainforest stretched unbroken from northern California, up through Oregon and Washington state, and on into British Columbia. Douglas was to be astonished by the sheer variety of cone-bearing trees, from cedars and pines, to hemlocks, spruces and firs.

It took him eight months to travel from Britain to the mouth of the Columbia River. If the journey had been terrible, Columbia was worse. At Cape Foul, the weather was awful. He was travelling along with some other Scots adventurers, when they found that their food supplies were beginning to run out. To save their porters, they sent them home. While they were bivouacking on a beach one night, the wind became a hurricane, whipping the waves so high that they had to move camp twice during the night to avoid being washed away. Their tents had long since blown down, and they had no protection from the storm other than wet blankets and a few pine branches. There was no food. The next day, they walked along the sandy beach for sixteen miles to a small deserted harbour. There was no food there either, and they had to resort to the roots of arrow-head (*Sagittaria*) and lupin. 'From continual exposure, I became much reduced,' Douglas noted. Starvation even reduced him to eating the berries and seeds he had collected, and his herbarium specimens were left behind as there was no one strong enough left to carry them.

The forests, though, were overwhelming. Douglas wrote that they were

grand beyond description; the high mountains in the neighbourhood, which are for the most part covered with pines of several species, some of which grow to an enormous size, are all loaded with snow; the rainbow from the vapour of the agitated waters, which rushes with furious rapidity over shattered rocks and deep caverns, producing an agreeable although at the same time a somewhat melancholy echo through the thick wooded valley; the reflections from the snow on the mountains, together with the vivid green of the gigantic pines, form a contrast of rural grandeur that can scarcely be surpassed.

The tree that most excited Douglas was the sugar pine (*Pinus lambertiana*), which reaches 250 feet in its native habitat and has cones 18 inches in length. He introduced this tree in 1827, together with the Douglas fir (*Pseudotsuga menziesii*), now one of Britain's tallest trees. The flora was so incredibly rich, and so beautiful, that he decided to extend his stay for a second season of collecting. Back in Britain, gardeners chafed impatiently to get hold of seed, though it turned out that many of his plants only did well on the mild west coast of the island, and especially on the west coast of Scotland.

But in the silent, eerie, green forests of Oregon, not all was going well for Douglas. He was beginning to have problems with his eyesight. He had had several harrowing brushes with Indians, renegades, wild animals and disease. He had suffered prolonged privations, quite often self-inflicted. He had had enough, and wanted to return to Britain. Rather than round Cape Horn again, he waited until late March of 1827 and joined a party of trappers making their way up to Hudson Bay. He must have been a picturesque figure; by now he was travelling with a live eagle caught for the London Zoological Society. He finally sailed home on an English whaler, triumphant but sick.

'Home' proved to be a mirage. Of course, honours awaited him. He was elected a fellow of the Horticultural Society but, oddly, he was only allowed to avoid paying fees and subscriptions for three years. He also became a fellow of those great London societies, the Linnean, the Zoological (who had got their eagle) and the Geological. Arrangements were made for his journal to be published. He was lionized, even asked to fashionable dinners and balls. Probably he never had been suited to that sort of life. He became discontented, ungracious, contemptuous and surly. None of these qualities was of use in the drawing room. His disgust had some cause. He found out that the salary he received from the Horticultural Society was lower than the one they were paying their doorman. Some of the animal skins he had collected, at great trouble, had been badly looked after, and were now quite ruined. He began to quarrel with almost everyone he came across, even those who could be most helpful to him. The only friend he seems to have made was a fiery Scots terrier, whom he named Billy.

It was soon clear that the wilds were the only place he could be, if not happy, then at least functional. He and those who had to deal with him were relieved when funds were put together, partly by the societies of which he was a fellow, to let him go off on another expedition to the west coast of America. The British Colonial Office had an interest. They wanted accurate maps of what was to become British Columbia. He was taught how to be a surveyor, and provided with all necessary equipment. He left Britain, the faithful and loving Billy by his side, in October 1829.

It took him eight months to reach Columbia again. His eyesight was getting worse. Old wounds ached, so he hired a rough, tough, deckhand to carry his equipment. His collecting trips were shorter than they used to be. Yet he could still hold out against a fever that wiped out whole Indian villages and twenty-four of a fur company's expedition, of which he was a part. He kept going by never giving in, treating himself badly by going on what he called 'healthful perambulations'.

At last, in late 1830, he was finished mapping. He paid off his servant, and set a course southwards. His list of provisions included shoes, shot, cod line, candles, ten pounds of tea, nine gallons of brandy, two large black silk handkerchiefs, a large moose skin and a jew's harp. He and Billy sailed to the milder south, to California. He'd never been anywhere like it. The spring was unbelievably beautiful. He immediately began to find wonderful plants, including the conifers *Garrya elliptica* with its astonishing catkins and the Monterey pine (*Pinus radiata*), and annuals such as wild heliotrope, blazing stars and Californian bluebells.

He sent duplicate specimens of much of his material on to St Petersburg, as Russian gardeners were as excited as those of London and Paris. The Tsar and the Russian governor of Alaska now wanted Douglas to botanize Alaska, Siberia and Russia before returning to Europe overland, a journey of 1,150 miles. He set off once more. By now he was completely blind in the right eye and had to wear smoked spectacles to protect the left. His temper was far worse; he quarrelled with a company trader, and had to refuse the offer of a duel. Seeing war parties of Indians ahead, he turned back, for the first time in his life, and disaster swiftly followed. Canoeing down the Frazer River, his party tried to shoot the rapids at Fort George Canyon. Douglas's bark canoe was gashed to shreds. He was swept off through the rocks and the foam, then carried into a whirlpool. He was there for an hour and forty minutes before he managed to scramble free. He lost a collection of 400 specimens of plants and his volume of field notes containing all his collector's information about what he'd found, and where. He was once again on the Columbia River, exhausted. He still had Billy.

He went south, eventually landing up at Honolulu. He did some desultory collecting, but realized that if a ship arrived that was bound for Britain, he would have to take it. One didn't come soon enough. During his voyage to the tropics he'd met a missionary who seemed to interest him. Douglas had said he'd show the man some of the sights of Hawaii. After all, it was a glorious place, and he had written of his exultation on climbing its volcanoes, 'one day there, is worth one year of common existence'. Their boat to the main island got becalmed before it reached their destination. Douglas, impatient, got himself put ashore, saying that he would go by foot overland to meet the missionary at the town of Hilo. He set off, carrying his own small bundle of clothes and collecting equipment, and stayed overnight at the house of a man named Davis. Early the next day, 12 July 1834, he called on an English ex-convict called Ned Gurney. Gurney warned him that the trail ahead was set with cattle traps: deep pits disguised with branches, leaves and earth, and often set with sharpened stakes.

A few hours later, two of Gurney's servants found that one of the traps had caught something. Inside, they found a wild bull, bucking and snorting with fear. Beneath the bull lay the gored body of a man. Beside the pit, a small black dog howled. There was eventually an investigation. It seemed impossible that Douglas could have failed to see the trap, even though he was partially blind. Some thought that Douglas' wounds were not caused by the bull. Some said he had quarrelled with Gurney. No conclusion was reached. Douglas, some of whose plants must be in almost every garden worldwide, and who had had a colossal impact not only on the American garden but on all gardens, left behind just fifty pounds, a bundle of plants he'd collected on the Sandwich Islands and Billy, who was sent back to England. Today, a simple memorial stands where Douglas died.

Overall, he introduced fifty species of tree and shrub, including *Abies grandis*, *A. procera*, *Picea sitchensis*, *Pinus radiata* and *Pseudotsuga menziesii*. Some, like the Douglas fir, the Sitka spruce and the Monterey pine, became important timber trees. The flowering currant (*Ribes sanguineum*) can be found in every garden centre. The snowberry (*Symphoricarpos albus*), on the other hand, has become a serious weed.

Douglas had not found everything that America had to offer. He had seen the coastal redwood (*Sequoia sempervirens*), a tree which he described as 'the great beauty of Californian vegetation . . . which gives the mountains a most peculiar, which I was almost going to say awful, appearance, something that tells us we are not in Europe'. But the greatest redwood – indeed the greatest of all the American trees – eluded him, and remained undiscovered for several decades.

In the summer of 1853, at a meeting of the recently established California Academy of Sciences, Albert Kellogg, an eminent local pharmacist and botanist, was giving a description of a strange giant conifer. He had recently been brought parts of it by a prospector called A.T. Dowd. In the audience was a stranger from England, a collector for the London Veitch nursery called William Lobb. Lobb dashed off in search of the fabulous tree. He stood, stunned, when he reached the area now called the Calaveras Grove. The trees towered 300 feet above him. Some had trunks 35 feet across. With his saddlebags packed with seeds, cones, even seedlings, he tore back to San Francisco and booked an immediate passage to England. He knew exactly what it was he had found – the ultimate tree for the ultimate American garden.

Two seedlings survived the journey, and rumour of this astonishing new plant soon spread. Seed was sown immediately and germinated quickly. By the summer of 1854 the Veitch nursery was offering seedlings for sale at the rate of two guineas each, six guineas for four or twelve guineas a dozen; eighteen months after Lobb had returned home, saplings of these potentially giant trees were being planted all across England. The plant was published in the *Gardeners' Chronicle* of 24 December 1853, under the name of *Wellingtonia gigantea*. Lobb's first-hand impressions made the front page. One can imagine astonished readers reading the article aloud to their nearest and dearest, at once wanting a young plant, for Lobb had written:

From 80 to 90 trees exist, all within the circuit of a mile, and these varying from 250 feet to 320 feet in height and from 10 to 20 feet in diameter. . . . A tree recently felled measured about 300 ft. in length with a diameter, including bark, 29 feet 2 inches at 5 feet from the ground; at 18 feet from the ground it was 14 feet; and at 200 feet from the ground, 5 feet 5 inches. . . . The trunk of the tree in question was perfectly solid, from the sap-wood to the centre; and judging from the number of concentric rings, its age has been estimated at 3000 years. . . . Of this vegetable monster, 21 feet of the bark, from the lower part of the trunk, have been put in the natural form in San Francisco for exhibition; it there forms a spacious carpeted room, and contains a piano, with seats for 40 persons. On one occasion 140 children were admitted without inconvenience. An exact representation of this tree, drawn on the spot, is now in the hands of the lithographers, and will be published in a few days.

'The mammoth tree grove in the Valley of the Calaveras': a plate from *Our Whole Country: the Past and Present, Historical and Descriptive* (1861) by Barber and Hare, showing the felling and tourism that sprang up after the discovery of *Sequoiadendron giganteum*.

With a sales pitch like this, how could any gardener resist its lure? The trees were, of course, a sensation everywhere. In California, the grove of giants became a tourist wonder. One hotel created a dance floor on the stump of a felled tree, and a bowling alley along a tree trunk. The bark of one tree was even shipped around Cape Horn for display in New York to feed the burgeoning American appetite for giant scale. The bark of another was shipped to London, and exhibited at the Crystal Palace at Sydenham. It must have added considerably to the heat when that building burned down in December 1866.

Fortunately, for such an amazing plant, the dawn redwood – as the tree came to be called – was, and remains, very liberal with its seed. One entrepreneur shipped a snuffbox full of seed to George Ellwanger's nursery business, Ellwanger & Barry, at the Mount Hope Nursery in Rochester, New York. The collector paid twenty-five dollars' shipping, but eventually got well over a thousand dollars back. The nursery raised thousands of seedlings, and shipped them to nurserymen throughout Europe. The dawn redwood is now widespread in Europe, whether as single specimens dwarfing country cottage or rectory gardens, or as whole avenues making an impact on the biggest of estates. Incidentally, Kellogg wanted to call the plant *Washingtonia*. However, a botanist called Buchholz seems to have been first into print, and, sadly, even *Wellingtonia* had to fall to the earlier *Sequoiadendron* – which does, however, have the merit of showing the tree's relationship to other huge redwoods growing in the same region.

Most of the redwoods were perfect for the American garden as then constituted. Mostly growing in a 500-mile region of wet, fog-drenched forest along the Pacific coast, from northern California and south-westernmost Oregon, they grew especially well in the wet western parts of Scotland. The new giant preferred hot, dry summers, and was much better suited to eastern Britain and mainland Europe. In their native land, most were felled for fence posts, vineyard stakes, roof shingles, and general building. Lobb must have watched his trees' destruction sorrowfully when, in later life, he returned to San Francisco to live.

It is surprising that, in spite of the American excitement about the tree, gardeners there did not seem keen to grow it, as big collections of native plants were springing up, initially in the eastern states. Bartram's son continued to collect native plants for his father's garden. Although he collected whatever attracted him, he was most interested in plants that had pharmacological uses in the Native American culture. Another member of Bartram's family, Humphry Marshal (1723–1801), farmer and stonemason, established what was to become another celebrated botanical garden. He also wrote about plants, and his *Arbustum Americanum: The American Grove or an Alphabetical Catalogue of Forest Trees and Shrubs, Natives of the American United States* (1785) was eagerly read by owners of American gardens in Europe, as well as many gardeners in North America.

The greatest early collection in America was at The Woodlands, the 300-acre estate of William Hamilton, on the banks of the Schuylkill River. Unlike the nearby Bartram gardens, The Woodlands was decidedly patrician, landscaped in the European manner. Hamilton liked all sorts of plants, and while there was every American plant he could lay hands on, he imported plants from Europe too, and had the largest collection of foreign shade and fruit trees in the country. Some of his imported trees, such as the Lombardy poplar and the Norway maple, eventually became important throughout America.

Following its discovery by the Lewis and Clark expedition, a nurseryman from Philadelphia, Bernard M'Mahon, sold the Oregon grape (*Mahonia aquifolium*). This quite modest plant soon became wildly fashionable, and he got staggering prices for it. By 1825, the Prince Nursery of Flushing, New York was charging twenty-five dollars each. Other New York nursery gardens such as Mount Hope soon followed. Indeed, the establishment of nurseries and seed merchants near the fast-expanding cities of America developed alongside awareness of the riches of the American flora. The American garden had at last arrived in America.

THE BEDDING
GARDEN

We are at Mr Stevens' splendid auction rooms at 38 King Street, Covent Garden, London, on a misty Thursday afternoon in October 1825. Thursday is plant day. Going under the hammer in an hour or two will be a large collection of lemon and orange trees, and dozens of their relatives. Many of the finer plants, especially some of the rare 'Hand of Buddha' lemon trees, have long been coveted by a number of knowledgeable London gardeners.

This room has recently seen collections of auriculas, orchids, recently imported oriental chrysanthemums, 'Indian' azaleas and florists' tulips going for a good price. Over the next few decades, the room will play an influential role in garden development, seeing, for instance, in 1861, the auctioning of the first consignment of ten bushels of monkey puzzle tree seed just arrived directly from Chile.

The owner of the lemon trees, fallen on hard times, is hoping for a good price, so he has ensured that catalogues of his collection have been placed in the hands of two rival ladies, both with fine gardens and fine glasshouses, who might well compete for some of the more delectable specimens. He has also ensured that many of their friends are present.

The rival ladies are the Dowager Duchess of Bedford and Lady Grenville. Their quarrel is already two seasons old and started on a warm afternoon in the spring of 1823. The grander of the two had noted with impatience the increasing fame of a nearby garden and decided to make a visit. To ensure that she had an expert on hand, she brought along her head gardener, John Caie. Lady Grenville's splendid gardens were at Dropmore Lodge, in Buckinghamshire. Her husband

A spectacular eighteenth-century planting scheme at the Trianon Palace, Versailles, showing how various sorts of plants were grown intermixed. By 1823, Lady Grenville was doing it very differently.

was William Grenville, now baron, and younger brother to the Marquess of Buckingham. Described by contemporaries as astonishingly handsome, he was also 'cold and unbending, even to great people'. Perhaps that was why his wife, very much younger and very much richer, had taken to gardening so much.

Lady Grenville specialized in the new 'rustic' style, a chic development of the 'picturesque' mode of gardening. This itself was a reaction away from the chaste smoothness of the classical English landscape garden style. But this was not what the Duchess wanted to see. Lady Grenville was especially famous for constructing rustic flower baskets out of garden and household detritus. These were said, by catty contemporaries, to be very beautiful, albeit very numerous. However, neither these floral baskets, nor the marvellous roses and rare trees, were the reason for the Duchess's visit. What she wanted to see was Lady Grenville's remarkable new way of planting flowers. In Mr Caie's pocket was a notebook.

The 'landscape' mode of gardening familiar to the Duchess, and splendidly displayed in her garden at Bedford Lodge, hardly allowed for flowers. Grass, smooth or shaggy depending on whether the garden was meant to be 'classical' or 'picturesque', surrounded all her houses. Most of the colour was banished to out-of-the-way places, very frequently the kitchen garden. Yet new flowers had been pouring into European gardens from the Americas and from Asia for much of the previous century. The Duchess and most of her contemporaries were desperate to grow them, but had nowhere to put them where they could easily be seen. When Lady Grenville, in exasperation, cut some large circles out of the lawn in front of her drawing-room windows, and filled them with scarlet bergamots, blue salvias or yellow cosmos, she broke a century's taboo, and started a colossal new movement.

By the time of the ladies' meeting in King Street, it had become clear to the gardening world that the Duchess's gardener, Mr Caie, had not only taken detailed notes of the revolutionary new flower beds at Dropmore Lodge, but had copied them at Bedford Lodge. He was even beginning to claim that the new way of planting flowers had been invented by him, and that Lady Grenville and her gardener Philip Frost were the plagiarists.

The Duchess, catalogue in hand, made a grand entry into Mr Stevens' auction room. Lady Grenville was already there. The entire room turned to watch. The great lady paused for a moment, imagining that the lesser one would not dare to do anything untoward. Lady Grenville at once turned her back on the greater woman and went to look at the plants. From the astonished bystanders, there was a sharp intake of breath.

At least, that's my story. There is, alas, no evidence that these two ladies really met in this way. Mr Stevens' auction room was real, and the two women, also real, did indeed have a quarrel about who originated the new way of planting flowers. It was important. When whichever spade first cut the turf at whichever garden, it was a defining moment. At one thrust, gardening was returned to all ranks of gardeners. The dull green grandeur of Le Nôtre and Brown was finally laid to rest. All the precious and convoluted theorizing about canons of chaste beauty, about the picturesque or the gardenesque, were sliced through like a Gordian tangle of worms. It was as if, through that first cut, gushed a vast arterial rainbow of flowers. The brilliant deluge was to wash away the chaste landscape garden, all greens, greys, misty blues. A moment later, it washed away the shaggy greenery of the picturesque. In its undisciplined exuberance, it made pompous marble temples and pavilions or faked-up cottages look as foolish and empty as they themselves had once made Chinoiserie pagodas and Gothick towers seem trivial and silly.

The gaudy tide of flowers swept over every country garden and through every city plot and poured out of London, taking over Paris in a season, New York and St Petersburg only a season or two after that. In a riot of cut-out stars and ribbons, plaited guilloches of colour, copies of parterres and magical Persian carpets, it greedily embraced the thousands of new flowers pouring into European gardens. At one moment the flood spawned strange pyramids of begonias and lobelias, at another, borders with drifts of asters and Japanese anemones. In some gardens, plaster Matterhorns arose as rock gardens far gaudier than Nature can ever have intended. Sometimes, it produced gardens that approached the heights of civilized taste, and sometimes it produced some of the most ghastly.

And what new flowers they were: brilliant annuals from the dry lands of Texas and Mexico; verbenas and petunias and a host of other half-hardy

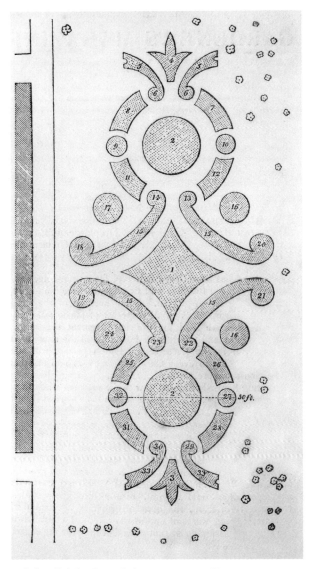

John Caie's plan of the parterre at Dropmore Lodge. Beds contained single sorts of verbena, lobelia, cineraria or pelargonium.

tropical roadside weeds from Brazil and Chile; geraniums from the veldts and mountainsides of South Africa, and echeverias and strange succulents from its deserts. They were all pouring into London, Paris, Stockholm and St Petersburg almost at the same moment as Lady Grenville was handed a perfectly polished spade.

The year of my fictional meeting of the Duchess and Lady Grenville, 1825, saw a real event that, over the next few decades, further fuelled its brilliance. It began in Glasgow, in that autumn, as a last mooring rope hissed across the greasy cobbles of the quay, and slipped into the murky greenness of the River Clyde. A ship began its journey out to sea. On board, watching his ungrateful homeland sliding away, was John Tweedie, gardener. He was bound for Buenos Aires. Already fifty, and something of a disappointed and frustrated man, he must have been unaware that he was also bound for at least one of the varieties of immortality.

Some of the plants he was soon to send home from South America would dominate the astonishing changes in gardening allowed by Lady Grenville's cut in the grass. Indeed, in 1850, the Duchess's gardener, Mr Caie – still trying to establish his old employer and himself as the great experts on flower bedding – published detailed planting plans of the flower beds at Bedford Lodge. For the summer plantings, and probably unwittingly, he chose flowers taken almost entirely from Tweedie's astonishing new South American material.

Although he became one of the most important collectors of Brazilian and Argentinian plants, Tweedie was not alone. There were hundreds of other plant collectors scattered over the globe also sending plants back to Europe. Some were searching for commercial products. Others were travelling for purely scientific ends. Most, though, were collecting new plants to assuage ordinary gardeners' almost frantic desire. It was no longer just the wealthy who wanted to collect them. Everyone with access to a piece of ground wanted the latest chrysanthemum from China, or the latest calceolaria from Chile. It was a huge revolution. Working-class gardeners, who had for a century or two largely populated the old florists' societies specializing in breeding plants that had been in the sixteenth-century wave of Turkish and Persian flowers, especially tulips, hyacinths, pinks and anemones, took up new introductions every bit as quickly as dukes. Indeed, they often found themselves centre stage in the new gardening. For instance, many began collecting the sumptuous new verbenas. By 1849, only a decade or so after Tweedie sent the first ones back to Europe, there were show classes devoted to them even among the humble cottage garden societies. Colours ranged from purest white, through an infinite number of pinks, roses and scarlets, to lilacs so deep as to seem almost black. In size they soon ranged from the minute 'Boule de Feu' to immense and vigorous varieties like 'Robinson's Defiance'. Large commercial nurseries started propagating vast quantities of plants. In 1861, John Scott of Merriott stocked 100 sorts of verbena, and took thousands of cuttings of each every season. Similar establishments were selling rooted verbena at two shillings and sixpence for a dozen. Another nursery had 80,000 verbenas for sale to suburban Londoners.

The verbena was acknowledged, even by contemporaries, as central to the whole bedding movement; William Thomson, head gardener at Dalkeith Palace near Edinburgh, commented in the early 1860s: 'Looking at Verbenas, I cannot help recording my conviction that the present principle of arranging plants in masses owes them very much . . . [Its introduction] had a very considerable share in the advent of the grouping style, and helped to establish it.' The verbena had come a long way in twenty-five years.

Tweedie was born in 1775 in Lanarkshire, where there were already a great many nurseries established to supply the rapidly expanding city of Glasgow. Of very humble birth, he worked his way up through the garden's ranks, eventually getting a job as head gardener at the Edinburgh Botanic Garden. He took to design, and left that institution to work as a landscape gardener on several Scottish estates. None of his designs was a success, and commissions dried up. That was when he decided to emigrate. He settled at Santa Catalina near Buenos Aires, became a shopkeeper, and landscaped a number of local estates.

He began travelling in 1832, first sailing sixty miles up the Uruguay River, then returning to the sea and sailing north to Rio. He next made a journey to Patagonia, but first starved, then became ill, and, when he had recovered, was trapped for weeks inside a fort by hostile Indians. For his third journey, Tweedie took fewer risks by joining a 'tropa': a caravan made up of 17 wagons, 240 cattle, 44 horses, 35 mules and 32 people, all bound for Tucuman. The journey was expected to last forty to fifty days but took very much longer. It was a hard trip and, at first, yielded almost no plants. One river was at full spate and the caravan had to wait a fortnight for the waters to subside sufficiently to allow them to the far bank. Passengers and baggage were then loaded into crude canoes each made of a single ox-hide with the corners tied together. These were towed across the torrent by Indian girls holding the tow ropes in their teeth. It took the expedition eight days to get entirely across. This gave Tweedie time to botanize, but it was already the dry season and he found little. Travelling all night to make up time, Tweedie dozed on a wagon loaded with bales of cloth. Towards dawn the driver fell asleep and the wagon overturned. Tweedie fell from a height and the bales of cloth came down on top of him. Perhaps unsurprisingly, the only surviving photograph of him shows a depressed-looking man. Even the eventual discovery of some exciting new plants did not prevent him from 'falling into a sort of melancholy fit', as he wrote on his sixtieth birthday, nine thousand miles from home and among people far removed in style from the couthy folks of his homeland. His depression lifted sufficiently to let him send a box of seeds back to William Jackson Hooker in Glasgow. He wrote: 'being from a strange country, they may be in request for your Botanic Garden'. One of the seeds turned out to be from a new species of passion flower (*Passiflora tucumanensis*). He also began sending seed back to nurserymen friends in Edinburgh. One such nursery, Handasyde of Musselburgh, was among the first in Europe to start crossing some of the new species of verbena to produce brilliant hybrids.

Tweedie continued to correspond with Hooker, who described many of his new species and genera. The one that bears Tweedie's name is the beautiful twining *Tweedia caerulea*, with speckled turquoise flowers that are like nothing else in the garden. He sent back dozens of verbenas. He found, too, *Petunia violacea*, which became one of the main ancestors of all the petunias in the garden today. He introduced the tree tomato (*Cyphomandra betacea*), which combines fragrant flowers and edible fruit. Most dramatic of all his finds, though, and still increasingly popular, was the great grass that gardeners either hate or adore: the silvery, rustling pampas grass (*Cortaderia selloana*). Seeds were first germinated in 1840 at Glasnevin Botanic Gardens, Dublin. The plants flowered two years later, and caused a sensation.

In his journal, Tweedie mentions an unnamed Prussian lady insect collector whom he met on his travels. She was obviously rather a wild one, commonly wading into dangerous lakes up to her armpits to collect something she thought interesting. Tweedie noted in a letter home that she would cheerfully do this in lakes so filled with alligators that the local people would not even go near.

Tweedie, whom one writer in the *Journal of Botany* of 1834 described as 'unassuming but indefatigable', was far less adventurous, although he was shipwrecked several times, including once when 400 miles up the Paranha River. In another storm, off Montevideo, his brigantine was completely destroyed and he saved himself by clinging to some rigging. He faced starvation on several occasions, once surviving for weeks on end eating the seeds of a new species of pine. His letters make rather little of these incidents. Finally, the *Weekly Standard* of Buenos Aires reported his death, at the age of eighty-seven. In Britain, his obituary appeared in the 28 June 1862 issue of *Gardeners' Chronicle and Agricultural Gazette*, among the lists of bankruptcies, in such unillustrious company as Noah Hodges, tailor; Thomas Tandy, needle maker; Robert Philips, wireworker.

As Thomson noted, Tweedie's new verbenas, and the hybrids that were rapidly developed from them, allowed a completely new sort of gardening. It was a rather ambiguous sort of gardening too. On the one hand, it ransacked the globe for plants that would suit it, and produced huge numbers of hybrids, many of beauty and some of value, apparently promoting diversity. On the other hand, it reduced the plants it adopted to a single quality, usually flower colour, but sometimes leaf shape. Uniformity was everything.

The great bedding genera of mid-nineteenth-century gardens – *Calceolaria*, *Petunia*, *Verbena* and *Geranium* (*Pelargonium*) – were popular not only because they were brilliantly colourful, assuaging the contemporary taste for gaudy and intense effects, but also because, being from the sub-tropics, they were 'seasonless'. As soon as the plants were growing, they also began to flower. They delivered no temperate nonsense about a burst of flower in late spring or early summer, and then a flowerless pause as seed production started. They were also very easily propagated. Huge swathes of entirely uniform colour were achievable. They also mostly had relatively flexible stems, which could be pegged flat if they were growing in an undesirable direction.

When Lady Grenville started the new movement, there was no fuss about plants not all being of the same height. As she largely planted a single species or variety as the only occupant of a bed, the effect was reasonably natural. However, a few decades later, gardeners wanted more complexity. In sufficiently large beds, why not have bands of different colours, supplied, if need be, by entirely different plants? Circular beds could have concentric bands; long beds bordering paths and walks could have stripes, and be called ribbon beds. For this to work, the plants showing the different colours had to be of uniform height. Victorian gardeners managed this either by constantly clipping and pinching out the plants, or by pegging down any branch that wanted to go its own way. Some plants refused to be so treated, and went on to form the herbaceous border, but the four bedding genera were entirely amenable and thereby hugely successful.

Gardeners are a diverse tribe though, and some felt that the blazing displays of colour were vulgar. They wanted something subtler, and, if possible, something without the nuisance of fleeting flowers. They developed what became called the carpet bed, the word 'carpet' being used as if it referred only to faded rugs from Persia. Grey-greens, soft browns, sages, bronze shades, earth reds and dusty purples were the colours they wanted. They tried planting with new sempervivums and sedums, echeverias and new aeoniums. However, the plant group that gave them everything they could possibly ask were the latest hybrid geraniums, not because of their flowers, which were suppressed, but because of their foliage. Hybrids developing mid-century had leaves patterned in the most extraordinary manner, with horseshoe markings of bronze upon a base of livid green, or white on emerald, or yellow on tan, and countless others. With these, bedding schemes of the utmost subtlety of tone and colour were easily built.

As with verbenas and calceolarias, most of the old geranium varieties are lost. It is hard to imagine that their huge diversity is scarcely more than a century and a half old. It is hard too, now that the bedding garden has relaxed its domineering hold on most gardeners' imaginations, to realise to what extent the genus underpinned all gardening from London's Great Exhibition of 1851, for almost the next century. And not just in London, but in Paris, Prague, New York and Toronto.

The genus's association with the garden had begun in the seventeenth century. It was first represented solely by the dingily flowered, but

Victorian hybridists created some startling pelargoniums, for their foliage, or, like these, for their flowers.

attractively perfumed *Pelargonium triste*, which had travelled from South Africa. When evening falls, the green and brown striped flowers pour out a clove-like perfume, which attracted European gardeners. A few decades later, the Dutch botanist Dr Paul Hermann sent home from the Cape *P. cucullatum*, and the ivy-leafed geranium *P. peltatum. P. inquinans* and *P. zonale* soon followed. Several of these species crossed, and by 1732 *P.* x *hortorum*, the garden geranium, began appearing in reference books. The 1754 edition of Philip Miller's abridged *Gardener's Dictionary* lists twenty-one sorts, but says there are many more. Miller, a man of his time, especially liked the ones related to *P. triste*, whose flowers only began to smell delicious after sunset. Thomas Jefferson liked them too, but it was not until twenty years later that he managed to take seeds home to America from France. Development continued slowly into the next century, but until glass became cheap in the 1820s, pelargoniums remained plants for prosperous gardens. However, once greenhouses could be owned by anyone with the tiniest garden, they took off.

By 1838, grand gardens had several varieties of scarlet-flowered zonals, as the patterned-leafed hybrids were called, some with variegated leaves. Ivy-leafed sorts were making an appearance in fashionable rustic baskets. By the 1840s, there were prize lists for new varieties at many local flower shows, though decent new sorts were expensive at two shillings apiece. Prizes seem to have acted as a spur to growers, breeders and collectors alike, and the genus spawned the first of the new florists' clubs. The Pelargonium Society was set up on 18 June 1842. By 1852, geraniums were used for every aspect of bedding. Leaf colour often clashed nastily with flower colour, but once the flowers had been pinched out, the leaf markings were often exceptionally subtle. Some matched the more interesting mid-Victorian colour fashions almost exactly: 'Lass o' Gowrie' has a white margin surrounding a jade green leaf with a reddish 'zone'; the lovely 'Crystal Palace Gem' has a green zone on a yellow leaf. Numbers were as prodigious as for verbenas. Scott's of Merriott overwintered several thousand plants of at least fifty sorts of the latest geranium. At the vast private garden of Shrubland in Suffolk, the gardener and writer David Beaton regularly overwintered 5,000 geranium 'Punch' cuttings, and several other varieties on top of that. None of this would have been possible without an extraordinary pair of men: Francis Masson and Carl Peter Thunberg.

Masson was a gardener by training, and was born in Aberdeen. Thunberg was a medical man, and was born in the same province of Sweden as his great teacher Linnaeus. Masson was quiet, stoical, even wise. Thunberg was excitable, foolhardy, boastful, rendered paranoid by rivalry, tiny yet strong. Masson died frozen in the wastes of North America. Thunberg died at home in his own bed, loaded with honours. Both men made huge contributions to gardening and botany, though Thunberg's were less important than he claimed. Both made their greatest contributions to gardening between 1772 and 1775, when their lives were entwined.

The Cape was already famed for its wild flowers. Officers of visiting ships often purchased collections of rarities to take home as souvenirs for their gardens in Europe. There had been other botanists there before Thunberg, the earliest being Paul Hermann. A Danish pupil of Hermann's developed the first botanic garden at Cape Town, and sent much of the early South African material to Europe. Things were then quiet until Johan Andreas Auge was appointed assistant gardener at Cape Town's garden, which he went on to turn into a proper botanic garden. However, Auge was a gardener, not a botanist, and mostly made collections for sale. He sold much to Governor Tulbagh (commemorated in the charming bulbs *Tulbaghia*), and sent material on to Linnaeus and others. However, some of the plants he collected were extremely beautiful, and whetted the appetites of gardeners, especially the great scientific entrepreneur Joseph Banks. On returning to London after his famous voyage with Captain Cook, Banks suggested to the King that a collector should be sent to South Africa to collect for the King's own garden at Kew.

The acclaim he received from this first voyage seems to have unhinged him slightly. He at once began to make plans for a second expedition, but the plans became increasingly grandiose. He wanted to have an entire entourage of naturalists, musicians and the best artists of the day. The British portraitist John Zoffany was a candidate. Cook wanted to sail in a handsome and stable Whitby collier called the *Resolution*. It did not suit Banks, who, partly at his own expense, had it torn apart and almost rebuilt. The captain's great cabin was extended into a room to house his naturalists, bigger even than the accommodation thought suitable for an Admiral of the Fleet. Captain Cook was to make do with a small shack built on the poop. Banks had a new deck built above the original main deck of the collier, and the new space was intended for Banks's party. The ship's officers were made dark quarters lower down, and packed, according to a report to the Admiralty, 'as close as herrings in a barrel'. Cook tried to sail the resulting ship to Sheerness, but the boat was so top-heavy that it nearly keeled over and drowned her crew. The *Resolution* needed extensive refitting before it was seaworthy once more. Cook refused to have anything more to do with Banks, and the Admiralty agreed. Banks, furious, retreated to his house in Soho. He must, though, have recovered himself fairly quickly, for he ensured that Cook's replanned expedition should have a botanist sail with it as far as the Cape. The King was to have the best that the Cape could offer. Banks's prescience, and the energy of a young Scottish gardener, was to change not only the King's gardens for ever.

The young man was the thirty-one-year-old Francis Masson. Though he later claimed that he was the only applicant for the post, he had already been working as a gardener at Kew and must have impressed Banks, who towards the end of Masson's life, was to call him 'indefatigable'. Banks must have impressed Masson too; Masson sent regular letters and specimens to him on all his subsequent travels. Many are now in the Mitchell Library in Melbourne, Australia. With a salary of £100 a year, payable on his return, and an expenses budget of up to £200 a year, Masson set sail on Captain Cook's voyage, which was to last from 1772 to 1775. After six months at sea, on 30 October 1772, the *Resolution* and her sister ship the *Adventure* anchored at Cape Town. Masson, wasting no time, at once set out on a two-month excursion, accompanied only by a Danish interpreter and guide. Instantly, he began finding marvels. He was hooked.

After this first trip, he met up with the extraordinary Thunberg. The inhabitants of the Swedish province of Småland, where Carl Peter Thunberg was born, are noted for frugality, as are Masson's Aberdonians. That may have been at the root of their bond. Carl's father was a bookkeeper for a local iron-foundry, and also had a small shop. The father died early, but Carl's mother managed to keep the shop going well enough to give him an education. Thunberg was soon recognized by his teachers to have great abilities. At the University of Uppsala he studied theology, law and then philosophy. Moving to study medicine, he spent the next two years working with Linnaeus. Linnaeus got him a tiny travel grant, and in 1770 he set off for Holland and France. Thunberg seems to have made some useful contacts. In Amsterdam, he visited the Burmans, a wealthy family fascinated by botany. They engineered a post for Thunberg with the Dutch East India Company, a commercial organization of immense wealth and power. Feeling that he was 'on the way', he began a diary, added to each day, and the source of his published memoirs. These contain some oddities. He noted, for instance, of Holland that 'water is the element that has permitted the Dutch to develop their shipping'. Of France, he wrote that 'it is highly disconcerting to note that the French language, held in such high esteem by the upper classes in Sweden and elsewhere, is spoken by both high and low members of society all over France'. In Paris, where he attended lectures in medicine and botany, he was astonished that the French were not permitted to bring their swords into the laboratories. He also disliked their habit of applauding during dissertations and autopsies.

Cape Town and Table Mountain, engraved in 1816. Many of Europe's finest bulbs,
bedding and conservatory plants were collected near by.

The Dutch East India Company thought that Thunberg should go looking for
horticulturally or commercially important plants in Japan. The Japanese were, with just
cause, highly suspicious of all foreigners. Only Chinese and Dutch traders were at that time
allowed in. Not being Dutch, Thunberg needed camouflage. He was asked to learn Dutch,
and the Dutch colony in South Africa was chosen as the most suitable place to study it. In
1772, he set sail as ship's surgeon on the East India windjammer *Schoonzicht*, destined for the
Cape. Many of the crew had been 'shanghaied' or 'press ganged', and were miserable and
in poor health. In spite of Thunberg's efforts, 115 of the crew died during the voyage.
Thunberg and the other officers almost died too when the cook baked them pancakes using
white lead powder for half the flour. Once recovered and on land, Thunberg was not
pleased by the arrival of another of Linnaeus's students, the brilliant, extravagant and
stylish Anders Sparmann, after whom the lovely and popular houseplant *Sparrmannia
africana* is named. They did some collecting together, but rather than be overshadowed by
him, Thunberg cast around for other less showy travelling companions.

In August, Thunberg made preparations for a long excursion with Johan Auge and two
soldiers, three men he thought might be suitable. They weren't. They travelled for four
months, along tracks from farm to farm. Their baggage was carried on an ox-wagon, which
was heavy and cumbersome, with a maximum speed of eight miles per hour. Lions were
ever-present. Water was scarce. By 7 September, they had obtained a saddlehorse each, and
the cart had three yoke of oxen, driven by two locals. On 3 November the party was

attacked by a rogue buffalo. It charged the sergeant's horse and slit its belly open. It turned to do the same to the second horse, but did not notice Thunberg's arrival. Thunberg leapt up into the branches of a tree. The buffalo, feeling mollified, wandered off. Thunberg clambered down and went to look for his companions. He found them, he wrote in *Travels in Europe, Africa and Asia* (1775), 'sitting fast, like two cats, on the trunk of a tree with their guns on their backs, loaded with fine shot, and unable to utter a single word . . . the sergeant at last burst into tears, deploring the loss of his two spirited steeds; but the gardener was so strongly affected, that he could scarcely speak for some days after.' The troupe eventually got safely back to Cape Town on 2 January 1773. The star turn of Thunberg's collecting on that trip was the bird of paradise flower (*Strelitzia reginae*), which he sent back to the botanic gardens of Leiden and Amsterdam. He still had not found a travelling companion. As for the fabulous plant, ironically, it is to Masson that it owes its scientific name, honouring Charlotte of Mecklenberg-Strelitz, the wife of George III.

How Thunberg and Masson met is not recorded by either man. Thunberg's salary had failed to arrive, and he was in financial difficulties. He had set up a small medical practice in Cape Town, but he did not want it to get too big, as he would have no time for botanizing. Patients' fees kept him alive, but he had to beg a loan from the secretary of the police to purchase a new wagon, and medicines to distribute in the interior. Masson, financially sound as King's Botanist, was in a much better position, and soon was 'well equipped with a large and strong wagon, tilted with sailcloth, which was driven by a European servant upon whom he could depend'. Thunberg felt that Masson was only a gardener, and not likely to upstage him. He was also much better equipped than him.

They started on 11 September 1773. At first, they travelled through the veldt. Masson was again enchanted. 'The whole country,' he wrote, 'affords a fine field for the botanist, being enamelled with the greatest number of flowers I ever saw of exquisite beauty and fragrance.' Among them he found dimorphothecas, ixias, lachenalias, gazanias, ornithogalums, romuleas and the white arum lily (*Zantedeschia aethiopica*). He started collecting some of the ever-present shrubby pelargoniums. Once they had crossed the veldt, they began the climb into the Blue Mountain range. Going was hard.

> *We climbed over the mountain's . . . even being obliged to lead our horses for three hours amidst incessant rain which made the road so slippy that the horses, stumbling among the loose stones, had their legs almost stripped of skin. And the precipices were so steep that we were often afraid to turn our eyes to either side. Towards sunset with great labour and anxiety we got safe to the other side where we found a miserable cottage belonging to a Dutchman, but however cold and wet as we were, we were glad of anything . . . There was only one room and the Dutchman gave us one corner to sleep in. He hung a reed mat and he and his wife slept there in the other corner. Just beyond a number of Hottentots lay promiscuously together.*

They found many more pelargoniums. Thunberg found the orchid *Disa caerulea*. Among the many new sorts of Cape heath Masson found *Ixia viridiflora*, a gorgeous bulb with sea-green flowers. On 19 November, riding back through the astonishing land, they had to cross the

Duivenhok River. 'Thunberg, without making inquiry,' wrote Masson, 'took horse and suddenly disappeared. He and his horse plunged head over heels into a pit made by a hippo, deep and steep on all sides, and for a few minutes I thought he might be dead, but his horse managed to get a foothold and scrambled out.' Thunberg wrote of the same occasion: 'I, who was the most courageous of the company and consequently always in the lead, had the misfortune to plunge into a deep hippopotamus-wallow, which might have proved fatal if I, who have always had the good fortune to possess myself in the greatest dangers, had not with the greatest calm and composure, guided the animal . . . and kept myself fast in the saddle.' After further hazards, the two men got safely home. Thunberg sent huge amounts of material back to Linnaeus in Sweden. Masson sent plants, seeds, bulbs and dried specimens home to Kew and Joseph Banks, including more than fifty species of Cape pelargonium. They were soon distributed to the nursery trade in London, and tried out for hybridization. Nurseries like that of Edward George Henderson in London's Edgware Road or the French firm of Jacques Calot were soon producing plants that immediately began altering the look of gardens throughout Europe and America.

Both men went their own ways. In March 1775, the Dutch East India Company decided it was time for Thunberg to go on to Japan. He travelled by way of Java, then a Dutch colony, where he had some smart uniforms made for his forthcoming stay in Japan, and also did some speculating: he bought up a supply of narwhal tusks which he knew would sell well in Japan. Japanese men thought them an aphrodisiac. On 13 August 1775, after a stormy seven weeks crossing from Batavia via Macao, the triple-decker *Stavenisse* anchored at the harbour entrance of Nagasaki. Thunberg was launched on a new career. He is still sometimes hailed as the father of Japanese botany, although his contribution to it would be outshined by Balthasar von Siebold, whom we will meet in Chapter Seven. He returned to Sweden three years later, once more aboard the *Stavenisse*. Calling at the Cape, he learned that he had been appointed lecturer in Botany at Uppsala University. After 1779, Thunberg hardly left Uppsala, and then only to travel to Stockholm. He was appointed to the Chair of Botany in 1784, and held it for forty-four years. His huge collections are still at Uppsala University, and they include thirty-six immense volumes of letters, to and from well over a thousand other naturalists and botanists. Thunberg was busy writing his autobiography when he died on 8 August 1828, at the age of eighty-five.

Masson, on the other hand, was unable to settle in one place ever again. He kept collecting, but without the same success as he had had on his Cape expedition. A few years later, he sailed to the Azores and the West Indies. In 1779, while he was a very unwilling British conscript in the army, trying to halt the fall of New Grenada in the West Indies, he was taken prisoner by the French in their attack on Grenada. Joseph Banks seems to have engineered his release. Masson went on to lose all his collections in a hurricane on St Lucia, though he did manage to hold on to material of *Cineraria cruenta*, the ancestor of the showy cinerarias that were such popular pot plants in the mid-twentieth century. He even returned to South Africa in 1785, but things had changed and it was not safe to travel more than fifty miles from Cape Town. Even when he was close to the settlement, Masson had some frightening times. On one occasion, a chain gang of escaped convicts tried to capture him to use as a hostage. They swept, chains extended, through the vegetation. He spent the night in the open, too terrified to move, crouched in hiding with a clasp knife in his hand, while the desperate convicts kept hunting him through the bush. By dawn, they had tired, and he escaped. On that trip, in spite of the difficulties, he collected over a hundred new species.

In 1795, he was granted permission to return to England to work on his most important work, a book on stapelias. Considering what astonishing plants he had found, and how influential some of them had already become, stapelias were an odd choice. He could have chosen gladioli, or aloes, or even pelargoniums. Stapelias are succulents, with strange finger-like stems, sometimes velvety or serrated. When they flower, their putrescent stink can as quickly clear a greenhouse of humans as fill it with blowflies. The five-petalled flowers, in browns, yellows and maroons, are often velvety, and are sometimes dotted with weird filaments that move in the breeze and resemble maggots. However uncongenial they seem to us, they plainly fascinated Masson. His monograph was called *Stapeliae Novae: or A collection of several new species of that genus, discovered in the interior parts of Africa* and was published in London in 1796. It was dedicated to the King, and began:

Sire,

Compelled to leave the Cape of Good Hope, lest I should lose, in an unexpected invasion, the Collection of living Plants that I had made, during ten years residence there, I returned to England; and was indulged, on my return, with your Majesty's gracious permission to remain a year at home. Unwilling to waste so much time in idleness, I resolved to render this vacation somewhat profitable to the science of Botany, by publishing observations made on that subject, in the interior deserts of Africa.

Twenty-four years I have enjoyed the honour of being, by your Majesty's command, attached to the Royal Gardens at Kew, as a collector of exotic plants. I have had the satisfaction of seeing several hundreds of those, collected by me in various climates, flourishing there, more beautifully, in some instances, than in their native soils. . . .

Let these circumstances, Gracious Sire, plead some excuse for the ambition that induced me to solicit the honour of laying my little work at your Majesty's feet.

Penetrated with gratitude for the uniform protection I have unceasingly received from your Majesty's bounty . . . anxious to recommence my employment as a collector, and still enjoying, though in the afternoon of life, a reasonable share of health and vigour, I am now ready to proceed to any part of the globe, to which your Majesty's commands shall direct me. Many are the portions of it that have not yet been fully explored by Botanists . . . all of them are equal to my choice. To extend the science of Botany, to enrich the Royal Gardens at Kew, and to obey your Majesty's gracious commands, are the only objects of ambition that activate the breast of

Your Majesty's
most humble,
most dutiful,
and most grateful Servant,

FRANCIS MASSON

By the time *Stapeliae Novae* was written, he was sixty-five. With no personal life and only a few close friends, he found no home. Banks obtained a commission for another journey, and he sailed for New York in 1797. 'We arrived here,' he wrote, in his usual neat hand

in great distress after a passage of four months from Gravesend during which period we experienced many difficulties. Regarding the Western Isles, we were stopped by two French privateers, one of which boarded us, examined our papers and let us pass. Nothing happened until the 5th of November towards night when we saw three sail bearing down upon us, one of which was a French privateer belonging to St Domingo who fired several shots and a volley of small arms into our ship and soon after boarded and took possession of us. The passengers were then put on board a Bremen vessel bound for Baltimore, and after having suffered many hardships from weather, want of water and provisions, were ultimately taken on board another ship and so to New York.

He travelled on from New York to Niagara, and then to the shores of Lake Ontario. From there, he went west to Queenstown, then to Fort Erie returning to Niagara and Montreal. Among the plants he sent home to Banks was the glorious wake robin (*Trillium grandiflorum*). For this plant alone, its triad of varnished and mottled leaves supporting the perfect white flowers, gardeners would always have remembered him. His beloved stapelias remain a collectors' fad. Most of the lovely but tender Cape heaths he introduced to Europe and North America have retreated into obscurity. The bedding garden, however, owed much of its popularity and ubiquitous appeal to the pelargoniums that he had collected in South Africa. At least some of the thousands of varieties bred using his introductions in their parentage were to be found in almost every garden, whatever its size, throughout the temperate regions of the gardened globe. Of this richness, little remains. Most of it was lost when gardening moved on from its obsession with bedding and pattern. Thousands of plant varieties upon which it depended became extinct as fashion turned away. A handful of nineteenth-century varieties survived as greenhouse or windowsill plants. Some of the survivors are beginning to be popular once again, now redefined as 'patio plants'. But among the tangled family background of dozens of the very latest pelargonium varieties to be bred will be substantial amounts of genetic material derived from plants first found by Masson among the ravines and desert scrub of South Africa so long ago. It was, and remains, an astonishing contribution. He died in Montreal, killed by the winter's cold in 1805.

Robert Thornton's *Temple of Flora* (1807) contained this magnificent plate of the South African *Strelitzia reginae*. Carl Thunberg sent plants to Amsterdam and to Leiden in 1773.

CLASSIC HERBACEOUS BORDERS

T he great age of the herbaceous border is largely over. Although virtuosic Edwardian designers such as Gertrude Jekyll could play with the splendid colour schemes that became possible as plant breeders developed ever-wider ranges of colour in delphiniums, asters, phlox and dahlias, very few gardeners now have the space or the time to plant and maintain huge borders. Gorgeous flowers like Oriental poppies, Japanese anemones, Russell lupins, astilbes, and the rest have had to find new roles in the garden. Nevertheless, the great Edwardian herbaceous border has a fascinating past, and has been resilient enough to evolve into new forms relevant to contemporary gardens.

The story of the delphinium, almost the archetypal flower of those great banks of colour, plots the border's rise and transmutations. It is also a prime demonstration of how plant introductions drive changes in the garden. Most gardeners now think of delphiniums as towering spires of blue, dove grey, soft pink or white, yet these splendid hybrid plants are only of very recent origin.

Perhaps their finest hour came in 1910, when Amos Perry, a famous British nurseryman, staged an exhibition of new delphinium hybrids, displaying 30,000 spikes of flowers. A few decades before that astonishing show, there had been almost no hybrids at all. It is an enormous genus, with species scattered over Asia as well as North

Achilleas, stachys, delphiniums and old apple trees in a watercolour by George Samuel Elgood (1851–1943). The *beau ideal* of herbaceous planting, it looks burgeoning and romantic but is very difficult to maintain.

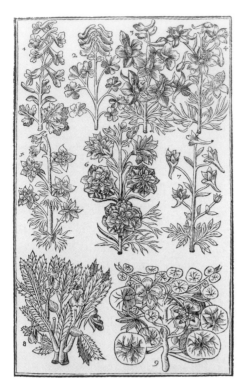

Delphiniums and 'larkesheeles',
illustrated in John Parkinson's book
Paradisi in Sole Paradisus Terrestris (1629).

America. Probably still evolving fast, it is unclear how many species there really are; estimates range between three and five hundred. The genus encompasses species with scarlet or yellow flowers, as well as ones in countless shades of blue. It is just the sort of genus that intrigues collectors and breeders.

Some native species of delphinium had been growing in European gardens since the fifteenth century. Probably the first of these was *Delphinium staphisagria*, the 'Staveacre', or louse grass, first grown to keep those creatures away from the gardener. Another species, *D. elatum*, from central Europe and central Russia, has had more influence on modern flower gardens. The seventeenth-century collector and author John Parkinson admired it, and noted that 'the tall and upright single kinds have been entertained but of late years. The double kinds are more rare.' With muddy blue flowers, and at most three and a half feet high, it found a place in eighteenth-century wildernesses. There were no other kinds until the early 1800s, when new species began to pour in from America and China. At first, the most exciting of these were the very similar Chinese species *D. chinense* and *D. grandiflorum*. Both would grow to six feet high if heavily fed, and caused great excitement.

By the late 1830s, a famous Manchester florist called Sam Barlow had started crossing the more dramatic of the new species. He described the first true garden hybrid, known as *D. barlowii*, in the *Botanical Register* for 1837. That august work stated: 'It is a most ornamental and beautiful herbaceous plant and very easy of cultivation: it appears to flourish in any soil and situation. We have had plants in bloom throughout the whole summer and autumn, the principal stems sometimes attaining the height of 7 and 8 feet and many branches.' The flowers were semi-double and intensely blue.

By 1850, one nurseryman in Norway had a vast collection of species in use as parent material. In 1860, some of the more interesting hybrids were taken up at Kelway's Nursery at Langport in Somerset, where delphinium breeding continues to this day. French nurserymen, such as the vastly influential company of Lemoine of Nancy, also did much of the early work. Though the firm is best known for its tremendous development of numerous cultivars of woody plants including *Syringa*, *Hydrangea* and *Philadelphus*, they did huge amounts of work on herbaceous genera too. Their delphiniums astonished gardeners; they were all of double or semi-double form, and in shades of lavender, sky-blue, mauve and

In the nineteenth century, the florists' societies shows like this one in Chiswick in the 1890s developed into spectacular flower shows that became great social occasions, and ones which created intense competition between nurserymen.

various combinations. Exhibited in London, one even got an Award of Merit from the Royal Horticultural Society in 1908.

Though gardeners were enthralled, the plants all had one awful drawback: none were reliably perennial. The first truly perennial one was British, called 'Millicent Blackmore'. Launched in 1910, she had a branched flower spike and individual flowers three inches in diameter. Appropriately, the flower was soon referred to as 'the Queen of the Border', and everyone wanted her, or something as grand. Breeders in France, America and Britain were happy to oblige. Amos Perry obliged on the grandest scale, while also producing magnificent day lilies, Oriental poppies, asters, kniphofias, huge numbers of herbaceous-border irises, as well as his delphiniums. His nursery became one of the most celebrated in the world, and his hybrids almost underpinned the whole of the development of the herbaceous border.

Amos Perry was born on 22 September 1841. His obituary says that he 'started life in the scholastic profession, but after serving his apprenticeship as pupil teacher, his health failed and his medical adviser advised him to leave this country. Instead of doing this he secured employment in Messrs. Wingfield's Nursery, Gloucester, adopting the profession of his forebears – his grandfather was a foreman at Messrs. Veitch's Nursery, Exeter, and his

This is one of the first double delphiniums, with the name *Delphinium barlowii*. Others followed, although the only one to survive to the present day is the rare and beautiful 'Alice Artindale'. This illustration is from *The Botanical Register*.

father was Rose-grower at Messrs. Ware's nursery, Tottenham.' He plainly had plants in his blood. He had independence in it too, and working for others did not suit him for long. Believing that as wealthy gardeners got bored with bedding plants a new market was forming, Perry started to collect hardy herbaceous plants, ones that would never fit into the bedding schemes of the day.

While a number of his finds were half-forgotten plants that had been in gardens for several centuries, far more of them were either recent introductions from America and China, or hybrids of recent introductions. And if there were no interesting varieties to be found, he bred them himself. No 'establishment' gardeners were interested. When he tried to exhibit them at a Royal Horticultural Society show, the superintendent almost refused to let the plants in, eventually letting them be displayed in an out-of-the-way corner, among gardeners' sundries. Perry persevered. In 1894, he left Wingfield's Nursery and set up on his own, growing alpines and herbaceous perennials. His most famous herbaceous plants include *Echinacea purpurea* 'Winchmore Hill', *Phlox canadensis* 'Perry's var.', *Spiraea rivularis* 'Gigantea', *Chrysanthemum maximum* 'Grandiflorum', *Achillea* 'Perry's White', *Sparaxis pulcherrima*, *Anchusa italica* 'Perry's var.', *Spiraea venusta*, *Helenium pumilum* 'Magnificum' and *Aster amellus* 'Perry's Favourite', the first pink variety of this flower. Even when he 'retired' from business, handing it on to his children, he couldn't stop hybridizing, and his garden was filled with thousands of seedling *Lilium*, *Sparaxis*, delphiniums and poppies.

The big lure in delphinium breeding eluded Perry, Blackmore and Langdon, Lemoine and the rest: scarlet delphiniums. Red flowers are found in two Californian species, *Delphinium cardinale*, discovered in 1885, and the orange-red *D. nudicaule*, discovered a few years later. Both species are worth growing in their own right.

America breeders such as Luther Burbank, an enthusiastic crosser of plants and avid promoter of their progeny, or N. I. Vanderbilt, a president of the now defunct American Delphinium Society, seem not to have tried using them, or if they did, got no seed. Frank Reinelt, a Czech gardener who emigrated to America in 1925, also tried. Although he was able to achieve a cross by artificial means between *D. cardinale* and the old *D. elatum*, there were no reds among his seedlings. Good purples were the best he could do. More recent attempts have taken place at Wageningen University in the Netherlands. So far, only pinkish-red semi-double delphiniums have been produced. Ultimately, scarlet delphiniums will arrive, and perhaps spark a rebirth of the border.

What was happening in the nineteenth century among delphiniums was far from unique. Many other plant groups were also expanding fast, as species newly in from China, America and India began to swap genetic material in the garden. That great standby for autumn flowers, the Michaelmas daisy, is an example. *Aster novi-belgii*, first identified in 1687 by a Belgian, had been introduced into England in 1710. Philip Miller, in the 1733 edition of his *Gardener's Dictionary*, gives three 'species', probably only variants of the 1710 species, which he says will flower till mid-November. The 1830 catalogue of the London firm of Conrad Loddiges lists the same ones, yet a hundred years later there were at least four hundred varieties of *Aster novi-belgii* alone.

The autumn-flowering asters in our gardens are American, and many that contributed to the vast increase in variation came from parts of America that were still unexplored by botanists in the early nineteenth century. These, and some of the new delphinium species too, were collected on the amazing journeys undertaken by a strange young man. He was incompetent, innocent, almost a 'holy fool', and yet seemingly protected by a zealous and extremely patient guardian angel. The young man was Thomas Nuttall.

Although he was to fall helplessly in love with the wilds of America, its plants and its birds, Thomas Nuttall (1786–1859), was born in Settle, a small village in Yorkshire. Life there was simple and safe. He couldn't swim, shoot or cook. He didn't need to. He didn't even need to consider a career, as his uncle owned a prosperous printing business. Thomas became a printer. Perhaps he and his uncle didn't get on, or Thomas wanted wider horizons. In any case, he set sail for America, landing at New York, then moving swiftly on. He arrived in Philadelphia on 23 April 1808, and set himself up in his accustomed trade.

In Yorkshire, he had had an intense love of nature. In Pennsylvania, the story goes, he began to walk the local countryside and came across a flower he had never seen before. A companion suggested he take it to Dr Benjamin Smith Barton, a professor at the University of Pennsylvania and author of the first American botany text. It was a momentous meeting between an Old World innocent and a New World cynic. It ended up creating a new Thomas Nuttall: botanist and naturalist. As a botanist he collected more new kinds of American native plants than anyone else, and no naturalist saw so much of America in its almost primeval condition. Barton, who was both too busy and getting too old to explore the unknown parts of his own country, seems to have suggested, almost jokingly, that Nuttall become his surrogate voyager into that unknown. He hoped Nuttall would explore the Northwest Territory and wrote a letter of introduction to the governor, describing Nuttall as 'a young man distinguished by innocence of character'.

Barton sent the young man on two collecting trips in 1809. The first was to the coasts of New Jersey and Southern Delaware, and was a disaster that haunted Nuttall for the rest of his life. He was bitten by mosquitoes so badly that he was 'all but driven away' from a house he approached for lodgings: the owners thought he had smallpox. From those bites, he also caught malaria, which recurred throughout his life, and almost killed him several times. The second journey took him to the shores of Lake Erie and the Niagara Falls. That journey was exciting. He was hooked.

He financed these first two trips himself. The next, in 1810, was financed by Barton. Nuttall was to have a salary of eight dollars a month and expenses. He was given a double-barrelled gun, a pistol and a dirk. He eventually used the gun for digging up plants and stored valuable seed in its barrel. Progeny from some of these we still grow in our gardens.

This time, Nuttall's proposed itinerary was completely impossible, and it is unclear whether Barton knew this. On 12 April 1810, Nuttall left Philadelphia by stagecoach for Pittsburgh. That was the last of comfort; from here he travelled on foot or by boat. His malaria kept appearing. His trunk got lost. A week later, he set out into the unknown, 'very weak and burthened', with the contents of his trunk on his back. He struggled through to Erie, until at last he got a boat for Detroit, and arrived on 26 June. Half dead, he holed up there for a month, then found a surveyor with a birch-bark canoe, who was going up the

Both Thomas Nuttall and David Douglas visited Niagara Falls. This dramatic view
was painted in 1818 by an artist known as 'Minott'.

coast of Lake Huron, to a settlement called Michili Mackinac. This place must have been
a shock after Yorkshire and the genteel life of Philadelphia. It was a fur-traders'
encampment, and one of the wildest and most raucous places on the continent. It was also
headquarters to John Jacob Astor's fur company, and a new expedition, the Astorian, was
about to leave. Nuttall joined it. His education had begun.

Nuttall left St Louis on 13 March 1811. He and his companions joined the main body
of the expedition 450 miles up the Missouri River, and the sixty men proceeded upriver in
four boats. Nuttall collected plants along the river banks whenever he could, delaying
everyone else. He can't have cared much, for he had soon found some notable things. These
included important future garden plants such as *Penstemon albidus* and *P. grandiflorus*, the
white-flowered evening primrose *Oenothera caespitosa*, a silvery saltbush called *Atriplex argentea*,
and various milkweeds like the *Artemisia longifolia* and the now widely grown *A. ludoviciana*.
The voyagers shook their heads but tolerated him. One described him as

*engaged in a Pursuit to which he appears singularly devoted and which seems to engross every thought
to the total disregard of his own personal safety and sometimes to the inconvenience of the party he
accompanies. When the boat touches shore he leaps out and no sooner is his attention arrested by a*

The conservatory at Liverpool Botanic Garden, c.1808, from *A Catalogue of John Shepherd*.
Many of Thomas Nuttall's American discoveries were housed here.

plant or flower than everything else is forgotten. The inquiry is made: Où est le fou? *(Where is the fool? – He is gathering roots). He is a young man of genius and very considerable acquirements but is too much devoted to his favorite pursuit and seems to think that no other study deserves the attention of a man of sense.*

If that is what he was like in company, he was far worse when left to himself. Further up the river, walking towards what he called 'the northern Andes', meaning the Rockies, he ran out of food and water a hundred miles from the nearest trading post. Turning back too late, he fell exhausted to the ground, unable to go further. He would soon have died had not a passing Indian found him, and recognized him as the mad medicine man who gathered plants that were of no use. He loaded Nuttall into his canoe, and paddled him down to the post. On another occasion, still with the fur trappers, he set out alone and got terribly lost. He seems, by now, to have been held in some affection. His companions sent out some Indians to bring him back. The Indians tracked him down, but fearful of his medicine-making powers, they dared not approach too closely. Nuttall, however, seeing them around him, was terrified. He tried to escape, ducking into ravines and hiding in the brush. The puzzled Indians followed. It was three days before he staggered back to the post, still herded by the faithful Indians.

For all the humour at his expense, he plainly knew the value of the plants he had found. Once the expedition was over, he sailed homewards to Yorkshire from New Orleans. Before sailing, he sent most of his herbarium material to Barton, but he took with him a large quantity of seeds and living plants. Once in Britain, much of this was planted at his uncle Jonas Nuttall's garden at Nutgrove, in Lancashire. Parts of the collection were given to the Liverpool Botanic Garden, but the rest was sold on by the Frasers, whom we met in Chapter Three. Their 1813 catalogue was written by Nuttall. Many of his gorgeous new herbaceous plants were illustrated in *Curtis's Botanical Magazine*. They included the evening primroses *Oenothera missouriensis*, *O. caespitosa* and *O. nuttallii*, the subtle blue-green *Penstemon glaber*, *Camassia fraseri* (now *C. scilloides*) and *Rudbeckia columnaris*. The bigger plants included *Yucca glauca*, the golden-flowered and perfumed *Ribes aureum* and *Shepherdia argentea*.

Nuttall returned to Philadelphia in May 1818, and in that year published his *Genera of North American Plants*, a book which he mostly typeset himself. This was the third American flora, André Michaux's (see Chapter Three) being the first. Nuttall's was naturally the most

The single-minded Thomas Nuttall, in an engraving by J. Thomson published in 1825.

complete, but it left him unsatisfied, and he set out on his travels shortly afterwards, this time financed by friends who were presumably going to get seeds or plants in return. It was to be yet another hair-raising voyage. On the banks of the Ohio, he bought a ramshackle boat, and hired a ramshackle old man and his young son as crew. They were at once engulfed in troubles: ice flocs, sand bars, floods, sunken trees, river Indians. Almost by chance they found the junction with the Arkansas River, and proceeded upstream. 'Nothing could at this season exceed the beauty of these plains,' Nuttall wrote, 'enamelled with such an uncommon variety of flowers of vivid tints, possessing all the brilliancy of tropical productions. I delayed behind the party for the purpose of collecting some of the new and curious plants interspersed over these enchanting prairies.'

Once again he got lost. He lost his horse. 'My botanical acquisitions in the prairies proved so interesting,' he wrote, 'as almost to make me forget my situation, cast away amidst the refuse of society without money, unprovided with every means of subsistence.' He set off once more through the grasslands of Arkansas, walking over prairies, 'gilded with millions of *Rudbeckia amplexicaulis*'. Amazing.

With a new companion, a hunter and trapper known only as Lee, he did more exploring. Malaria and depression were never very far away. Green blowflies filled their blankets and personal linen with maggots. 'To compensate for these disgusting and familiar visitors,' he later wrote, 'we had the advantage of the bee and obtained abundance of excellent honey, on which, mixed with water, I now almost entirely subsisted.' Later, they almost wandered into a hostile Cherokee camp, but escaped just in time. The trip yielded new portulacas, new eriogonums, grasses and gentians. The prairies were now 'enamelled with innumerable flowers . . . and charming as the blissful regions of fancy'; these flowers included *Coreopsis tinctoria*, *Oenothera speciosa*, yet more penstemons and rudbeckias. He reached New Orleans on 18 February 1820, and returned to Philadelphia by sea.

The botanical knowledge Nuttall had accumulated brought him the appointment of curator of Harvard University's Botanic Garden at Cambridge, Massachusetts, a post that he held from 1822 to 1834. He made a few small sallies into the unknown, and revisited England several times, taking seeds, especially of Arkansas flowers, to be grown on by friends and nurserymen. Finally, he went on a joint trip with some naturalist companions, and crossed the Rockies, finding the lovely shrub that remains his widely planted memorial: *Cornus nuttallii*. He was so eager to go travelling again that he resigned his chair. The party went over what was to become the Oregon Trail. One of the party wrote that they 'traveled over one of the most arid plains we have seen, covered with jagged masses of lava and twisted wormwood bushes. We saw not a drop of water and our only food was dried meat . . . in these regions, the air feels like a sirocco, the tongue becomes parched and horny, the mouth, eyes, and nose are incessantly assailed by fine pulverized lava.' Even in this desert Nuttall found new plants. Finally, he reached California. He was the first botanist to visit the region, and found some more delphinium species, though neither of the red ones.

The boat he had chosen to take him back to the east coast was the *Alert*. It was the same one on which the former Harvard student Henry Dana was serving his celebrated *Two Years before the Mast*. Dana at once recognized Nuttall, and was astonished. 'I had left him quietly seated in the chair of Botany and Ornithology in Harvard University,' he wrote, 'and the next I saw of him, he was strolling about San Diego beach in a sailor's peajacket, with a wide straw hat and bare-footed, with his trousers rolled up to his knees, picking up stones and shells.' Like the Canadian boatmen years before, the sailors did not know what to make of the white-haired naturalist; they called him 'Old Curious', but thought his madness harmless.

On his eventual return via a wild rounding of the Cape of Good Hope, he was without income, and now ageing fast. Fortunately for Nuttall, his old uncle Jonas had died. He was left his estate of Nutgrove, but on the inconvenient condition that Thomas live on it for nine months of the year. He was in no position to do anything else, and so sailed once more to England. In his new garden, he grew his favourite American plants in memory, perhaps, of the extraordinary escapades during which they had been collected. He died in 1859. Almost every European garden and many American ones still grow many of his flowers.

Routes through the Rockies were becoming increasingly of interest to Americans and maps were needed. A collector who carried out some immensely important mapping of 'the wild west' was a surprising and complete contrast to the crotchety bachelor Thomas Nuttall. Unlike Nuttall, he was fabulously handsome but also a rascal, a catastrophic speculator, an estate owner, a gold miner, a pauper and completely *au fait* with civilized society as it was developing in America. He was once court martialled, and once even in the running to be President of the United States. He was also exceedingly tough in the field and found nearly a thousand new plants. Unfortunately, one of his guides on an early expedition said of him:

Morally and physically [he] was the most complete coward I ever knew, and if it were not casting an unmerited reproach on the sex, I would say that he was more timid than a woman. As an explorer, I knew more of the unexplored region fifteen years before he set foot on it, than he does today. They tell me that Stonewall Jackson whipped him in a battle, and it was no credit to Jackson, for an old squaw could whip [him]. . .'

This extraordinary person, eventually widely hated, was John Charles Fremont. He was born on 21 January 1813, in Savannah, Georgia. His was not an auspicious start, for he was the son of a 'dashing French émigré of the town' named Charles Fremon. (John Fremon later added a 't' to the end of his surname to make it sound more French.) His mother was a Mrs John Pryor, described as 'an ardent and beautiful young woman, the picture of animation and energy'. She was, perhaps because of those qualities, a discontented wife with an elderly husband. Her beautiful and intelligent young son seems to have worn his illegitimacy lightly, and found approving patrons with great ease. Supported by several (in particular the diplomat Robert Poinsett, after whom the familiar plant is named), he entered Charleston College in 1829. He was expelled two years later 'for irregular attendance' but, having done well in mathematics, talked himself into a job teaching mathematics on a warship. He rapidly left the navy to become second lieutenant in the United States Topographical Corps, later the Army Corps of Engineers. He started his travels in 1838, and in 1839 was mapping terrain around the upper Mississippi and Missouri Rivers. By 1841, he was heading his own expedition into Iowa and along the Des Moines River. The purpose of these expeditions was not primarily to look for plants. Settlers were moving west in increasing numbers – some to Oregon, where the United States had a legitimate claim, and others to California, where the claim was less clear – and there were, as yet, almost no decent maps to facilitate this movement.

Nevertheless, science was important too. The first expedition yielded more than twenty new plants, but in the second, the number was nearly eight hundred. The final tally was over a thousand. The expeditions themselves were constantly beset with problems. They were staffed by rough and ready Creole and French Canadian adventurers, paid around a dollar a day; these recruits were young, but had already spent time in the difficult lands of the western frontier. They knew how to survive in primitive conditions, could shoot and ride, and were already selected for hardiness. That was as well, for during the course of the journey they needed to be able to eat anything. At one point, all they could find for the pot was a dead skunk. Bivouacking in Sierra Nevada in 1844, they cooked the expedition dog Clammet. The expedition surveyor, squeamish at first, eventually realized that even a mule's head, stewed gently overnight, was fine if it had plenty of salt. The rest of the mule was not very appetizing, for it, like the men, was starving. At least there were good smoky fires when they were cooking; the men spent as much time as they could wrapped in the smoke. Whatever it did for their lungs, it freed them from the ever-present clouds of biting flies and mosquitoes. On parts of some of the expeditions, conditions got so bad that the carcasses of starved and desiccated cattle and horses, all no doubt headless, acted as waymarkers for the exhausted expedition.

John Fremont – 'a handsome buffoon and a rascal' – in an 1860 portrait by John George Nordheim.

Still, Fremont responded to the magnificence of the continent. One of his party wrote, crossly, 'Fremont is roaming through the mountains collecting rocks and is keeping us waiting for lunch. I am hungry. . . . That fellow knows nothing about mineralogy or botany. Yet he collects every trifle in order to have it interpreted in Washington and to brag about it in his report. Let him collect as much as he wants – if he would only not make us wait for our meal.' Fremont was oblivious. His journal for 1845 recorded: 'The depths of this unexplored forest were a place to delight the heart of a botanist. There was a rich undergrowth of plants, and numerous gay-colored flowers in brilliant blossom. . . . We wandered about among the crags and ravines until dark, richly repaid for our walk by a fine collection of plants, many of them in full bloom.' On 20 July, he wrote:

We continued our march up the stream, along a green sloping bottom, between pine hills on the one hand and the main Black hills on the other, toward the ridge which separates the waters of the Platte from those of the Arkansas. As we approached the dividing ridge, the whole valley was radiant with flowers; blued yellows pink, white, scarlet, and purple vied with each other in splendor. Esparcette was one of the highly characteristic plants, and a bright-looking flower [now thought to be Gaillardia aristata*] was very frequent; but the most abundant plant along the road today was* Geranium maculatum, *which is the characteristic plant on this portion of the dividing ground. Crossing to the waters of the Platte, fields of blue flax added to the magnificence of this mountain garden.*

The men slept in a large single lodge of buffalo hides. Fremont had a smaller version to himself. The camps were surrounded with all the mess of a plant-hunting expedition: drying paper hung in any available breeze, open plant presses, press straps, boxes of dried material. Not all of it got back to the relevant institutes and their botanists. On the second expedition, a pack mule carrying some of the plants fell into a chasm, and its entire cargo was lost. On another occasion, a camp and all its materials were swept away down the Kansas River during a sudden flood. Fremont noted that the Indians were the toughest members of the expedition. Winter, 1854: 'The Delawares all came in cold, but the whites of my party were all exhausted and broken up, and more or less frost-bitten. I lost one, Mr Fuller of St Louis, Missouri, who died on entering this valley. He died like a man, on horseback in his saddle, and will be buried like a soldier, on the spot where he fell.'

The party was attacked by hostile Indians. On 25 October 1853, Fremont's artist Richard Kern and botanist Frederick Creutzfeldt were both slain. Two seasons later, an expedition member wrote that the whole party was on foot. Lack of food made them weaker each day, and the cold was killing men and animals. They decided to dump part of the baggage to lighten all their loads. The men could at least all ride again. Whenever a horse or mule died, or was killed for food, the man who had been riding it had to walk. Killed animals were divided into twenty parts, ten for the Indians and ten for the rest. Each portion had to last for two days. The hungry consumed theirs in one day, then had to go without until the next horse or mule was killed. Each day the surviving men and animals became more gaunt and nearer starvation.

The tough travelling clearly did not diminish Fremont's social charm, and on leaving Iowa, after his first journey of discovery in 1841, he secretly married Jessie Benton, the headstrong and intelligent seventeen-year-old daughter of Senator Thomas Hart Benton. Over the next few years, she took over the writing of his expedition reports, several of which sold well. They bought an estate at Mariposa in the Sierra foothills. By chance, it had a good seam of gold, and Fremont was suddenly a millionaire. With both money and contacts, he became a senator for California in 1850 and later became the first Republican candidate for president. The American Civil War dislocated his life, as it did more terribly for so many others. He got a command in the Western Department of the Union Army, but his incompetence forced President Abraham Lincoln to get rid of him.

Worse was to come. After the war Fremont lost his fortune through ill-conceived promotions of railroads, and his wife had to support the family with her writing. Finally, her connections got him the job of territorial governor of Arizona. He tried to use that position to regain his fortunes, and spent most of the time running his own personal mining schemes or land development. Nothing worked, and under some opprobrium, he returned to California in poverty. A few months before his death he was restored to his army rank of major general and was granted retirement pay. He died on 13 July 1890 in New York City.

His contribution to the garden included some notable shrubs such as *Carpenteria californica*. The herbaceous border has blood from many of his plants. The bicoloured flowers of lupins are indebted to species he found. Sidalceas, liatrises, oenotheras, penstemons, mimuluses, cleomes, salvias, all have more. He found the silvery yellow *Lysimachia ciliata*, the smoky red *Sphaeralcea coccinea*, many sorts of milkwort and the lovely golden-foliaged *Carex aurea*.

Meanwhile, in Europe, the bedding garden was evolving fast, and all sorts of plants were being forced into its overriding need for uniformity of height (see Chapter Four). As gardeners were unwilling to give recalcitrant plants up, they had to be grown somewhere else. The area devoted to them became the herbaceous border. Something similar had sometimes been planted around the perimeter of early eighteenth-century parterres, often in a long bed against the surrounding walls, if the garden were grand enough to have them. Such beds had survived into the early nineteenth century, when John Claudius Loudon in his *Encyclopaedia of Gardening* wrote of the 'promiscuous' planting schemes of these old-fashioned gardens. He uses that word to mean a planting scheme where no two plants of

The pale yellow *Lysimachia ciliata* was one of Fremont's greatest contributions to the herbaceous border.

the same sort were planted next to one another. Some of his suggested plants included the very latest arrivals: *Anemone japonica* (now *A.* x *hybrida*), *Zauschneria californica*, *Dicentra spectabilis*. Now it was plain that every garden had to have a herbaceous border. All that was needed was some way to make them look less of a mess.

At the same time, the bedding garden began to look, at least to some enquiring gardeners, lurid. It was an artificial system that reduced plants to being merely the providers of undifferentiated colour. The tiniest gardens had stars and scrolls of scarlet pelargoniums, purple verbenas and yellow calceolarias, lobelias and petunias. Stylish gardeners shuddered and hoped for something different. William Robinson was to be the most audacious critic of the bedding garden. In his book *The Wild Garden*, of 1870, he inveighed against what gardening had become, with its insistence on intense maintenance and colour saturation. He began to push the sort of plants that were hardy, wanting the reader to grow thalictrums, anemones (such as *Anemone apennina*, as well as the new *A.* x *hybrida* 'Honorine Jobert'), and a vast list of hardy herbaceous flowers.

The new herbaceous border needed space. It had to display eupatoriums, plume poppies and the increasingly tall delphiniums. Borders needed to be at least six feet deep to allow sufficient space for banks of colour, and they could hardly be less than thirty feet long to register at all. Their plants needed spraying, staking, dividing, manuring: all of which were time-consuming and very expensive. Their season only ran from mid-summer to mid-autumn, which was insufficient in small gardens where the border was the only element. The herbaceous border swiftly became one of the great artifices of the garden, hinting at the abundance of nature, but also at the abundance of the owner's purse. It allowed the wealthy to differentiate their sort of garden from the gardens seen on seafronts or in front of boarding houses. That it was also becoming increasingly wealthy in botanical terms too merely added to its attractions.

This wealth was not just derived from the flora of North America. The Treaty of Nanking of 1842 had opened China to foreigners for the first time. Botanists already knew that the seaboard of China was filled with exciting and economically important plants. They wanted to see. What they initially failed to realize was that western China, with its colossal system of mountain chains and narrow valleys, was infinitely richer still. It took another few decades for that area to be explored, and it turned out to be exceptionally dangerous. The coastal regions too were hazardous. One explorer's tale, of a trip made in the late 1840s, ran:

About four o'clock in the afternoon the captain and pilot came hurriedly down to my cabin and informed me that they saw a number of Jan-do [pirates] right ahead, lying in wait for us. . . . I therefore considered it prudent to be prepared for the worst. I got out of bed, ill and feverish as I was, and carefully examined my fire-arms. . . . I also rammed down a ball upon the top of each charge of shot in my gun, put a pistol in each side pocket, and patiently waited the result. . . .

All was now dismay and consternation on board our junk, and every man ran below except two who were at the helm. I expected every moment that these also would leave their post; and then we should have been an easy prey to the pirates. 'My gun is nearer you than those of the Jan dous,' said I to the two men, 'and if you move from the helm depend upon it I will shoot you.' The poor fellows looked very uncomfortable.

The pirates now seemed quite sure of their prize, and came down upon us hooting and yelling like demons, at the same time loading their guns, and evidently determined not to spare their shot. This was a moment of intense interest. . . .

The nearest junk was now within thirty yards of ours, their guns were now loaded, and I knew that the next discharge would completely rake our decks. 'Now,' said I to our helmsmen, 'keep your eyes fixed on me, and the moment you see me fall flat on the deck you must do the same'. . . . We had scarcely done so, when bang! bang! went their guns, and the shot came whizzing close over us, splintering the wood about us in all directions. . . . 'Now, mandarin, now! they are quite close enough', cried out my companions, who did not wish to have another broadside like the last. I, being of the same opinion, raised myself above the high stern of our junk; and while the pirates were not more than twenty yards away from us, hooting and yelling, I raked their decks fore and aft, with shot and ball from my double barrelled gun.

Had a thunderbolt fallen amongst them, they could not have been more surprised. Doubtless many were wounded, and probably some killed. . . .

They were so completely taken by surprise that their junk was left without a helmsman . . . and, as we were still carrying all sail and keeping on our right course, they were soon left a considerable way astern. . . . Another was now bearing down upon us as boldly as his companion had done. . . . I determined to follow the same plan with this one, and to pay no attention to his firing until he should come to close quarters. The plot now began to thicken; for the first junk had gathered way again, and was following in our wake . . . and three others, although still further distant, were making for the scene of action as fast as they could. In the mean time, the second was almost alongside, and continued giving us a broadside now and then with their guns. . . .

My poor fellows who were steering kept begging and praying that I would fire into our pursuers as soon as possible, or we should all be killed. As soon as they came within twenty or thirty yards of us, I gave them the contents of both barrels, raking their decks as before. This time the helmsman fell and doubtless several others were wounded . . . their junk went up into the wind . . . and was soon left some distance behind us . . . Two other piratical junks which had been following in our wake for some time, when they saw what had happened, would not venture any nearer; and at last, much to my satisfaction, the whole set of them bore away.

Lilium auratum, the golden-rayed lily of Japan, was one of the many sumptuous garden plants brought back to Europe by Robert Fortune and other plant collectors after their visits to the Japanese capital in the 1860s. This illustration is from the *Botanical Magazine*.

The explorer in question was Robert Fortune (1812–80), and his herbaceous plant haul included the marvellously beautiful white-flowered form of *Anemone* x *japonica* which he had found growing on the graves of Shanghai. Over several journeys in China and Japan, his contribution to the herbaceous border was enormous. From China alone it included, apart from the anemone, *Adamia versicolor, Arundinaria sinensis, Callistegia pubescens, Chirita sinensis* (later to win awards as a great garden plant), endless chrysanthemums, *Dielytra* (now *Dicentra*) *spectabilis, Platycodon grandiflorum* and *P. grandiflorum* 'Album', huge numbers of peonies, many ferns including the handsome *Cyrtomium fortunei, Statice fortunei*, as well as campanulas, farfugiums, *Aster turbinellus, Eupatorium fortunei, Gentiana scabra* var. *fortunei* and more. From Japan he introduced yet more chrysanthemums, a variegated lily of the valley, the parasitic *Lastrea standishii, Lilium auratum* and *L. lancifolium, Saxifraga fortunei*, the gaudy-leaved *S. stolonifera* 'Tricolor' and *Primula japonica*.

Fortune was born on 16 September 1812, near Duns in Berwickshire, the son of a hedger on the Kelloe estate. Showing plenty of talent, he went to work at the Royal Botanic Garden, Edinburgh from 1839, then in 1842 sailed for London to become Superintendent of Hothouses at the Horticultural Society's garden at Chiswick. That was the year of the Treaty of Nanking and the Society was eager to obtain its rumoured botanical riches. By February 1843 Fortune had got the job of Collector for the Society at a salary of £100 per year. He was thirty-one years old. Then as now the Society was divided up into committees. The minutes of the Chinese Committee for 1842–3 drew up a job description. He was 'to collect seed and plants of an ornamental or useful kind, not already cultivated in Great Britain . . . and to obtain information upon Chinese Gardening and Agriculture together with the nature of the Climate and its apparent influence on vegetation'. The Society asked him to find all sorts of exotic plants, some entirely mythical like 'Peaches of Pekin', and the legendary yellow-flowered camellia. He was also to find 'Plants that yield Tea of different qualities', 'the plant which furnishes Rice Paper' and 'The Orange called CumQuat'. The Society issued him with the firearms that saved him from the pirates, and many letters of introduction.

He may already have seen a 'Wardian case' in a house overlooking the Botanic Garden in Edinburgh, and he was to make extensive use of these cases throughout his career. They were, in essence, small glasshouses. Young plants could be shipped around the globe, needing scarcely any watering, and being free of sea spray, rats and interfering sailors. They were kept in the light, on the poop if possible, or on deck, or, if there was no room, 'in the Main or Mizzen-top'.

Fortune's account of his first visit to China was published in 1847 as *Three Years' Wanderings in the Northern Provinces of China*, and was very popular. He took some remarkable risks for his plants. As no foreigners were allowed to travel more than thirty miles from the main ports of Amoy, Fuchou, Ningpo or Shanghai, Fortune used a disguise. He had his head shaved, wore a wig and tail, dressed in local clothes and, he wrote, 'made a pretty fair Chinaman'. British officials certainly knew of this, and approved. It was astonishing that he was not discovered, for he visited endless Chinese nurseries, got followed around by Chinese children, even Chinese thugs, yet must have remained mute through all these encounters.

Robert Fortune increased Europe's garden flora by nearly two hundred new plants from China and Japan.

Still, his collections grew, though at one point, near Ningpo, he tumbled into a pit dug to catch wild boar. He managed to grab a twig on the way down, and saved his life. Had any Chinese been near, his cover would certainly have been broken. He later mused that had the twig not held, he would have suffered the 'fate of my predecessor, Mr Douglas, who perished in a pit of this kind on the Sandwich Islands . . . his melancholy end naturally coming to my mind at the time, made me doubly thankful for my escape'.

To make certain that his material reached Europe, he divided his collections into three or four consignments, sending them home on different boats, and by different routes. Travelling home with one of them, he wrote: 'As I went down the river I could not but look around me with pride and satisfaction; for in this part of the country I had found the finest plants in my collections.' When he returned from Japan, he turned out to be on the same boat as the nurseryman John Veitch. Veitch was amused to see the boat loaded 'so that the whole of the poop was lined with glass cases crammed full of the natural productions of Japan. Never before had such an interesting and valuable collection of plants occupied the deck of any vessel, and most devoutly did we hope that our beloved plants might be favoured with fair winds and smooth seas.'

Many of Fortune's and Veitch's plants from the east of China had long been known, even domesticated, in Chinese gardens in the great centres of Chinese culture, all in the eastern parts of the country. However, the plants of the far reaches of the west were unknown even to the Chinese. There the mountainous terrain made communication and cultivation difficult, and the indigenous peoples spoke strange languages. China raised what taxes it could, but left the inhabitants otherwise to themselves. Over the centuries, Christian missionaries had had mixed fortunes in China but in 1860, the Chinese were forced to agree to allow missionaries to travel throughout their entire land, and towards the end of the nineteenth century, French missionary societies sent substantial numbers of priests. These men, some of exceptional energy and imagination, fanned out through the country, some into the country's remote western regions. When the French missionaries interested in Chinese plants began to send material back to Paris, it was at once clear that they had stumbled into a treasure trove.

That area of the country, bordering on Myanmar (Burma) and Bhutan, is part of the eastern system of mountains thrown up as India crashes formidably into the great tectonic

This mode of transport, illustrated in Robert Fortune's *Three Years' Wanderings in the Northern Provinces of China* (1847), is called a 'mountain chair'. The seat was a rough plank of wood.

plates to the north and east. The Yangtze River penetrates to their very centre. As with all new mountain chains, the valleys formed are deep and steep-sided. The climate in them can often run from humid and sub-tropical at the base, to plantless and permanently snowed up at the top. This change can be encompassed in less than half a mile of horizontal difference. Plant communities even in adjacent valleys are genetically completely isolated from one another as pollinating insects cannot cross the topographical barriers. Either through haphazard events, or through environmental and climatic pressures, plant species change rapidly. Without the stabilizing influence of large amounts of their original genetic material from distant populations, plant populations quickly alter to become, as far as plant taxonomists are concerned, new species. Western China is also astonishingly rich, as it lies at the junction of three huge floristic regions, those of the tropic south, the Indian continent and the Middle East.

The first French missionary to send material home was Abbé Armand David (1826–1900). In 1862, at the age of thirty-six, he received a posting to the Mission of Lazarists in Peking, where he was to teach science and natural history. Born in Espelette, a small Pyrenean town, he was one of the three sons of Fructueux David, the local doctor, mayor and magistrate. Fructueux had three passions: medicine, good food and natural history; he had a son for each. Young Armand became the natural historian, walking the Navarre foothills for eleven or twelve hours in a day hunting for interesting things for his collection. It was a good training. Once in China, he couldn't help but continue. His beautifully prepared specimens from remote regions of Mongolia, central China and the Tibetan border caused a sensation in the scientific circles in Paris. He was given leave from his missionary duties so that he could concentrate on collecting.

He made three huge journeys in the late 1860s. All of them were undertaken with a remarkable disregard for comfort or safety: he said that if he were to take notice of such things he would never get anywhere. He was often ill, became caught up in local wars, almost always in places where he was the first westerner ever to be seen, and was the object of intense suspicion by local monks. He found transport hard to find, and difficult to keep. Once, having obtained an obliging donkey, he found it necessary to allow it to share his tent to protect it from hungry local wolves. Sometimes he was so weak and exhausted that he fainted and couldn't go on. Sometimes he was stuck on a river bank for months, waiting for a spate to subside. Even when rivers were navigable, conditions were hard; once on the upper reaches of the Yangtse, in a region of rapids and gorges, it took eighty hauliers to get his boat up through the current. The tow rope broke several times; the gorge's shallows were littered with the ominous remains of previous wrecks. There were huge compensations. He was the first westerner ever to see a panda. He found rare wild silkworms. He saw an astonishing new tree, with white bracts the size of handkerchiefs, which was to be named *Davidia involucrata*. He saw countless other new plants.

David caught malaria and had severe bouts of 'intestinal irritation', even symptoms of typhus, with terrible pain and swelling in the legs. Chinese doctors called it 'bone-typhus' and treated him with ginger and onions moistened with brandy. He was obliged to cut short his travels and leave for more civilized regions. After years in the field, he journeyed back to Shanghai in a sedan chair, but his malaria got so bad that he was given the last rites. He didn't die, and made it back to Paris, where he was to find over eighty species of plants growing in the garden of the Musée d'Histoire Naturelle, from seeds he had sent home.

These were but a fraction of his botanical discoveries. Many were eventually brought back to European and American gardens by others. His botanical collections were sumptuously published as *Plantae Davidianae*, the first volume of which appeared in 1884, containing forty-five illustrations, hand-coloured in some copies. A second volume, devoted to the plants of eastern Tibet, followed in 1888. In spite of the ills he had suffered in China, he lived to see his seventy-sixth year, lecturing to prospective missionaries in the rooms of his own museum.

Here is an astonishing list of more sumptuous plants from the same region, all now widely grown: *Thalictrum delavayi*, *T. dipterocarpum*, *Anemone delavayi*, *Paeonia delavayi*, *P. lutea*, *Meconopsis betonicifolia*, *Rodgersia pinnata*, the lovely *Primula delavayi*, *P. malacoides*, the wildly coloured and popular *P. vialii* (named after a M. Vial), *Clematis chrysocoma*, dozens of the first *Nomocharis* species, *Roscoea*, several sorts of *Trollius* and vast numbers of species of *Delphinium*, *Corydalis*, *Draba*, *Saxifraga*, *Sedum*, *Gentiana*, *Androsace* and *Lilium*, not to mention *Incarvillea delavayi*.

As many names in the list suggest, the collector of many of these was Père Jean Marie Delavay (1838–95). Little is known about his early life. Born in Abondance, Haute-Savoie, France, he doesn't emerge from the shadows until he is a missionary priest recently arrived

Tombs near the ancient city of Amoy c. 1843; an engraving after Thomas Allom.
All Chinese tombs were planted with species designed to show the status of the occupant:
Koelreuteria paniculata for high officials, *Sophora japonica* for lesser ones.

at the Chinese region of Guangdong, already with an obsession for hunting plants. He first started collecting in a small way in order to oblige Dr Henry Fletcher Hance, a member of the British Consular Service in Canton and Hong Kong. However, in 1881, Delavay went home to France on leave, and while in Paris he met Père David. David introduced him to Adrien René Franchet, the Director of the Musée d'Histoire Naturelle and immediately Delavay agreed to send his future collections to Franchet. Franchet had no idea what he was setting in motion. He proved unable to cope with the flood of material that Delavay soon started to send.

Franchet had managed with David's plants, describing more than 250 new species and ten or eleven new genera. He had even managed to publish *Plantae Davidianae*. But Delavay sent him some 200,000 beautifully prepared specimens, constituting 4,000 species, about 1,500 of them new. In 1885, Franchet tried to write an alphabetical summary of Delavay's plants, but got no further than the letter A. He made a start on compiling a *Plantae Delavayi* in 1889, but died before it was finished. Some consignments of Delavay's material were not even opened until decades later.

Unlike Père David, who was released by his order from any attempt at gaining Chinese souls for Christianity, Delavay had missionary work to do as well. He seems to have managed both strands of his life by exploring a relatively small area of China with great intensity: he is said to have climbed Mount Tsemei Shan, which he called 'his garden', sixty times from all sides and at all seasons. Contemporary plant collectors increasingly find this an important approach, for the flora of the region is so rich, that even a month can bring into flower an entirely new range of species. Even with such an intensive cover of a small area, Delavay realized that he had hardly tapped the resources of the rich Chinese alpine flora.

He seems to have been as blind to danger as David. He could not, however, avoid one of the scourges of Asia. In 1888 he contracted bubonic plague, and though it did not kill him, he lost the use of his right arm and was in bad health for the rest of his life. He brought one more load of specimens and seeds back to France, then returned to China in 1893. He reached Yun-nan-sen in February 1895, and died in December of that year. Few of the seeds he had collected did well back home, although *Deutzia purpurascens*, *Incarvillea delavayi*, *Iris delavayi*, *Paeonia lutea* and *Rhododendron racemosum* soon reached the garden. His herbarium material entranced gardeners. It launched dozens of collectors, anxious to be the first to bring home, and establish, marvellous herbaceous plants such as *Meconopsis betonicifolia*, *Primula malacoides*, *Thalictrum dipterocarpum* and the genus *Nomocharis*.

Once established, these marvels were an overnight success with gardeners. The herbaceous border was the obvious place for the larger plants. Some of the new genera and species allowed new effects. No one had ever seen anything like the purple haze of the *Thalictrum delavayi*, or wondered what to plant with the exotic pink trumpets of *Incarvillea*. Using new marvels from China, and the new hybrids fast developing in dozens of other genera, designers such as Gertrude Jekyll were able to start playing with painterly ideas. She began by inventing the colour scheme for a border, then looked for plants to fill the roles needed. In effect, planting design was turned back to front. Many of her plans survive, but are often so sumptuous that they can hardly be recreated today. Other designers used simpler schemes which are much more relevant to contemporary gardeners. One excellent designer was Miss Hope, a spinster of Edinburgh, who wrote frequently for the magazines of the day, notably *Gardeners' Chronicle* and *The Garden*. She liked combining the new red or creamy white peonies with the perfumed lemon yellow flowers of *Hemerocallis lilioasphodelus*. For smaller plantings, she combined *Delphinium formosanum* with the greeny pink and thread-like petals of *Tellima grandiflora*. For larger ones she mixed white spires of *Aruncus sylvestris* with the cold yellow *Aconitum vulparia* and the cream-variegated leaves of gardeners' garters (*Phalaris arundinacea* 'Elegantissima'), or glittering rust-red *Papaver orientalis* with straw-coloured irises.

However, many plants specially created for the herbaceous borders of the early twentieth century face extinction. Purism among gardeners is on the increase, and fancifully named and flamboyantly over-developed hybrids are seen as less admirable than pure species collected from the meadows of the mid-west or the valleys of Yünnan. Yet what has happened to the flowers at the hands of the nurseryman and the gardener is only what can happen in nature, but vastly speeded up. Continents no longer need to collide, or valley systems erode or be scoured clean by glaciers. We gardeners bring plants together. We gardeners get hooked by our plants. Our weakness for them hugely enhances their evolutionary possibilities. They win.

THE GLASS
GARDEN

On a frozen late afternoon in December 1843, at the Duke of Devonshire's stupendous garden at Chatsworth in Derbyshire, England, the Great Conservatory's vast central aisle was lit by 12,000 tiny lamps. Their light shone softly on the foliage and flowers of plants gathered from the jungles of Guatemala and Gabon, from the dripping foothills of the Himalayas, and from the swamps of the Malayan archipelago. Footmen rushed to the great glass doors, opened them, and an equipage of jet black horses harnessed to an open carriage clattered in. The landau bore the young Queen Victoria and Prince Albert. They had come to look at one of the most astonishing glasshouses ever built, and one of the greatest collections of fabulous rarities ever assembled. Yet, for all the orchids, many of which had been collected especially for the Duke, the twining palms from South America, the gaudy bougainvilleas, the colossal ferns, the new begonias and pandanus and passion flowers, the Duke's conservatory was destined to house more extraordinary plants still. And what he had growing in his epitome of glasshouses, everyone wanted. They would soon have a good part of it.

Houses for exotic 'greens' had appeared in the gardens of the wealthy in the sixteenth century, but they were little more than a spare room in the garden quarters, with minimal heating, usually an open fireplace, for winter. Among their winter inhabitants were lemons, myrtles and oleanders. The orangery, popular well into the eighteenth century, was hardly much of an advance, being solidly roofed and often

The Great Conservatory at Chatsworth, Derbyshire, in 1843. Here, fabulous orchids and tropical water lilies flowered for the first time in Europe, among Brazilian ferns, palms and pandanus.

with only one wall fully glazed. Nor were the heated 'green' houses at botanic gardens such as those at Leiden in Holland or those built at Oxford in England between 1680 and 1687, apart from having glazed roofs. Sub-tropical and tropical plants sent home by seventeenth-century collectors such as Dr Paul Hermann, from his voyages to South Africa and the Far East, stood little chance of survival.

Things changed gradually. The growers of exotic greens looked to the kitchen garden, where gardeners had long been aware of the heat given off by fermenting farmyard dung and had used it to bring on early vegetables like asparagus and peas, or to induce melons to fruit in northern Europe. Bell jars, glass cloches or even whole frames were placed on hotbeds built of horse manure, and the plants were grown in pockets of soil. Glass became gradually cheaper through the eighteenth century, and glasshouses of the sort we would recognize today began to be built in the kitchen gardens of the wealthy, still heated by fermenting manure beds. Even in northern climates, this technology could give prodigious crops of pineapples, early cherries, strawberries, asparagus and so on. As well as heat, the dung gave off large amounts of water vapour and a degree of smell. Glasshouses were clearly not suited to all plants, nor all people. Alternatives were needed. At first, the back walls of lean-to glasshouses were built containing winding chimney flues. With a furnace fed from the back of the house, hot air and fumes wound up through the wall, heating the air in which the plants grew. The level of heat depended on the skill of whoever fed the furnace. However, the heat given off was very dry, and this encouraged pests like red spider. Any leakage of fumes into the glasshouse rapidly killed the plants. A better method of heating greenhouses was becoming more and more urgent, as tropical plants were arriving in increasing numbers, and gardeners were getting the itch to grow them.

In the early nineteenth century, and especially during the Napoleonic Wars, the art of casting iron became far more refined. Iron tubing to hold hot water or even steam became very much cheaper. Coal was plentiful. The scene was set. The repeal of Britain's 'glass tax' in 1845 was, in that country at least, the trigger to a huge increase in the ownership of glasshouses. It enabled them to be moved from the kitchen garden, and to be attached, even to modest homes, as conservatories. Suddenly, there was a colossal market for the exotic vegetation of the tropics.

Soon glasshouses ranged from backyard lean-tos for the culture of calceolarias from Brazil, to Decimus Burton's Palm House at Kew or Prince Potemkin's vast conservatory at the Tauridian Palace in St Petersburg, containing his own private jungle. His gardener, Mr Gould, had this heated with hot-water pipes. 'Great emulation now exists in this department of horticulture not only among country gentlemen but among commercial Gardeners,' wrote John Claudius Loudon in the edition of his *Encyclopaedia of Gardening* published in 1828. In London, the firm of Conrad Loddiges was renowned among nurserymen for its palm house, 45 feet high and 60 feet wide, and for its plant house 18 feet high, 23 feet wide and upwards of 100 feet long, which stood without a single rafter or column.

All this excitement was the result of a series of great expeditions, mostly French, to South America. One of the first was that of Charles-Marie de La Condamine. His basic aim was to measure the diameter of the globe, but he was accompanied by Joseph de Jussieu

(1704–79), the expedition botanist. He was one of three famous French botanist brothers, their joint enthusiasm for botany encouraged by their pharmacist father. They sailed from La Rochelle on 16 May 1735. The whole trip was a drama. While at sea, they seem continually to have been wrapped in storms, or long calms when men got sick and died; when on land, they were caught up in riots and war. Botanically, though, the expedition was vastly influential. Jussieu sent home the first cinchona trees, the first coca plants and the first heliotropes, and when La Condamine noticed Indians using a strange resin that could be moulded and bounced, the rubber tree (*Hevea brasiliensis*) was on its way to the West. These discoveries were all made under terrible difficulties; several members of the expedition went mad, some were slain, some died of disease. La Condamine lasted it out for ten years, returning in 1744. Jussieu seems to have become deeply, even morbidly, mesmerized by the jungles and was unable to tear himself away. He stayed on in Peru, earning a living as a doctor. His brothers entreated him to return, and once they even managed to get him to the dockside. He vanished back into the wilderness just as the ship was to sail, and ended up ministering to the miners of Bolivia, especially in the notorious Potosi silver mines. At last, in 1771, his surviving brother Bernard sent friends, who fetched him home. On his homeward journey his notes were lost at sea or mouldered, and in Paris, crushed, he sat mute in a darkened room until death released him.

While Jussieu was busying himself in the wilds of Bolivia, another Frenchman, Philibert Commerson (1727–73), was in a hurry to get to South America. He was late. In his hectic life, this was not unusual, but on this occasion he was in danger of missing a boat, one on which he very much wanted to sail. It was the *Étoile*, docked at Rochefort, an ungainly 480-ton storeship, 111 feet long, and with a complement of 8 officers and 108 men. The captain was the kindly François Chenard de la Giraudais. The companion ship to the *Étoile*, the *Boudeuse*, was docked at Nantes, and together they were to embark on one of the first great global scientific expeditions. The expedition's prime mover was the rakish, handsome and immensely civilized Louis-Antoine Bougainville (1729–1811). Commerson, a botanist, had been taken on as the ship's naturalist and doctor. He was also a man escaping private unhappiness.

As he journeyed to Rochefort, he pressed the postillion to drive faster. He later wrote:

I had to traverse the dangerous part of the Luberon . . . to find that no postillion would agree to go, because four or five days before this a chaise had been robbed on this road. I exhibited the King's order, for I was travelling on his service, and so forced the postmaster to obey me. Yet, in spite of this, the only person willing to ride the posthorse was a young rascal of eleven or twelve years old, who indeed was both skilful and courageous, for his beggarly comrades did all they could to discourage him, crying 'Go and get yourself killed.' He replied quite cheerfully 'Oh, no, I'm too young. The gentlemen will pay for the two of us.' All this commotion was foolish, for we met nothing more alarming than a hat lying by the roadside. Seeing the hat the young imp had stopped and was preparing to dismount. I asked what was the matter. He answered, 'A hat, Sir. I must pick it up.' 'Go on, leave it, and I will give you a crown.' 'Oh, no, sir,' he replied, 'I would lose by that, for it has gold embroidery.' And so the young rascal mounted and rode on with the hat on his crupper.

The strange Philibert Commerson in a portrait by P. Pagnier.

Commerson travelled as fast as he could manage, clattering through both night and day, travelling more than eight hundred miles in less than three days. He didn't even give himself time to take off his boots. He reached Rochefort just in time for the right tide, but after all his haste, the *Étoile* was delayed. It remained in the harbour for another couple of weeks, though the *Boudeuse* had set sail on 5 November 1766. The two ships were to rendezvous at the Malvinas (Falkland Islands), where Bougainville, to his great chagrin, was to hand over to the Spanish the colony which he had founded there.

Commerson's enforced wait at Rochefort gave him time to collect himself. He carried out administrative chores, such as reconsidering his will. Much of it was concerned with his infant son, left in the care of relatives. Commerson also took care of his servants, especially the housekeeper he had engaged. He left her the furnishings and contents of his Paris flat at M. Le Gendre's, Fauxbourg St Victoire, rue des Bolangers, and allowed her a year's tenancy, during which time she was to administer his natural history collections before giving them to the state.

He was a strange man with a strange childhood. He was born, a second son, on 18 November 1727, at Chatillon-les-Dombes (now Chatillon-sur-Chalaronne), in Ain, France. His grandfather had been a Michel de Commerson, Chatelain of the Seigneurie de Romans. It was an ancient family, and the stump of their medieval castle still stands. However, he was so poor that he held no pretensions of grandeur, sold what was left of the estate, and became a lawyer in Macon. Philibert's father followed the same profession, though perhaps nursed regrets for the family's loss of status. He seems to have been very hard on his many children. Our Commerson wrote to his own son's guardians,

I wish you to draw the conclusion that children must be brought up hardly. That was the system of my poor father, and I owe him many obligations for having put it in practice in my own case. He made me go about in winter without special winter clothing, and also in summer without taking my clothes off. So, in spite of the tender affection which I bear to my child, and of the kindness which I have asked you to show in his moral education, my intentions are that you subject him to hard gymnastics and the greatest sobriety. Let him never wear hat or bonnet, gloves or mittens; keep him in winter as far away from the fire as is possible without his suffering too severely. Let him become strong by chopping wood, carrying successively heavier burdens, jumping hedges and ditches, and using both left and right hand. The value of this last accomplishment is not sufficiently understood.

Such an upbringing seems to have produced in Philibert a sense of insufficiency rather than self-sufficiency. Philibert's father was successful enough as a lawyer to provide all his children with small incomes. He saw that Philibert had an obsession with botany, and sent him to Montpellier University. There, the young Commerson was quickly recognized as brilliant. It was equally clear that he was a compulsive, indeed maniacal, collector of plants, herbarium specimens, botanical treatises, books and catalogues. His local expeditions around Montpellier were filled with hair-raising exploits, and were often undertaken with no thought for his preservation. He travelled with neither money nor provisions. He would return home ill, scarred by accidents, worn out by the intensity of his enthusiasm. He was completely dominated by the need to collect, and accepted his friends' calling him a 'botanomaniac'. Nothing stopped him, not even morality; he sometimes stole plants from other collectors, and got into considerable trouble. After one trip, he returned home shaking with fever, and wondered if he could find a cure at the baths of Bourbon-Lancy. Even when there, he couldn't stop plant hunting, and began visiting the curé of a nearby village. Perhaps the curé knew something about plants. Certainly, he had a pretty sister. She and Commerson were soon married. His new wife brought him a fortune, and her influence seems to have calmed the fires that burnt within him. She also bore him a greatly loved son whom they christened Archambault. Two years later she died. Grief set Philibert once more ablaze.

In Paris, he had come to the attention of Bougainville and young Archambault was consigned to the care of an uncle when Commerson set off to travel the world. At Rochefort, on 2 January 1767, the *Étoile* was ready to sail. Amid the muddle of departure, just as the gangway was about to be pulled aboard, a young man pressed forward, begging to be taken on the voyage. Commerson needed a valet. In the rush and haste, the man was waved up the gangway with no questions asked, no answers given. The Fates must have smiled behind their hands.

Commerson seems to have been a trifle cocksure. He wrote, soon after the French coast vanished below the horizon: 'Once on board, the slight experience I have so far had of the sea has not been particularly trying. I believe that I shall soon get my sea-legs, and I have not yet suffered from sea-sickness.' In a later letter, he wrote: 'What repentance everywhere. A ship is like a mousetrap wherein each perceives his piece of cheese. Once the sails are spread, the trap falls.' He was to become almost mortally seasick, and was never a good sailor. He did, though, recover quickly at each landfall, and his usual obsessive pattern started up. He collected whatever he could find. He wrote: 'Often I do not know where to begin. Often I forget to eat and drink. Indeed, the captain, an excellent friend of mine, has gone so far as to forbid me any light after midnight, because he perceived that I was injuring my health in thus robbing myself of sleep – for I need the whole night to examine properly all that comes before me.'

Meanwhile, on board the *Boudeuse*, Bougainville had reached Montevideo, now capital of Uruguay, then the only good harbour in the whole of the Spanish colonies in South America. He had to meet up with the future governor of the Malvinas, then sail back to those islands for their official exchange. When he had accomplished all that, still the *Étoile*

An 1881 engraving, after a painting by
Edouard Riou, showing the
Esmeraldas jungle in Ecuador.

had not appeared. Not giving it up for lost, on 21 June 1767, Bougainville anchored in the harbour of Rio de Janeiro. The *Étoile* was waiting for him. The ship had been there for six days, and already its chaplain had been murdered ashore. For gardeners, something more important had happened. Commerson had been collecting. At their first anchorage of Montevideo, he saw why the Spanish explorers of 1513 had called the river the Rio de la Plata, not from its silver, but because on its banks grew endless millions of white zephyr lilies (*Zephyranthes candida*). It's a lovely thing to grow. He was enchanted; indeed, the whole exquisite beauty of Brazil delighted him. Of the area around Rio de Janeiro, he wrote:

This country is the Loveliest in the world; in the very middle of winter oranges, bananas, pineapples continually succeed one another. The trees never lose their greenery. The interior, rich in every sort of game as well as in sugar, in rice, in manioc, etc., offers, without any labour of cultivation, a delicious subsistence to its inhabitants, as well as to thousands of slaves who have but the trouble of gathering its fruits . . . You know my mania for observing everything: in the midst of all these troubles, in spite of a formal prohibition to go outside the town, and even notwithstanding a Fearful sore on my leg which had appeared at sea, I ventured to go out twenty times with my servant in a canoe, which was paddled by two blacks, and visited, one after another, the different shores and islands of the bay.

He found another species of zephyr lily, and also a rather showy violet-flowered scrambling climber. Perhaps he thought it would make an ironic tribute to the expedition's flamboyant leader. Without telling him, Commerson wrote home, describing it scientifically as *Bougainvillea*. Once the plant reached Europe, it went suddenly onwards from its erstwhile habitat in the margins of South American forests to get an almost planet-wide distribution and was to make his name live for ever.

More scuffles having broken out between his crews and the Portuguese settlers, Bougainville thought it prudent to leave straight away. His plan was to circumnavigate the globe while carrying out scientific investigations. A pattern developed whereby whenever possible the ships would find safe harbour, and let the scientists get on with their observations. Commerson was indefatigable. His exertions were vastly helped by his faithful valet, Jean, whom he often mentions in his letters, and who carried all the equipment that was necessary. Commerson took to calling the boy his 'faithful beast of burden', and was very obviously grateful for his fortitude, for his ingenious attempts to make both their lives more comfortable, and for his endless willingness to carry firearms and the substantial amount of collecting equipment.

In April 1768, the ships anchored in a coral-ringed bay on the shore of one of a group of beautiful islands in the South Pacific. Bougainville, as he had been doing throughout the expedition, at once claimed them for France, naming the island Nouvelle-Cythère, and the whole group of islands Archipel de Bourbon. The local name for the island was Tahiti. On 7 April, Bougainville met the local chieftain and somehow managed to establish permission to set up a camp near the beach. The ships' sick were brought ashore, and fresh water was given them from the nearby stream. They found rest in a land of plenty. For iron, earrings and other baubles, they bought pigs, chickens, pigeons, bananas, shells, strange cloths, and native weapons and fishing gear. The French entertained the Tahitians with music and a fireworks display. Commerson was, of course, soon furiously busy, describing and dissecting new and rare fishes, and gathering many new plants. His valet accompanied him. The local chief, Ereti, took a strong interest in the young man, and, with a group of followers, made off with him. French sailors set up a pursuit. In the following scuffle, the young man's clothes were ripped apart. He turned out to be a young woman. She was, in fact, Jeanne Baret, Commerson's Paris housekeeper. She was hurried back to the *Étoile* and interrogated by Bougainville. Bougainville's cool account is as follows:

> *There had been a rumour that M. de Commerson's servant (Baret by name) was a woman. His features, the tone of his voice, his beardless chin, the scrupulous care which he took never to change his linens etc., before anybody, as well as other indications, seemed to confirm this suspicion . . . When I was on board the* Étoile, *Baret confessed to me, her eyes streaming with tears, that she was a woman. She told me that at Rochefort she had deceived her master by presenting herself before him in men's clothes at the very moment when he was about to embark. She said she had already been a lackey in the service of a Genoese in Paris, she was an orphan born in Burgundy and had been rendered utterly destitute by the loss of a lawsuit, so that she has chosen to disguise her sex. Moreover, she knew that it was a case of Voyaging round the world, and this had aroused her curiosity for she would be the first of her sex to do this. I must, in justice, say that on board she had always conducted herself with the utmost propriety. She is neither ugly nor pretty and is not more than twenty-six or twenty-seven years of age.*

Commerson's will suggests that he had no idea that she would follow him. Yet, fiercely observant by nature, can he really have failed to notice his new servant's features? Was she in the carriage as it clattered through the Luberon? Commerson named a genus of plants after her. Alas, unlike *Bougainvillea*, it has become submerged as a synonym for another genus. She was faithful to her master until his end. Commerson was not well. The *Étoile* sailed out of the Tahiti anchorage on the 14th. The *Boudeuse* managed to raise its anchors and leave the next day. Though, later, many of the sailors began to show signs of syphilis, the French, who had only been on the island for nine days began, in their writings and memoirs, to create a picture of an earthly paradise. In spite of the thieving, the constant quarrels, the episode of abduction, the Tahitian people were depicted as proof that Rousseau's 'noble savage' really did exist, and that with the right climate, the abundant crops and game, the irrelevance of work, Utopia was possible. But Utopia had its dangers. Like many of the crew, Commerson had got dysentery.

The expedition continued onwards, with Jeanne in her usual 'valet' role, until it eventually arrived on the shores of Mauritius on 8 December 1768. The island was then a French possession and known as the Île de France. Several of the crew were ill, among them Commerson, who was still suffering agonies of seasickness on top of dysentery. Jeanne Baret went ashore with him. He could go no further. He decided, together with the expedition's astronomer, to leave the expedition, recuperate and return to France by a separate route. Before they parted, Commerson told Bougainville about the climber he had discovered in Brazil, and the name he had given it.

Commerson seemed to recover gradually, and made a trip to Madagascar between October 1770 and January 1771. While leaving the island, he was seriously injured and, though desperate to return to France, had to remain on the Île Bourbon (now Réunion). He didn't even get back to Mauritius for a whole year. France had become a mirage. He wanted to see his son. He wanted to describe scientifically some of the huge number of plants he had collected, and to receive some of the recognition he felt was his due. After all, he knew around 25,000 plants, and had found around 3,000 species, and perhaps 60 genera that were new to science: a truly astonishing haul.

Fame waited, but there were endless delays and disappointments. Finally, he was forced to buy a house in Port Louis in which to store his baggage, especially the forty cases of plant and animal specimens. Jeanne made him comfortable, but his health was failing. He wrote to his old friend Lalande on the 19 October 1772, that he had

> scarcely strength to write to you, and it is an equal wager that I shall succumb, owing to my excessive night-watchings and severe labours. After an attack of rheumatic gout which kept me in bed for nearly three months, I thought I was convalescent, when, in addition, dysentery attacked me; up to the present it has been incurable – and it has brought me to the very edge of the grave. My strength is almost utterly exhausted and I am already more than half worn out. If country air and a diet of rice and fish do not cure me of this attack, you may as well, as you once said (prophetically, no doubt), begin to work on the history of my martyrology.

However, at last, he had permission to return and a comfortable berth assured, to make his seasickness less dreadful. But he became too ill to travel. The ship sailed without him. He rallied slightly, and had enough strength to reach the cooler windward side of the island, sixteen miles from Port Louis, at Flacq, in a house called La Retraite. Jeanne stayed behind to look after their collections. On 13 March 1773, her master died. He was buried in an unmarked grave. Eight days later, in Paris, he was elected a member of the Academy of France by a unanimous vote in a full assembly. It was an unprecedented honour, for no other man had ever been elected while absent from France. He was also given the Cordon of the Order of St Michael.

A late-eighteenth-century lithograph of Port Louis, Mauritius, by S. Beaufoy.
Commerson arrived in 1768, unable to continue with Bougainville's expedition.
He bought a house here, and died near by.

Jeanne Baret eventually guided many of the cases of material still on Mauritius back to
France. She had, by then, married a soldier, but seems to have returned to France alone. She
settled down near her master's family at Chatillon-en-Dombes. When she herself died, in
1816, without children of her own, she left all she owned to Commerson's son,
Archambault. She was, as she had hoped, the first woman to circumnavigate the globe.

Many of Commerson's and Baret's herbarium specimens still exist. The Linnean Society
of London possesses about 1,500 specimens. The Delessert Herbarium in Paris has 3,000.
Far more are scattered through museum collections in France and elsewhere. Archambault
followed family tradition and became a prominent local notary. Bougainville went on to
have an extraordinary career, survive the Revolution, find a perfect wife and die in August
1811 of the dysentery he had once caught in Tahiti. He was given a state funeral on 7
September and his ashes were buried in the Pantheon. His heart, though, was removed and
placed next to his wife in the cemetery of St Pierre at Montmartre. The symbol of his
friendship with Commerson grows in at least half of the glasshouses across the entire globe.

It was by now abundantly clear that South America was packed tight with economically
important plants, and plants of the greatest beauty. The French government and the ageing
Bernard de Jussieu thought that another expedition should be mounted to replace the
material that had so tragically gone missing during the return journey of his brother Joseph.
Bernard suggested a pupil of his, Joseph Dombey (1742–96). He had a personality very

different from that of Bernard's brother, being gay, charming, extravagant and quite deeply in debt. He loved gambling and loved women. He was also quite a good botanist, and a good doctor. But although his expedition increased the glasshouse flora with many cactus, including the fascinating white-haired *Cephalocereus*, with many new begonias, many new orchids, and the ineffable bedding plant *Salvia splendens*, he should never have set off. He needed the consent of the Spanish government if he was to visit Spanish South America, but lacking Jussieu's or Bougainville's diplomatic and aristocratic connections, he had to meet some ridiculous conditions. The best of his material was to go to Madrid, not Paris. He had to travel with two Spanish pharmacists who would oversee his work: Hipolito Ruiz Lopez (1754–1816) and José Antonio Pavon (1754–1840). Draughtsmen were to be included in the personnel too, but their drawings were not to be available to Dombey. He was made to wait for two years in Madrid before the expedition even set off.

They sailed at last at the end of October 1777, and arrived at Callao on 8 April 1778, proceeding the following day to Lima, which was to be their base for nearly four years. Curiously, though paid much less than the Spaniards, Dombey seemed to have inexhaustible funds. He himself travelled with several servants and bought Inca antiquities, including an Inca robe costing nearly seven months' salary, which he wanted to give to Louis XVI. He lent money to his companions, spent much of his time treating the sick for free, and dispensed free medicines, even setting up, at his own expense, hospitals for the needy.

During their travels, Hipolito Ruiz Lopez travelled over mountain ranges, and through virgin jungles, with a full wardrobe that contained five suits (one of silk), three pairs of velvet breeches and seven of plain white, two dressing-gowns, sixteen pairs of stockings, fourteen shirts, twelve pairs of shoes, three cloaks, hair-nets and sleeping-caps; his camping equipment included four tablecloths, many pieces of plate, a chintz bedspread and a silver chamberpot. In 1785 he lost them all during a brush fire at a camp in the jungle at the hacienda of Macora (now Huanco), the oldest Spanish settlement in Peru. He and José Pavon lost tents, equipment, collections, three years' journals, and even the garden where they had been growing plants for dispatch to Spain.

Within a few months of his arrival Dombey sent his first duplicate collections to France and Spain. The following year, he sent off an even larger amount of material, both plants, seeds and bulbs, and Peruvian antiquities. Spain, France and the American colonies were now at war with England, and this consignment had the misfortune to be captured by the British. His collections were ransomed by Spain, who then claimed the whole contents as its own. The war ended in 1783, making it possible for the botanists to return home. Like his predecessor Joseph de Jussieu, Dombey became obsessed with the strange pyramidal ruins in the jungle. He was equally absorbed even by their Jesuit replacements, such as the cathedral that was built on the ruins of the Temple of the Serpent in the ruined Inca quarter of Macora. Once lighthearted and frivolous, he was now obsessed by the sense of death that they emanated. But he was getting ill with scurvy and suffered from dizzy spells. With permission received, and a free passage home, at which he never ceased to marvel, he sailed for Cadiz on 4 April 1784. He had with him his French share of the collections: seventy-three cases of minerals, manuscripts, dried plants, antiquities, wood and bark samples, fish, birds, insects, reptiles and shells. He handed the Spanish share over to Ruiz and Pavon, who dispatched it with their own collection on board the *San Pedro de Alacantara*. There were fifty-five cases and thirty-one tubs of living plants, together with bulbs and seeds. But the *San Pedro* was lost at sea, and the Spanish government insisted on holding on to all Dombey's material when it reached Cadiz. After a terrible journey, he finally arrived there on 22 February 1785, but ignorant and obstructive officials ensured that plants died, and specimens and manuscripts mouldered away. Spain acquired thirty-seven boxes out of his seventy-three; an exact copy was taken of all descriptions and field-notes. His property was not released, nor his departure allowed, until he had promised not to publish anything before Ruiz and Pavon's return. He reached Paris on 13 October 1785 with the scant remnants of what he had hoped would bring him fame. It is hardly surprising that the once happy and confident Dombey became a misanthrope and a recluse.

A glorious bromeliad (*Aechmea paniculata*) illustrated in Ruiz and Pavon's *Flora Peruviana*.

What happened next is still a matter of accusation between French and Spanish botanical historians. It was undoubtedly Dombey's botanical knowledge that made the expedition possible. It was undoubtedly carried out on what was then Spanish soil. There was a race to publish. On 14 January 1786, the *Journal Général de France* published the news that Charles Louis L'Héritier de Brutelle would take charge of studying and describing the plants. The celebrated naturalist Buffon himself presented the Dombey Collection to L'Héritier and arranged the publication of the work. Cheekily, L'Héritier smuggled the specimens to England to be published in order to circumvent the condition set by the Spanish Court. It almost became a diplomatic incident. The first volume of the *Flora Peruviana et Chilensis* by Ruiz and Pavon appeared in 1798. Eight volumes and an appendix were planned, but only three were published. The book was largely based on Dombey's work; his name appeared in the preface, but there was no further reference to him.

The Revolution hailed him, but Dombey couldn't bear to see the upheaval and violence it caused. He obtained a permit to go to back to America to buy corn and other commodities for a needy France. When he landed at Guadeloupe in the West Indies, he found that revolution had spread there too, and was imprisoned for a while. In a further mishap, he fell into a river, and consequently caught acute fever and was told to leave the island. He did, but his ship was then attacked by two corsairs, who found him disguised as a Spanish sailor. He was then imprisoned as a French agent by the British on Montserrat, where he died, in 1796.

The immense tropical water lily *Victoria amazonica* has reddish leaves so heavily ribbed and spined below that they can support the weight of a child. They commonly reach six feet in diameter.

Ruiz and Pavon got back from South America in 1788; it was January 1793 before suitable accommodation was found for them, and their cases could at last be unpacked. Lopez afterwards wrote that he had suffered

heat, fatigue, hunger, thirst, nakedness, want, storms, earthquakes, plagues of mosquitoes and other insects, continuous danger of being devoured by jaguars, bears and other wild beasts, traps of thieves and disloyal Indians, treason of slaves, falls from precipices and the branches of towering trees, fording of rivers and torrents, the fire at Macora . . . the separation from Dombey, the death of the artist Brunete, and the most touching of all, the loss of manuscripts.

The surviving material is now at the Botanical Garden of Madrid, and the Office of Natural History. It contained 150 new genera and around five hundred new species. Ruiz died in 1816, and Pavon, impoverished, was reduced to hawking round his spare herbarium specimens. He died in Madrid in 1840.

Whatever human wreckage there was, nothing could stop the rise of the glasshouse mania in the garden. In 1846, three years after Queen Victoria and Prince Albert had made their dramatic visit to the Great Conservatory at Chatsworth, the royal couple heard of

Once seeds of *Victoria amazonica* were in commerce, the plant caught gardeners' imaginations. This is the Victoria pool at the Botanic Garden in Adelaide, illustrated in a newspaper of October 1869.

even more astonishing things that the Duke's gardeners were nurturing. It took several seasons before some extremely precious seedlings grew into young plants and flowered in their extraordinary ducal foothold. Even so, they had already become a legend, and had spawned, among the very rich, large numbers of new glasshouses built especially for them. The blooms were soft pink, many petalled, pineapple-scented, and over eighteen inches across. They rose above leaves that were often six feet in diameter. The plant was a water lily.

Then named *Victoria regia* after the Queen herself, what is now called *Victoria amazonica* remains one of the world's most extraordinary plants. It had first been discovered growing in that river on 1 January 1837 by Sir Robert Schomburgk, an explorer for the Royal Geographical Society. Although he collected and sent home orchids and other exotics, he didn't manage to collect seed of the water lily. His stories of it, though, created a sensation in Europe. Rich gardeners had to have it, even though it was obviously going to need huge pools and warm water in which to flourish. If the wealthy dreamed of growing it, collectors worldwide dreamed of harvesting seed. The first to do so was Aimée Bonpland (1773–1858), but that he survived long enough to do so was a miracle.

One day in 1821, the skies above an old Jesuit college in northern Argentina, recently converted to a botanic garden, were thick with smoke. The newly restored buildings and the surrounding village were in flames. Its fields were burning. Badly wounded and wrapped in chains, the garden's director, Bonpland, was dragged away, past the bleeding corpses of his beloved Indian workers. He must have thought his own last day had come. By then he had already contributed hugely to gardens worldwide, and to European glasshouses in particular. His most extraordinary contribution was yet to come.

Aimée Jacques Goujaud Bonpland was born on 28 August 1773, in a house on one of the lovely arcaded streets in the ancient seaport of La Rochelle, France. His father was a prosperous surgeon who was also a fanatical gardener, and whose private conversation was filled with plant names. The young Aimée took on both his father's interests, and studied to be a physician, though all the while being more fascinated by plants than humans. Studying in Paris under Lamark, Bernard de Jussieu and Desfontaines, he gravitated towards the more scientifically orientated 'salons' of that exciting city. In particular, he was drawn to the circle that surrounded Louis-Antoine Bougainville, who had by now returned from his celebrated circumnavigation of the globe with Commerson and Baret. As he had helped the young Commerson, Bougainville was to play a vastly important role in Bonpland's life too.

One evening in Bougainville's company, Bonpland met a man who was to completely alter his life, who was to remain a constant and involved friend until death parted them, and with whom he would travel on an epoch-making journey to tropical South America. Their names will be linked for as long as mankind likes plants. This was Alexander von Humboldt. Always seen as the brighter star in the partnership, Humboldt was an aristocrat. He was, when he met Bonpland, rich. He was voluble and sociable, and found it easy to make influential connections. Yet, it was Bonpland who was to make the largest contribution to the garden, and whose own personal journey became a quite extraordinary story.

Friedrich Wilhelm Heinrich Alexander von Humboldt had been born in Berlin on 14 September 1769. His father, a minor aristocrat, was an officer in the army of Frederick the Great. His mother, a French Huguenot, a cold and bigoted woman, raised her two sons in a rigorous way intended to fit them for high public positions. Alexander did not thrive under her regime, and spent fruitless years trying to study economics at Frankfurt and Berlin. Then, apparently out of the blue, he became passionately interested in amateur botany, and began to collect local plant specimens and to classify them. Brandenburg's flora is not rich, and he was soon dreaming of travel to the jungles. He embarked on a career in mining, but also began to develop an odd theory that the rich flora of the world's jungles was due to magnetism of the area in which they grew.

On his mother's death, he was left substantial means. Resigning his mining job in 1797, he moved to Paris, a city then in intellectual and political ferment. He was twenty-nine. Believing that all the sciences were interdependent, he passionately wanted to go to South America, thinking that the luxuriant and primitive jungle there would bear out his theories. Once he and Bonpland met, it was immediately apparent that a very strong friendship would develop. Like Dombey, Humboldt too needed Spanish permission to visit South America. Unlike Dombey, he was well connected. Through Baron Forell, Ambassador of Saxony, he and Bonpland were introduced to Carlos IV and received direct permission from him to explore Mexico and South America, though at their own expense. Bonpland had no

Alexander von Humboldt (looking suitably Byronic) and Aimée Bonpland (working) under a canopy by the Orinoco River during one of their first trips to the Venezuelan jungle. The painting, by Ferdinand Keller, dates from 1877.

private means, and the French state was similarly embarrassed. Humboldt decided to finance the whole expedition himself, paying all of his friend's expenses too. In the early summer of 1799 they set sail from Marseilles, and landed near Caracas on 15 July 1799.

The impact the tropics made on them was enormous. They were both overwhelmed by the sheer size and exuberance of the vegetation, and realized that no European could conceive, from written descriptions, what it was like. The very European Humboldt was equally astonished to find that man was not in the least central to all this raw nature, but just one of a myriad of peripheral animals. Rather than rejoicing, as he should have done, he found that 'this animated nature, where man is nothing, is both strange and sad', as he wrote in *Ansichten der Natur* ('Views of Nature, or Contemplations on the Sublime Phenomena of Creation') in 1808.

The two men spent five years, from 1799 to 1804, in Central and South America, covering more than 6,000 miles on foot, on horseback and in canoes. It was a life of great physical exertion and serious deprivation. They proved that the Casiquiare River formed a connection between the vast river systems of the Amazon and the Orinoco. In the dense tropical forests, tormented by clouds of mosquitoes and stifled by the humid heat, they became exhausted. Their provisions were destroyed by strange insects and incessant rain. They subsisted on ground-up wild cacao beans and river water, never ceasing to be amazed by the marvellous plants and exotic animals, even though on one trip they lost seven horses, electrocuted by electric eels. When the two men and their party arrived at San Carlos de Rio Negro near the Brazil/Colombian border, Humboldt was at once arrested on the Brazilian side by the Portuguese on suspicion of being part of a Spanish border survey, but he managed to convince them that that was not the case, and after some harassment, they were all released.

In spite of the privations, both travellers, buoyed up by the excitement of their collections, remained healthy and in the best of spirits. Only once they reached civilization, at places like Cuidad Bolivar, did they both succumb to a severe bout of fever. Bonpland became seriously ill. Once he had recovered, he sent yet more plants back to France, and as Humboldt had agreed, to Spain. These already included around fifty new species of passion flower, countless fuchsias, cinerarias, zinnias and new genera of orchids. He had also become entranced by the hundreds of sorts of palms, and the roles that they played in the lives of the jungle Indians. Some of these palms would find new roles in the drawing rooms and glasshouses of Europe. Some found their way to Chatsworth.

Humboldt was very anxious to visit a correspondent who had become a serious collector, and also an expert on the cinchona tree, the source of quinine. José Celestino Mutis, whom Linnaeus had grandly named 'Phytologorum Americanorum Princeps', had an estate in Mariquita, near Bogota. Mutis had studied medicine at Seville and Madrid and, from 1757, practised as a physician at Madrid, where he became fascinated by plants. Soon afterwards, he went to South America as physician-in-ordinary to the newly appointed Viceroy of New Granada. He rapidly tried to develop the scientific world in Spanish South America. He taught mathematics. He became an astronomer and set up an observatory. He became a priest too, even while planning to write a flora of New Granada. Humboldt and Bonpland decided to make the journey to see him by land and a long fifty-five-day river trip up the Rio Magdalena. Upon arrival, they were welcomed by Mutis with great cordiality, and lodged in a house adjacent to his own.

The travellers stayed in Bogota for three months, partly to allow Bonpland to recuperate after another bout of fever, contracted on the journey. They set off once more on 8 September 1801. Sometimes, they hacked through virgin jungle; sometimes, they rested in towns such as Popayan, where the botanizing was good and the climate delightful. They climbed volcanos such as Purace and Chimborazo, where they both suffered from mountain sickness, which Humboldt correctly attributed to lack of oxygen. They survived the rainy season in the paramos, where the gales were bitterly cold and, far above the treeline, there was no shelter. Finally, in the spring of 1803, the two travellers sailed from Guayaquil to

Acapulco, Mexico, where they spent the last year of their expedition. After a short stay in the United States, at President Jefferson's invitation, they arrived back in France in August 1804.

As Humboldt had sent back accounts of their travels and discoveries throughout the journey, they were both now famous. They had enriched the known flora of the world by an astonishing 5 per cent of the number of plant species then known. There was a huge demand not only for their scientific results, but also for their travellers' tales. The scientific material eventually took up twenty-six volumes of notes and stories, which were a huge success. The translated volumes of *Voyage aux régions équinoctiales du Nouveau Continent* were published in Philadelphia in 1815, and in London soon after. While Humboldt settled back naturally enough, though with a much reduced income, into the sophisticated society of Paris, Bonpland needed a job. Fortunately, as something to occupy her mind during Napoleon Bonaparte's Egyptian campaign, Napoleon's wife, Josephine, had bought the Château de Malmaison, near Choisy, with 5,000 acres of land. Her huge plant collections there, including most of Masson's cape heaths, the newly imported dahlias, cactuses, orchids, roses and Bonpland's passion flowers, needed a botanist. Bonpland went to work for her. He compiled, with the artist Redouté, the *Description des plantes rares cultivées à Malmaison et à Navarre* (1813). He was consulted by every grand gardener in Europe, and was in touch with great nurserymen like Vilmorin, Perregaux, Noisette and Cels. But the job wasn't enough to satisfy him. He was also at the mercy of other people's lives. When Napoleon at last rejected the extravagant Josephine, Bonpland lost his job, and was once more as depressed as he had been on his return from the Americas. He had also married unhappily.

A meeting in England in 1816 with Joseph Banks at the Royal Botanic Garden, Kew, seems to have made him realize that he had to get back to South America. By chance, one evening at Humboldt's modest attic apartment in the Latin Quarter of Paris, he met Simón Bolivar. Bolivar was fascinated to meet someone who knew so much about South American crop plants and their local uses. Bolivar also knew that the botanist's personal life was miserable and unsettled, and that he had detested the sometimes shoddy glitter of Josephine's entourage. When Bolivar suggested that they both travel back to the wilds of Argentina, Bonpland's dream of escape was realized. Leaving his wife behind, he set off back to South America. Bolivar had found an abandoned former Jesuit college in the north of Argentina, near the Paraguayan border. It had a large estate, and Bonpland at once started its restoration. It was soon magnificently productive.

Bolivar wanted him to create a botanic garden and experimental farm. Argentina being poor, Bonpland financed the new institute by growing and selling maté plants, a profitable tea crop. It was a great success, but this made it dangerous. Across the Parana River, José Gaspar Rodriguez Francia, the despotic '*el supremo*' of adjacent Paraguay, wanted to set up a monopoly of maté for himself. Argentinean growers had to be destroyed, among them Aimée Bonpland. In 1821 he organized the raid at whose end we first met the hapless Bonpland.

Though the Indians were murdered, Bonpland was too famous throughout Europe and the Americas to be killed. Nevertheless, despite an almost immediate flood of threats and

An *Epiphyllum* from the forests of Central America, illustrated in Bonpland and Redouté's *Plantes de la Malmaison*.

pleas from around the world, including the United States, Francia kept Bonpland in chains for several months. Surviving this treatment, the botanist was then placed in detention in a remote Paraguayan village. He remained there for ten years. With no financial support, but an extensive knowledge of local medicinal plants, he became a doctor in order to earn a living. Ironically, with his simple life and his care for the Indians, Bonpland became universally loved throughout Paraguay, and gradually became a political, rather than an economic, challenge to the dictator. To his immense surprise, Bonpland was banished back to Argentina.

Aged fifty-eight, he began to form another botanical institute, this time near Corrientes, a trading town on the banks of the Parana River across which he had once been dragged. He began, once more, to send plant material back to France. He even tried marriage again, this time to an Indian woman. The new institute, and the new marriage, were both successful, and while he was most especially absorbed by the study of Indian food crops and medicinal plants, he found time to search for seeds of the gorgeous but useless *Victoria amazonica* growing in the Parana River system. Once he had found them, he sent seed back to the famous Parisian firm of Vilmorin. French grandees, as well as the English Duke of Devonshire, were soon busily redesigning their conservatories to enclose suitably large pools.

Bonpland and Humboldt never forgot one another. Every so often, Humboldt would beg his friend to return to Europe, but Bonpland now had a great mission of his own. However, nothing for Bonpland was easy. He was accepted by neither the Indians nor their rulers, and his children turned out to be uninterested in what he was trying to accomplish. Money was always a difficulty, but he struggled on. On the death of his wife, he finally lost heart. He retired to a two-room shack on the estate, and without his leadership to guide the estate, weeds, however desirable some were in European glasshouses, began to encroach on the fields and plant beds. Humboldt begged him once more to return to his care, and getting no reply, sent a Dr Lallemand to see how Bonpland was doing. The doctor found a radiant but frail old man, muddling dates and endlessly returning to thoughts of his terrible captivity in Paraguay.

There was one final strange touch. Bonpland died in hospital on 11 May 1858. His fame was so great that his body was to be embalmed, awaiting a great state funeral. As it lay on its bed, awaiting the process, a passing Indian, a close acquaintance of Bonpland's in life, drunk, passed the time of day. Receiving no reply, he stabbed the corpse in a frenzy. It had to be buried immediately. Humboldt died the following year. He was ninety, and had just finished his great work, based on his and Bonpland's travels of all those years ago: *Kosmos*.

The new glasshouses could house a huge flora, and that was part of their vast appeal. Their owners could share in the excitement of the great expeditions, could have a tiny piece of orchid- or fern-filled jungle, could marvel at carnivorous plants, the strange succulents from the Cape or the even stranger *Opuntia, Cereus, Echinops, Epiphyllum, Selenicereus* or *Melocactus* from the deserts of the Americas. Perhaps it is still the orchids that tease and seduce gardeners most. Certainly, in the latter half of the nineteenth century, they spawned some tremendous plant nurseries in every capital in the Western world, and the nurseries employed some tremendous collectors, several hunting some species of orchid to extinction.

The craze for orchids had started with a sensation in 1818. William Swainson, a visitor to Brazil, sent off a consignment of tropical treasures to William Cattley of Barnet, packing them round with some dull plants which had an orchid's 'pseudobulbs' but no flowers. Cattley got them to flower: they had blooms five inches across with mauve petals and a trumpet-like lip with frilled edges, a purple base and a yellow throat. It was by far the most beautiful orchid then known and no more of its kind were found for the next seventy years. Hugh Culling, another unknown, was in the Philippines in the 1830s and managed to send back live orchids. They were gorgeous too. There was then almost a gold rush of orchid prospectors. Karl Theodor Hartweg spent nearly seven years in Mexico collecting for the Horticultural Society. He made one of his most valuable finds when he noticed an unusually fine bloom in the hat of a Quichole Indian. He found the original plant and half a dozen other new species. The Duke of Devonshire started his Chatsworth collection in the early 1830s when he saw *Oncidium papilio* at an orchid show.

Collecting became so competitive that some collectors became quite paranoid. One such was the strange, silent, Thomas Lobb (1820–94), the brother of William Lobb who collected the giant dawn redwood. He signed a three-year contract in 1843 with the Veitch nursery to collect orchids in Malaysia and the islands. He sent home marvels like the moth orchid (*Phalaenopsis amabilis*) with its broad white petals, and *Vanda tricolor*, the cowslip-scented orchid with cream or pale mauve petals spotted with brown, and with a rosy pink lip. He also sent home misleading telegrams to his employers, disguising where he was so that fellow collectors could not duplicate his travels.

Also collecting at this time was the extraordinary Benedict Roezl, who had an iron hook for a left hand, and who collected orchids all the way from California to Patagonia. He was born in 1824, worked as a nurseryman in Vienna, then emigrated to Mexico in 1854. At first, he sold Mexican conifers. In 1861 he introduced the cultivation of a Mexican textile plant called ramie (*Boehmeria nivea*), which he hoped to develop as a fibre for the European market. Later, he began to send orchids to the nursery of Henry Sander of St Albans in England. He almost pillaged Central America, sending home 10,000 orchids from Panama and Colombia in 1869. He went across the Isthmus of Panama to Guayra and Caracas and sent eight tons of orchids and ten tons of other plants back to London. In Mexico, near the volcano of Colima, the Indians learned that Roezl would pay for orchids and they brought him 100,000 plants, all rare masdevallias or miltonias. There were sometimes huge losses. Of 27,000 plants dispatched by Roezl in one consignment from New Granada, just two plants survived the long journey to England. In the 1850s, nurserymen started hybridizing orchids when John Dominy, working for the Veitch nursery, crossed two species of *Calanthe*. That was just the start. It was soon found that wide crosses between different genera were also fertile, giving rise to some of the most popular of today's orchids, given strange generic names such as *Doritaenopsis* or *Vascostylis* that relate to nothing ever found in a real wild environment.

And what about *Victoria amazonica*? Appropriately, it was at Chatsworth, in 1849, that the great water lily flowered in Europe for the first time. Though hardly a plant suited for a backyard glasshouse, astonishingly it has developed a backyard following. There turned out to be two species, *V. amazonica* in quiet parts of that river, and *V. cruziana* from rivers in cooler Argentina, Bolivia and Paraguay. The latter species is hardier and has white flowers. Recently, gardeners have discovered that they can be crossed, producing hardier plants than *V. amazonica*, with pink or red flowers, and a heavier perfume of pineapples. Once the plant of plutocrats or the showiest botanic gardens, they are now grown by ordinary enthusiasts in the United States from Oregon southwards. While some gardeners swear by 200-gallon tanks, some have flowered their victorias in 40-gallon plastic buckets. Clearly, one of the most astonishing plants in the world, having been known for less than two hundred years is, at the hands of gardeners, set to increase its range further still.

The orchid *Anguloa superba*, found in the jungles of Ecuador and Peru, belongs to a genus first described by Ruiz and Pavon. This illustration, by Turpin, appears in Bonpland and Humboldt's *Voyages aux régions équinoctiales du Nouveau Continent*, published between 1805 and 1834.

FROM THE WILDERNESS TO THE ROSE GARDEN

T he remarkable way in which an ancient element of the garden called the 'wilderness' both survived and developed into modern times has been driven, since the eighteenth century at least, by some marvellous plants introduced by brave men. The fact that it is today, in one form or another, one of the most vigorous and exciting areas of the garden is due to two quite extraordinarily brilliant and tenacious individuals, and to a whole dynasty who owned and ran an immensely important nursery which brought some of the most thrilling plants of the East to the 'wildernesses' of Europe and America.

It is early summer, 1835. Across Russia, America, France and England, on tables of rough planks or tables of marquetry and ormolu piled with books, crisp paper sheets bearing pressed flowers, ebony-handled lenses, inkpots and quills, space has been cleared for a large, flat package. Elsewhere, similar packages have already had their wrappings torn open and the contents eagerly scanned, kindling a new desire.

At the same moment, in a sunlit garden on one of the smartest streets in Leiden, the ancient and picturesque university town in

The royal palace of Hampton Court, Middlesex illustrated by John Kip in his *Survey of London* (1730). To the left of the palace is the 'wilderness', containing formal and informal walks.

In official portraits, Siebold preferred to be depicted wearing the many medals he had received from William II of Holland.

Holland, Philipp Franz Balthasar von Siebold strolls past bushes of mountain peonies bearing their last flowers, Chinese roses just starting to unfurl and huge clumps of chrysanthemums yet to produce their flowers, which will prove to be far more splendid than anything any European gardener has yet seen. He wears a splendid kimono, has sandals, and is sipping tea from a rough earthenware cup.

The packages, some still travelling rough roads in creaking wagons, others already lying empty on Persian rugs, contain or contained the first batch of engravings of Siebold's long-projected *Flora Japonica*. This describes some of the most beautiful trees, shrubs and herbaceous plants that Siebold collected and grew in that exotic country. It is to become a vastly influential work. Similar packages will leave Leiden for the next nine years, though the entire project will never be completed in his lifetime. He himself will continue to publish major works on the culture and history of Japan, and will briefly return to his beloved garden there. Though he will be loaded with honours for his contributions to science, the most intense years of his life are over. He is thirty-nine years old.

However, on this summer morning, some of the plants upon which much of the botanical work for the *Flora* has been based are only just beginning to flourish. Enchanting small trees like the Japanese crab apple (*Malus floribunda*), in a Japanese spring a billowing mass of palest pink flowers, are as yet little more than single branches. These horticultural riches, on which Siebold is starting to build a business, are but a fraction of the ones that he loaded on to the ship at the Japanese island of Deshima. Yet it was neither the immense variations of climate of the voyage, nor the hazards of being at sea, that decimated them.

Philipp Franz Balthasar von Siebold (1796–1866) was an extraordinary and energetic man, arrogant, callous, perceptive, foolhardy, but with a quite perfect eye for a good plant, or a piece of porcelain, when he saw it. He was born in the Bavarian town of Würzburg, into a family of strong-minded, often distinguished, men and women. His father and his grandfather were well-known doctors, and an aunt, trained in obstetrics, attended the Duchess of Kent at the birth of the little girl who was to become Queen Victoria. Philipp's future must have seemed mapped, and he did indeed enter the medical school at Würzburg. Once qualified, he set up a small practice. It provided him with enough money to live, but not enough excitement. As a student, he had become interested in natural history and fascinated by the wonderful plants and animals that the planet supported. Wanderlust gripped him. He set out for Rotterdam, intent on launching a new career as a scientific explorer. An attractive, well-qualified and persuasive young man, he soon found a post as surgeon major in the Dutch East Indies Army, and was, by September 1822, aboard a ship setting sail for the Dutch outpost in Java. However, Fate took hold of him, and he was hardly in Java before he was swiftly moved on towards Japan.

The Dutch had first reached Japan much earlier. In 1600, a ship called the *Liefde* drifted ashore in Usuki Bay in Bungo Province (now the Oita Prefecture). It was the only survivor of a fleet of five sailing ships that set out from Rotterdam in 1598. Most of the men on the expedition had suffered cruelly, freezing to death in the Straits of Magellan, starving, being killed in skirmishes with the Spanish and Portuguese on the Pacific, or drowning in terrible storms. The *Liefde* suffered too, with only 24 of the original 110 crew living to see Japan. Six of those died within two days of landing, and only six could walk unassisted to shore. Two of the survivors went on to earn important places in Japanese history: William Adams and Jan Joosten. Adams became an adviser on diplomacy and trade, Joosten on military matters. Both were to prove so important that the Dutch trading company was granted extensive trading rights.

That privilege was gradually reduced, and by the time of Siebold's arrival, the company's only settlement was the tiny man-made island of Deshima, built by the shogunate in Nagasaki Harbour so that they could keep the barbarians at arms' length, and under constant supervision. Generation after generation of Dutchmen and a scattering of other Europeans signed on with the Dutch East India Company and were assigned two-year stints at Nagasaki, but they were forbidden to look at the country or converse with its inhabitants. The inquisitive found that an overwhelming lure. The company's employees were virtually prisoners on the island, allowed to trade, but in only a few commodities. Knowing how profitable trading with Japan could be, Holland was anxious to re-establish secure trading as soon as possible. They were even keener to outflank other European trading nations who had their eyes on Japan. A special embassy to Tokyo was planned, to negotiate better conditions. A skilled physician was an asset, and Siebold was especially suitable. He had graduated as an eye-specialist, and could operate on cataracts. His ability to make the blind see gave him immense prestige almost as soon as he began to work at Deshima. His Dutch employers must have been very pleased. It may be that they asked him to take on subtler duties, perhaps extending to espionage.

With his almost demonic energy, he took every opportunity to learn as much about Japan and the Japanese as possible. He plainly wanted to become the leading European authority on every aspect of the culture. It turned out to be easier for him than any previous foreigner: the cataract operations, for which he refused money payments, brought him not only gifts, but also disciples. He treasured the gifts and taught the disciples who, at his bidding, began to act as explorers and researchers into the parts of the countryside that were forbidden to him. Japanese artists were trained to make illustrations of plants and animals. Siebold even asked the governor general in Java for additional help in this task, and a highly skilled draughtsman and artist was soon sent to his aid.

However much it seems as if Siebold was intent on exploiting Japan and its inhabitants for his own ends, and those of the Dutch, the fact is that he was captivated. Like many other collectors, he 'went native'. He fell in love with Japan's culture and history. He also fell in love with an eighteen-year-old Japanese girl whom he met at the house of a client. After much difficulty, they were allowed to marry, though to do this, his new wife had to register as a prostitute for the use of all the Dutchmen on Deshima. She must have loved him. She went to live with him, and in 1827 a daughter, Ine, was born.

Deshima already had an overgrown botanic garden, set up by Siebold's Swedish predecessor, Carl Peter Thunberg (see Chapter Four). Siebold refurbished it, and filled it with more Japanese plants, both wildlings from the hills and plants from the huge numbers of Japanese gardens and nurseries in and around Nagasaki and the capital. The garden soon expanded, and he became such a favoured foreigner that he was allowed to move his base of operations to the mainland and to occupy a house on a hillside above Nagasaki. The surrounding grounds were transformed into another botanical garden and arboretum.

His world must have seemed glorious. A wife. A child. A teaching school filled with pupils eager to learn whatever they could about Western medicine. An obviously immensely important collection of plants which he knew would fascinate Western gardeners. A house filling with lacquer, porcelain and bronzes. But he overreached himself. He knew perfectly well that the Japanese state was paranoid about its military weakness in the face of Western technology. He knew that there were certain things it was forbidden for him to own. Yet in the autumn of 1828, he met, and charmed, the court astronomer at the capital. This man, presumably knowing the immense danger of the act, gave Siebold secret maps not only of Japan itself, but of important adjacent regions such as the province of Amur, the island of Saghalien, and the Liu Kiu islands that lie between Japan and Formosa.

Siebold had been amassing huge numbers of plants from the nurseries of Tokyo, and the collections were already packed on the vessel that was to take them from the capital back to Deshima. Disastrously, the ship was beached in a storm, and before she could be refloated, the forbidden maps were discovered. When the news reached Tokyo, the astronomer killed himself. Several of Siebold's Tokyo pupils and friends were imprisoned and brutally tortured. Undeterred, Siebold fought hard to retain the maps, only giving them up once he had made hasty copies by torchlight and hidden them among his zoological collections.

Fate had turned against him. He was imprisoned from 18 December 1828 to 28 December 1829. His Dutch employers were too wary of the scandal to give him any great support, though they presumably got hold of the copied maps. When he was released, it was only to discover that he was sentenced to permanent banishment from Japan. On 2 January 1830, after six years and three months spent in the country which had enchanted him, he set sail for Holland, driven from Eden. Unlike Adam, he left his wife and daughter behind.

He took with him a collection of about five hundred new garden plants, which he hoped to unite with a shipment he had already sent to Europe the previous year. That seems to have happened, but Fate dealt him another blow. The whole collection fell foul of war. After the defeat of Napoleon, Holland and Belgium had been uneasily united. History proved strong, and neither could forget language or religion. Belgium wished to regain her independence, and war broke out between the two states in the summer of 1830. It is unclear what exactly happened, but Siebold's plants seem to have been growing in a garden either at Antwerp or Ghent. War engulfed the collection in August, and he tells the story that the garden was used to house a cavalry regiment. The collection was already subject to the intense envy of local horticulturists, and they seized the opportunity for pillage. Eager gardeners scuttled, doubled up, between the milling horses and shouting riders, gathering what they could of Siebold's Japanese flowers in the middle of the noise and stench of war.

Among the plants that changed ownership so dramatically were many brilliantly coloured azaleas from the nurseries of Japan. In later years, Siebold claimed, and the nurserymen of Ghent acknowledged, that the whole prosperity of that city was based on the prodigious popularity of what became known as 'Ghent' azaleas. Once the fighting died down sufficiently, Siebold fled to Holland. When he tried to reclaim his property, the local inhabitants, sensibly claiming that they had saved his collection, made some attempt at recompense, giving him back at least one plant of everything they had managed to propagate. However, that only amounted to about eighty or so of the many hundred species that had set out from Deshima. Even with that reduced number, Siebold soon established a 'Jardin d'Acclimatisation' at a new home in Leiden.

He seems to have kept most of his earnings and his zoological and ethnographic collections intact, and also his Japanese household goods. He bought a fine house on the Rapenburg, one of the town's most fashionable thoroughfares, and with it a large garden. It must have been the first house in Europe to be furnished in the Japanese style, though forty years later, it was quite common to show off at least a Japanese fan, or a Japanese-inspired 'Art Nouveau' vase. By the early 1830s, he was selling plants created from his introductions. He was himself a sight of some considerable interest for the town's conventionally minded inhabitants. He wore Japanese costume while out in the town, took off his shoes when entering houses, used chopsticks to eat his food, and slept on tatami mats; there was also the shocked whisper of his abandoned wife and child.

His 'Japonism' was perhaps a marketing tool for promoting his business and his many other books about the customs, animals and history of Japan. For all these, he became much honoured and was awarded an official post in the Dutch East India Company, and a patent of nobility, with the title of 'Jongheer'. Payment for the maps, perhaps.

The whole gardening and botanical world, into which the *Flora Japonica* found its way from 1835 onwards, was undergoing great change. This was partly a result of the colossal number of new plants pouring into Europe. They not only made new sorts of gardening possible, but their immense diversity was beginning to alter how people thought of Nature itself, causing them to question how some plants were identical even when found growing on continents separated by vast oceans, and indeed, more radically, how species and varieties were created. The *Flora Japonica* had an important part to play in this. With a large format, the work was sumptuously illustrated with elegant, hand-coloured engravings showing marvellously drawn Japanese plants, often life-sized, on folio-sized plates. The engravings alone made the *Flora* worth purchasing by middle-ranking gardeners, and gave a wide range of horticulturists, nurserymen and gardeners their first exciting view of an array of the decorative plants of Japan. Better still, many of the engravings retained the

Japanese feel for plant form and placing on the page, which alone must have intrigued the subscribers. The plates include illustrations of very double pink forms of *Anemone hupehensis* var. *japonica* (Robert Fortune was only to bring back the single white form in 1847), arisaemas in quantity, gorgeous peonies, an edible tulip (*Tulipa edulis*) and *Lycoris*. His plate of *Iris ensata* shows a flat-flowered variant that every gardener must have instantly desired.

But it is among the small trees and shrubs that gardeners found plates that made them throw the *Flora*'s wrappings impatiently to the floor and carry the engraving to the window to get a better look at them. Several of the shrubs had entirely new properties, such as perfumed flowers in winter. Japanese allspice (*Chimonanthus praecox*) with yellow bells on bare branches; the astonishing *Mahonia japonica*, with its spiky and glittering foliage, and arching sprays of yellow flowers that have one of the most bewitching perfumes in the whole garden; viburnums (*Viburnum carlesii*, with a ravishing smell in early summer); and many more. Siebold illustrated the strange flowers of clerodendrums (whose foliage has one of the nastier garden smells), camellias, hydrangeas, the lovely *Styrax obassia*, the first *Forsythia* to be illustrated in Europe, and on and on, even including roses that would go on to become vastly influential in the garden, such as *Rosa rugosa*, *R. multiflora* and *R. banksiae*. There are marvels among the trees too: new maples with exquisitely shaped leaves and blazing autumn colours, new magnolias to offer relief from the American species already long familiar, new oaks, new cherries, including a fine soft pink form of *Prunus pendula* var. *ascendens*.

None of these plants was suitable for the American garden, now filled and shady with big trees. None could mar the crisp and colourful beds of annual flowers now being copied all over Europe and gardened America, using Lady Grenville's ideas as a base. The only place for the maples and viburnums, the hydrangeas and peonies was the 'wilderness'.

The wilderness is an ancient aspect of the garden. The gardens of ancient Rome often had, beyond the elaborate schemes of topiary, a few areas of supposedly naturalistic *nemus* or 'grove', such as can be found at the Fishbourne Roman Palace in Sussex. There, plants were allowed to grow as they pleased, the emphasis was on the natural and the native, and wild Pan and his ilk were supposed to take refuge there, though statuary of rustic gods such as Terminus or Bacchus were acceptable. With their shade and murmuring springs, these wildernesses were never quite forgotten by European gardeners, and whenever the ancient world was remembered, and space permitted, artificial wildernesses formed an important part of the garden.

Many grand Renaissance gardens, especially in Italy, developed a system of design that was supposed to be Roman, whereby the formal, high-maintenance and highly artificial gardens were close to the main building, and the wilderness began beyond the reach of formality. Wildernesses were still unashamedly artificial, containing statuary, fountains, pavilions and seating. Villa Lante has a well-known example. In some gardens the wilderness was optimistically paganized and referred to as the *sacro bosco* ('sacred wood'); even if the ancient gods did not return, at least the trees were allowed their head, and formed shady walks and rides which were impossible nearer the house.

By the seventeenth century, when the passion for building gardens engaged the owners of vast and flat estates in France, the wildernesses were penetrated by formal rides which stretched, if the owner could afford it, to the horizon. The rides naturally radiated outwards from the house and its flower-filled parterres, while lesser rides joined features of interest such as a hunting pavilion, a pool or a statue of Diana the Huntress. To make the division between formal axes and wilderness suitably clear, the rides were given substantial hedges. The contrast between clipped greenery and wild makes for great visual excitement. In large estates used for hunting, the division may also have helped steer both quarry and hunt into open country. Neither of these had time to admire the plant species used.

The English tried to catch up on French developments. In the 1690s at Hampton Court, the great Tudor palace on the bank of the Thames, William of Orange began to garden again after the death of his wife, Queen Mary. Old medieval garden features like the mount were swept away, and although a wilderness was planted, it merely re-used shrubs from the old privy garden. In 1732, John Loveday, visiting the Duke of Devonshire's vast house at

The Japanese *Rosa rugosa*, introduced by Siebold, is now widely grown in various forms throughout the world.

Chatsworth in Derbyshire wrote: 'When we had satisfied our curiosityes within doores . . . we walk't out into the Gardens, which fill'd our Eyes with fresh Objects of delight and admiration . . . There is a large Grotto . . . and a Willow tree in the Centre of a Wilderness which spouts out of every branch and leafe, there are also severall basins with Jet d'eaux . . . the whole Wilderness guarded with Satyrs . . . also a charming long arbour . . . and a Firr Wilderness . . . from thence we entered a walk with Statues on each side.' Clearly, the plants themselves were rather dull.

Another garden visitor of the age, Celia Fiennes, was not an especially educated gardener, but she was a snob. Had there been something rare and valuable to see, she would have at least noted the cost. She did sometimes notice the difference between 'firrs' and broadleaf trees, and sometimes even how they were pruned. She visited Tixall Hall in Derbyshire late in the seventeenth century, and found 'just by the Bowling-green is a very fine wilderness with many large walkes of a great length, full of all sorts of trees . . . and so shorn smooth to the top which is left as a tuft or crown, they are very lofty in growth which makes the length of the walke look very nobly'.

Most wildernesses, including those at Tixall and Chatsworth, seem to have been botanically unexciting. It is hard not to feel that they were merely the unloved and untrodden interstices between the walks and rides. Contemporary garden writers and designers threw up their hands. Stephen Switzer's book *Ichnographica Rustica* of 1718

William Robinson, in *The Wild Garden* (1870), recommended the Chinese plant *Hemerocallis fulvis.*

suggested that 'We must cashier that mathematical stiffness in our gardens, and imitate Nature more', largely by growing a diversity of plants. A decade later, Batty Langley, in his *New Principles of Gardening*, aimed at gentle rather than aristocratic gardeners, suggested that a wilderness should be of 'shady walks and groves, planted with sweet briar, white jessamine and honeysuckle, environed at the bottom with a small circle of dwarf stock, candytuft and pinks'. Such a wilderness would have been very pretty, but early eighteenth-century plantings often included the smaller types of fruit and nut trees, because these were often decorative in leaf, flower and fruit. They were grown in orchards for produce.

The Scottish architect Sir William Chambers, the designer of the exotic Chinese pagoda in the Royal Botanic Gardens at Kew, whatever his other sophistications, was something of a plant dunce. He described a Chinoiserie wilderness-cum-shrubbery in his *A Dissertation on Oriental Gardening* published in May 1772. This consisted 'of rose, raspberry, bramble, currant, lavender, vine and gooseberry bushes; with barberry, alder, peach, nectarine and almond trees'. He seems unaware of the new trees and shrubs fast appearing from the Americas at the hands of collectors like André Michaux and John Bartram, let alone new ones actually from China itself.

Even by 1754, when landscapers were busy sweeping them away, there is a long section on how to design, plant and manage wildernesses in that year's edition of Philip Miller's *Gardener's Dictionary*. He says, in his rather stuffily worthy manner, that 'if rightly situated, artfully contrived, and judiciously planted, [wildernesses] are very great Ornaments to a fine Garden', and then, equally garden-worthily, goes on both to complain about how bad most are, and how they ought to be when well done. Not surprisingly for the curator of the Chelsea Physic Garden, he gives generous planting lists.

In the Distribution of these Plantations, in those Parts which are planted with deciduous Trees may be planted next the Walks and Openings, Roses, Honeysuckles, Spirea Frutex, *and other Kinds of low flowering Shrubs, which may be always kept very dwarf, and may be planted pretty close together; and at the Foot of them, near the Sides of the Walks, may be planted Primroses, Violets, Daffodils, and many other Sorts of Wood flowers; not in a strait Line, but rather to appear accidental, as in a Natural Wood. Behind the first Row of Shrubs should be planted Syringas, Cytisus,* Althea Frutex, *Mezereons, and other flowering Shrubs of a middle Growth; which may be back'd with Laburnum, Lilacs, Gelder-roses, and other flowering Shrubs of large Growth: these may be back'd with many other Sorts of Trees, rising gradually to the Middle of the Quarters, from whence they should always slope down every Way to the Walks. By this Distribution you will have the Pleasure of the flowering Shrubs near the Sight, whereby you will be regaled with their Scent, as you pass through the Walks.*

Most of these plants had been perfectly familiar to gardeners since the late sixteenth century, but elsewhere he suggests some more adventurous shrubs, almost all American in origin, and often introduced in the previous century. They include fine things like the snowdrop tree (*Halesia* species, from North America in the 1750s), the beautifully flowered indigo trees (*Indigofera* species), various sumachs (*Rhus glabra* and *R. typhina*, both from America in the seventeenth century), coluteas, the spicily scented benzoin tree with its fine autumn colours (*Lindera benzoin*, also from America in the seventeenth century), as well as the azaderach (*Melia azadarach*, from either India or China in the seventeenth century). Of middling-sized trees, there were many acacias (*Gleditsia* and *Robinia*) and numerous maples. There was also the American *Styrax*, now rare in spite of its lovely flowers, five species of *Celtis*, as well as many hollies, bays, laurels and the three then-known types of lilac, including the too rarely seen (or smelled) Persian lilac.

The wilderness flora was now richer than ever, but the scene was set for much faster changes. Pierre Nicholas le Cheron d'Incarville (1706–57), an abbé trained in botany by the French botanist Bernard de Jussieu (see Chapter Six), was in Beijing for sixteen years after joining the Chinese mission of Jesuits in 1740. It was direct to Jussieu that he sent his herbarium collections; his seeds had a much more complex route. Seeds of the pagoda tree (*Sophora japonica*) went to friends in Moscow. From there, they were forwarded to Paris, and some seedlings finally reached Philip Miller in 1753. It took another fifty-eight years for plants to reach New York. D'Incarville also introduced to Europe *Ailanthus altissima*, the 'Tree of Heaven', which began to colonize America soon after. He also sent out the golden rain tree (*Koelreuteria paniculata*), from its traditional plantings around the graves of high officials. This little wave of new introductions was the merest taste of what was to come.

The owners of small gardens had been disenfranchised from 'garden taste' for much of the previous century, as both the high French style and the English landscape style that developed from the 1720s needed large amounts of space. But with all these small trees and large bushes, the wilderness was becoming a suitable garden element for small gardens, such as those found around the new and unpretentious villas that were beginning to appear in prosperous regions. Philip Miller was watching developments. Here he is giving advice on small gardens:

Where there is not room for these magnificent Wildernesses, there may be some rising Clumps of Ever-greens, so designed as to make the Ground appear much larger than it is in Reality; and if in these there are some Serpentine walks well contriv'd, it will greatly improve the Place, and deceive those who are unacquainted with the Ground, as to its Size . . . but if there is a distant Prospect of the adjacent Country from the House, then this should not be obstructed, but rather a larger Opening should be allowed for the View . . . and on the back part from the Sight, may be planted the several kinds of flowering Shrubs, according to their different Growths, which will still add to the Variety.

The 'rustic seat' at Montgomery Place in New York showed a taste very much abreast of the latest European fads.

Variety was plentiful, and as wildernesses were seen as being adaptable to small gardens, they were soon very popular. They were even espoused by the public tea gardens in the major cities, often places that set the very latest styles of gardening. One at Enderby, near Leicester, had a strawberry garden, a plant nursery and a wilderness with serpentine walks, all being advertised for sale in 1849.

Even in the settled states of North America, where there was a terrifying amount of real wilderness, some grander gardens followed European tastes and built themselves artificial ones. Blithewood, at Annandale-on-Hudson in New York state, with its manicured lawns, was also admired for its wild and picturesque ravines; Montgomery Place near by had a wilderness with rustic seats, as well as a lake and flower gardens. The area of the garden suited to Siebold's new plants was beginning to appeal to a wide range of gardeners, wealthy and middling, European and American. Perhaps they had been waiting for a signal, and the *Flora Japonica* provided it.

Siebold's nursery was a success, but he couldn't forget the plants he had lost or left behind. After much negotiation, he managed to get back to Japan in August 1859. By the time he reached his old haunts in Nagasaki, including the school he had set up, he found that things were very different, and his happiness was short. Six years earlier, in 1853, a rather threatening squadron of American ships, under Commodore Matthew Perry, had entered Edo Bay, and the Japanese authorities decided to open their country to foreign trade. Japan could never be the same again.

He moved with great caution, collecting plants as fast as he deemed wise, but this time he fell foul of intrigue between the various foreign powers that had established themselves in Japan since 1853. The Dutch were, perhaps understandably, anxious that his presence would create more problems than it might solve. However, he was much more eminent now than in his previous sojourn and so, in 1862, in a dastardly act, they tricked him into leaving Japan, by promising him that he would soon return as the main Dutch adviser in Japan. It is unclear whether or not he believed them. The deck of the vessel on which he sailed, again without his Japanese family, was a veritable nursery. He returned to Leiden with yet more marvels, and this time no war stopped their introduction. His catalogue for 1863 listed an astounding 838 species and varieties of Japanese plants. These ranged from *Forsythia suspensa* var. *sieboldii* – the first of the genus to be introduced into European gardens – and the fabulous Japanese wisteria (*Wisteria floribunda*), with its masses of lavender or white pea flowers in the familiar long racemes, to the popular climbing hydrangea (*Hydrangea anomala* subsp. *petiolaris*) and the garden-centre stalwart *H. paniculata* 'Grandiflora', with its immense late-summer flowerhead, cream at first and later ageing to weird shades of bronze-greens. There were some marvellous small trees too, including more forms of the most beautiful of all ornamental crab apples, the Japanese flowering crab (*Malus floribunda*), and the handsome *Sorbus* known as the Korean mountain ash (*S. alnifolia*), though it is indigenous to Japan and central China.

Curiously, however, he had brought back no Japanese flowering cherries. He had written a substantial report on them, and had clearly seen the hundreds of types being grown in

The lake and pavilion at Montgomery Place. The estate was much admired by the first American landscaper, Andrew Jackson Downing.

Japanese gardens in the 1820s, when they were at the peak of popularity. Most of the double-flowered ones he saw he called the 'temple cherries', as they had become popular gifts to monks and their gardens. Yet none of this seems to have influenced him. It seems, with hindsight, an odd lapse. Perhaps the market wasn't ready; a double pink cherry had been received and described by a French nurseryman called A. Jacques in the autumn of 1832, but it did not create a sensation. Even by 1877, Siebold's nursery showed only one at the international horticultural exhibition held in Amsterdam, and yet by then almost everything Japanese was in fashion. The cherries had to wait.

The sudden, glorious discovery of all these new small trees enriched not only the mid-nineteenth-century wilderness, but also the possible look of suburban gardens, freeing them, if their owners wanted, from annual and half-hardy bedding schemes and the constant work and expense that they entailed. All of a sudden, small gardens could have trees that did not overwhelm them, and which could provide abundant colour for the hungriest of eyes.

When Siebold returned to Japan, he was no longer the only collector there. Wonderful things were pouring into Europe and North America from many other hands; glorious things like the katsura tree (*Cercidiphyllum*). In the West this is one of the delights of summer, with oval jade-green leaves, and one of the wonders of autumn when the leaves turn butter yellow; in Japan it grows to a much larger size and is used for cabinet making and panelling. It was first collected by Thomas Hogg, an American citizen, but one with a famous name in British floristry. His father was a well-known Scots-born London nurseryman-cum-florist who had given his name to some successful auriculas, pinks and carnations such as 'Mrs Siddons' and 'Queen of Roses'. However, he seems to have found London not to his taste, and set out for New York in 1822. Finding few nurseries in that city, he set up his own.

Hydrangea paniculata 'Grandiflora', published in *The Garden*, 1876, was brought to Europe from Japan by Siebold in 1862. It is now a much admired shrub worldwide.

Thomas Hogg's New York nursery was a success. One of his two sons, our Hogg, seems to have made some interesting friends, for he was sent out to Japan by Abraham Lincoln, and was in Tokyo from August 1862. Like Siebold, he became fascinated by Japan, and when his American work finished, he remained in Tokyo to work for the Japanese customs service. While there, his brother was looking after the family nursery on 23rd Street and Broadway, and it soon grew some handsome Japanese plants. While *Cercidiphyllum*, *Stewartia pseudocamellia*, *Styrax japonicus*, the now widely grown *Symplocos paniculata*, first described by Siebold, were triumphs introduced by Hogg junior, he also sent home some disasters like the kudzu vine (*Pueraria lobata*), now a vicious American weed.

Though his shrubs are lovely inhabitants of the northern garden, as far as the wilderness is concerned, his splendid achievement is overshadowed by that of Joseph Dalton Hooker (1817–1911), yet another of the plant collectors who started his professional career as a doctor. He became one of the most influential botanists and travellers of his age, Director of the Royal Botanic Gardens at Kew and publisher of a mountain of scientific works and of fascinating travelogues illustrated with his own lively drawings.

He was born at the family estate of Halesworth, Suffolk, on 30 June 1817, almost into the centre of the botanical world. His father was William Jackson Hooker (1785–1865), at that time teaching botany at the ancient University of Glasgow, and to become, in 1820, its Professor. From there, he was to move south to become Director of Kew Gardens.

Joseph was immersed in botany throughout his childhood. Even as a small boy he had found some rare mosses surviving in the smoke of industrial Glasgow. While some sons rebel against their father's enthusiasm, plants and exploring became part of him; as a teenager, his bedtime books were travel adventures such as those of Mungo Park and Captain Cook. He became an avid reader of Darwin's *Voyage of the Beagle*, and a chance meeting with the great man later in his life led to a lifelong and very productive friendship. Joseph nourished dreams of being a great collector-explorer, of having his own hair-raising tales to tell. Fate decided to fulfil his fantasies. Nature, too, took a useful hand. He proved to have formidable energies, quite astonishing powers of physical endurance and superb luck in the face of frightening odds that many other collectors might have envied.

He graduated as MD in 1839. Unlike Siebold, he didn't even try building a private practice, but was at once appointed as assistant surgeon aboard the HMS *Erebus*, for a proposed expedition with the HMS *Terror* to the Antarctic, under the command of Sir James Clark Ross. Its most ambitious aim was to find the South Magnetic Pole, and later to call at the Falkland Islands, New Zealand and Tasmania. As Ross sailed north from Antarctica, the weather worsened. Gales were so extreme that eight- and ten-inch hawsers snapped like threads, causing the ships to shudder. The sails were shredded and both ships nearly capsized. They got embroiled in dangerous floes of ice, and sailed dizzyingly between icebergs that lay so close to each other that they themselves often collided. The cold was so intense that the foam on the wave crests froze, and the ships' decks, spars and ropes were top-heavily weighted with ice. One night, the two ships, normally in constant sight of one another, found that they were alone in the storm. It was days in the ice before they found one another. On another night, on board the *Terror*, a swaying lantern started a fire below

Joseph Dalton Hooker was assistant surgeon and naturalist on board the *HMS Erebus*.
In this coloured lithograph, *Erebus* and *Terror* negotiate the Antarctic ice.

decks which blazed for two hours until finally extinguished. Later, a wild blast of wind sweeping down between cliffs of ice caused the *Terror* and the *Erebus* to crash together with such force that the masts and frozen riggings became enmeshed. Spars and rigging had to be sawn free, leaving the *Erebus* almost totally disabled.

Ross was a superb seaman, and he managed to manoeuvre the *Erebus* away from the ice, and the ship was repaired sufficiently to make it to the quieter waters of Berkeley Sound in the Falkland Islands on 6 April. Hooker's dreams of excitement were being amply fulfilled. And so were his dreams of collecting fine plants, for over the next arduous few months, he found *Lapageria rosea*, the beautiful, waxy-leaved climber, with drooping bells that look as if they have been cast from the drippings of a pink candle. Though fairly hardy, it rapidly became a favourite in Victorian conservatories. Another famous plant from that trip is the strong holly-like *Desfontainia spinosa* with coral red flowers, an exotic-looking inhabitant of the more sheltered shrubbery. He found the flame-flower, *Tropaeolum speciosum*, now entwined through every yew hedge in northern Europe. He also brought back a new berberis, *Berberis darwinii*, which, with its brash orange flowers, now hangs over every suburban fence. Most spectacular of all, and unsurpassed in cool countries as a tree with the most brilliant flower colour, was *Embothrium coccineum*. One Scottish landowner, the Earl of Stair, was so enraptured with it that he replanted his magnificent seventeenth-century avenues with it, alternating the trees with those of the dark green, dulled leaves of *Quercus ilex*. The effect is still quite remarkable.

It was Hooker's next big collecting trip to the then unknown parts of Sikkim and Nepal, a journey that lasted from 1848 to 1851, that had the greatest effect on the European garden, because of the new rhododendron species to which he brought the world's attention. Even while travelling, he managed, characteristically, to organize their illustration, publishing his magnificent *Rhododendrons of the Sikkim-Himalaya*, most of which he himself soon introduced into England. He returned to Kew, together with his co-collector, Dr Thomas Thomson of the Bengal army, with specimens of around six and a half thousand species. They included twenty-eight entirely new rhododendrons, many new orchids, balsams, ferns and mosses, and over three hundred specimens of different timbers for his father's Museum of Economic Botany at Kew. Gardeners will be either horrified or grateful that, of the many plants he introduced, bergenias must now be among the most widely grown.

The sumptuous *Lapageria rosea*, collected by Joseph Dalton Hooker, was given Empress Josephine's maiden name.

In 1854, he published two volumes of his *Himalayan Journals*, and the following year, *Illustrations of Himalayan Plants* as well as the beginning of the colossal *Flora Indica*. His appetite for work was clearly prodigious. He was appointed Assistant Director of Kew Gardens in 1855 and, on his father's death in 1865, Director. He held that august and influential post for twenty years, still travelling extensively, and publishing ever larger projects. His father had edited the *Botanical Magazine*, founded in 1786. It was, and remains, a widely read periodical that illustrates a number of new plants in each issue, together with a page of notes on the plant's history and botanical relationships. For over thirty years, starting from 1865, all the plants introduced into Kew from China were described by him, and illustrated with his own coloured drawings. Parallel with that magazine, he also took over from his father the periodical *Icones Plantarum, or Figures with short descriptions of new and rare plants*. While none of these were quite as glamorous to look at as Siebold's *Flora Japonica*, they were very much cheaper, and reached a much wider audience.

Nothing could stop the flood of plants from the East. Max Ernst Wichura, a German collector, found in Japan the eponymous rose that has given rose fanciers so many gorgeous climbers. The Russian Emil Bretschneider scoured the Western Hills of China, sending seed to Charles Sprague Sargent at the Arnold Arboretum in Boston, to Kew, the Jardin des Plantes in Paris, and the botanical gardens in Berlin and St Petersburg. One tattered tin reached Sargent containing the first seeds of a widespread northern Asian rhododendron

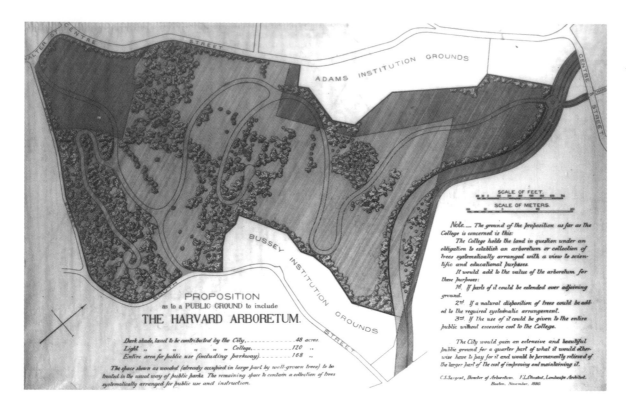

A plan of the Arnold Arboretum at Harvard in 1880. As American gardeners became
passionate about new plants, the Arboretum became an important engine
driving the search for new species.

(*Rhododendron mucronulatum*), the purple flowers of which are now the bane of early spring
gardens throughout the temperate world, and look particularly dreadful amongst daffodils.
The Russian Carl Maximowicz arrived in Japan in 1860 and stayed for three and a half
years. His Japanese assistant, Tchonoski, is immortalized in that perfect wilderness tree,
Malus tschonoskii. The American collector George Rogers Hall even met Siebold in Japan,
and sent some of the great man's plants directly back to the United States.

By now, the wilderness was becoming a popular garden element in new American
gardens too. The idea was being promoted by several writers, most notably by the
nurseryman George Ellwanger. To grow the new tree flora, the Arnold Arboretum was
founded outside Boston by a wealthy, comfort-loving, yet immensely energetic patrician,
Charles Sprague Sargent (1841–1927). It swiftly became a gardener's paradise. Sargent
publicized its development, thereby promoting the new garden flora, in a newsletter called
the *Illustrated Weekly Journal of Horticulture, Landscape Art and Forestry*. One of the genera he
championed in its pages had been present in European wildernesses since the sixteenth
century, and in Middle Eastern gardens for probably a thousand years before that. Just as
those ancient lilacs must have travelled the ancient trade routes from China, the new species

of *Syringa* arrived as new trade routes from China were being forged. Many of them had been collected by Emil Bretschneider. The issue of the *Illustrated Weekly Journal* dated 26 June 1889, reported: '*Syringa villosa* has, now that the plants are thoroughly established, and of large size, flowered here more abundantly than it ever has before. It is certainly an ornamental plant of the first-class and one of the most important introductions of late years among flowering shrubs.' *Syringa pubescens* was another species which Sargent tipped for future garden grandeur: 'This species is one of the most beautiful lilacs in cultivation. The individual flowers are not large, and the clusters are smaller than those of other species; they are produced, however, in the greatest profusion, and quite cover the branches. The flowers are at first a delicate rose-colour, but, before fading, become almost white; they are deliciously fragrant.' Both are still producing hybrids at the hands of American breeders.

The final development of the wilderness in the average suburban garden was due to the vastly influential London nursery of Veitch and Co., run by a long dynasty of Veitchs, most of whom were gardeners and two of whom did some collecting. Overall, the Veitch nurseries were instrumental in bringing in endless astilbes, birches, *Clematis* species, *Corydalis*, many cotoneasters, the fabulous handkerchief tree (*Davidia involucrata*), deutzias, *Dipelta*, endless gentians, *Kolkwitzia amabilis* (now a staple shrub in temperate American suburban shrubberies), dozens of lilies and honeysuckles, magnolias aplenty, *Malus* species, mountain and herbaceous peonies, hundreds of primulas and rhododendrons, the new *Rodgersia*, many lilacs and viburnums. It is an astonishing list.

Perhaps in response to the plethora of plants, the Veitch family seemed to like a limited number of Christian names, and the relationships between the various Jameses and Johns take some working out. James Harry Veitch (1868–1907) had the most influence on the wilderness garden, being instrumental in introducing to Europe and America some of the most sumptuous forms of Japanese cherry.

James's father, John Gould Veitch (1839–69), was born at Exeter, just as the first Veitch nursery was being set up there. He was a devoted horticulturist, but the business's prosperity gave him wider horizons, and he became an intrepid voyager. In April 1860 he set off for Japan and China. He stayed briefly at Siebold's old haunt of Nagasaki, but soon moved on. He was among the first party of Europeans ever to climb the sacred Mount Fuji, and he cheered wildly when the party's leader had the temerity to implant that sacred mountain with a Union Jack. Later, in Tokyo, he met Robert Fortune (see Chapter Five), and did some collecting in nearby nurseries. He wrote very lengthy reports and aspects of his trips made heavily edited copy for the *Gardeners' Chronicle and Agricultural Gazette*. The clamber up Fuji is described in the issue for 22 December 1862, among adverts for 'Surplus Stock of Imported Dutch Bulbs', 'Scarlet Rhododendrons, Kalmias (and other plants for the American Garden)', 'seedling Cedrus deodara', and entrancing articles on topics as diverse as 'Peach Trees and Weevils', 'Holly Tea' and 'The Show of Dogs at Birmingham'.

In the first of John Gould Veitch's letters, dated 15 December, he is visiting gardens in Nagasaki, where he finds *Cryptomeria japonica*, *Aralia sieboldii*, viburnums and camellias, and is getting Wardian cases built by local carpenters, who are amazed by his needs. He ships home ferns such as *Gleichenia dichotoma*, and collects many acers, variegated aucubas, azaleas,

The glazed plant cases first described by
Dr Ward kept plants in perfect health
through astonishing vicissitudes.

variegated bamboos, a buddleia of which the Japanese use the bark to make paper (*Buddleia davidii*), *Cephalotaxus*, deutzias, *Euonymus japonica*, the first variegated hosta, *Hydrangea japonica*, *H. bracteata*, *H. hirta*, new gardenias, new spireas, weigelas, pernettya (now gaultheria), pines, podocarpus and oaks. This letter alone contains an amazing list.

Viburnums were a Veitch speciality, and perfect for the Victorian wilderness. John Gould Veitch found some good ones. However, one of the most famous species, *Viburnum farreri* (first introduced as, and sometimes still called, *V. fragrans*) had to wait until 1911, when the English collector William Purdom sent seed to Messrs Veitch. This seed came from plants in the Temple Gardens in Gansu, where Purdom actually found two forms, one white flowered, the other pink. The seedlings did not flower in their new gardens until 1920, which was, sadly, six years after the nursery itself had closed. Here is the English collector Reginald Farrer, writing of its discovery in *On the Eaves of the World* in 1917:

Shallow scrub and coppice descended here to the track-side, and here we came on the Viburnum, at first isolated and suspicious, but soon in such quantity and such situations that one could no longer doubt that here this most glorious of flowering shrubs is genuinely indigenous. Its place of origin had long been in doubt, though all over North China it is probably the best-beloved and most universal of garden plants; so that there was real satisfaction in thus having traced it to its home, in the wild hills immediately to the south of Shi-hor [Xi he] and probably elsewhere in this narrow belt, though after this day we never set eyes on it again in nature.

Later he refers to its 'gracious arching masses, ten feet high and more across, whose naked boughs in spring before the foliage, become one blaze of soft pink lilac-spikelets, breathing an intense fragrance of heliotrope. The white form, indeed, is pure and lovely as the best of forced white lilac, but my own heart goes out yet more specially perhaps to the commoner pink type, whose blushing stars glisten as if built of crystals after the pleasant fashion of so many spring flowers.'

James Harry Veitch, eldest son of John Gould Veitch, was also responsible for the introduction of some marvellous things, especially the beautiful *Rhododendron schlippenbachii*, first discovered forty years earlier on the coast of Korea. During travels in Japan, India and Australia between 1891 and 1893 he shipped home the Japanese lantern vine (*Physalis alkekengi* var. *franchetii*), for the delight of children, gardeners and endless numbers of flower arrangers. To his regret, though, he missed the flowering of Japan's fabled cherry orchards. Presciently, he arranged for local nurserymen to send young plants to his nursery at Chelsea. From the early 1890s the business began to receive some of the huge numbers of Japanese *Prunus* species and cultivars. Almost all of the 150 sorts introduced were an instant success, and it is no wonder that 1930s suburban gardens were still full of them. Rows of red-brick houses have them as street trees, sometimes alternating pink and white, all over Europe. Design-conscious gardeners pride themselves on growing only *Prunus* 'Taihaku'. The parks of great American cities grow them with a sense of scale that is entirely Japanese in inspiration.

These cherries have an immense and august history, and have long been a favourite in the gardens of Japanese noblemen. In *The Tale of Genji*, a romance written around AD 1000, the garden of a prince has 'a very pleasant arrangement of lakes and hills. The hills were high in the southeast quarter, where cherry trees were planted in large numbers. The pond was most attractively designed. Among the plantings in the forward parts of the garden were cinquefoil pines, red plums, cherries, wisteria, Kerria, and rock azalea . . . and far away in the private gardens a willow trailed its branches in a deepening green, and cherry blossoms were rich and sensuous.'

A Japanese scholar called Rassho Naba (1595–1648) was the first person to write a book devoted entirely to cherries. It covered Chinese and Korean types, as well as those of his own hillsides. After it appeared, a knowledge of cherry varieties became as much part of intellectual culture as was an appreciation of painting, music and poetry. His garden contained well over two hundred varieties of flowering cherry, and even in 1822, an illustrated catalogue of the trees growing in a seventeenth-century cherry garden near Kyoto, and romantically entitled *A Paragon of Bowers*, shows many of them. Like nineteenth-century roses, their names alone are rich and poetic, making the gardener want to plant them almost for the name itself. Certainly, Western gardeners, taking up Japanese ideas in a way that even Siebold can hardly have dreamed, fell instantly in love with them. With the introduction of Japanese cherries planted in their millions, the ancient European 'wilderness' finally transmutes into the way we garden today.

Around the middle of the nineteenth century, the wilderness begins to show very clearly how garden elements evolve in response to incoming plants. Phylogenetic diagrams have illustrated how, for example, small mammals and the first birds evolved from different branches of reptiles, and botanists have had endless fun and feuds exploring similar processes in the plant world. Garden historians can easily copy zoologists and botanists, and observe the branching evolution of gardens. The wilderness sprouted one amazingly vigorous evolutionary branch, and one which now, like the mammals and birds, has a powerful and independent life of its own.

In his discussion of the wilderness in the mid-eighteenth century, Philip Miller suggests that wilderness walks be bordered with roses. Of Europe's wild species, only the eglantine rose (*Rosa eglanteria*), with its deliciously apple-scented leaves, was much grown in the garden. Most of the rest were ancient garden plants, often so old and of such complex parentage that they had lost complete contact with any known wild species. All these old garden roses are doubles, sometimes with so many petals that they have been called 'Centifolias'. In double flowers like these, the pollen-bearing anthers have been transformed into petals, and therefore the plant is male-sterile. There does seem to have been some rose breeding going on in Holland in the early seventeenth century, although quite what plants were involved, and how it was done, is unclear. In any case, the total number of roses in cultivation at that time was still only around fifty or so.

In Britain, the Society of London Gardeners published a catalogue in 1730 in which only forty-three roses are listed as being 'available to the public and recommended for being intermixed with flowering trees and shrubs in small wilderness quarters'. The 1754 list of William Joyce, who had a nursery at Gateshead, near Newcastle contains thirty-two roses, including the ancient *Rosa mundi* and various 'cabbage' and centifolia roses, as well as a double yellow and a musk.

Things were soon to change. André Michaux (see Chapter Three) was collecting roses from Persian gardens in the early 1780s. Plants were coming in from China too. In its warm southern regions, species had evolved that, like many sub-tropical plants, bloomed throughout the entire season of growth. European and Middle Eastern roses only had a single, evanescent, flowering. This had engaged the sympathy of the poetically minded since the dawn of Western literature, but had always irritated gardeners. The Chinese admired roses too, and that rich and ancient garden culture had gradually selected a number of roses that were almost perpetual flowering, were reasonably double, but were rather scrawny shrubs, or rampant climbers. Screen paintings around AD 1000 show the delicate, slightly nodding flower and distinctive foliage of what became known in the West as the 'China Rose' (*Rosa semperflorens*).

There is a slight possibility that this rose had been grown in Europe in the sixteenth century, for something very similar to this group of plants appears in the Florentine artist Bronzino's famous *Allegory with Venus and Cupid*. It may have reached Venice as an item of trade, but its owners probably did not realize that it would die out in a cold winter. The first European herbarium specimen in existence is dated 1733. Linnaeus seems not to have known of that sheet when he described the species, using a specimen probably from the garden of Peter Osbeck, a pupil of his who was collecting in Canton in 1751. Living plants reached the West soon after, and a China rose was grown at the Chelsea Physic Garden in 1759. From there, cuttings being easy to root, it was soon at the Princess Augusta's garden at Kew, and, following social precedence, soon after that in the garden of the redoubtable Dr John Fothergill at Upton House, London, who, with an immensely lucrative practice, built a greenhouse reported to be the largest in the world. It reached the pages of the *Botanical Magazine* in December 1794, where it was described thus: 'We are induced to consider the rose here represented as one of the most desirable plants in point of ornament

Exhibited in 1804, this painting by Jan Frans van Dael shows the ancient cabbage rose, soon to be superseded by new types, and many other old garden flowers. Also depicted, however, is a flower truss of *Hydrangea quercifolia*, just in from Louisiana.

ever introduced . . . its flowers, large in proportion to the plants are semidouble, and with great fragrance; they blossom during the whole of the year, more sparingly indeed in the winter months; the shoot itself is more hardy than most greenhouse plants.'

Unlike European doubles, it proved to be highly fertile, and by 1798, enthusiasts such as Thory and Redouté were raising seedlings in their Paris gardens. Soon, all gardeners realized that if they could combine new China roses' long season with the robust habit and heavily petalled flowers of the current European ones, they would achieve an extraordinary horticultural and commercial 'coup'. French nurserymen seem to have been the first to notice that the old European roses, if grown in very starved conditions, produced fewer petals, but the occasional fertile anther. Rose breeding was possible; nurseries were soon springing up. One in London was specializing in roses from the 1780s, and one in New York soon followed. But the French gardeners began rose breeding in earnest. M. Dupont sold the best of his seedlings to the first major rose collector, the Empress Josephine. M. Descemet did the same. Soon there were so many marvellous new sorts that it was clear the old wilderness couldn't do them justice. Gardeners had to create a brand-new part of the garden to hold them all: the rosarium.

The Empress Josephine began her collection of roses at Malmaison in 1804. By 1814 it contained all the species and varieties then known: well over a thousand different plants. With her English gardener, Howatson, she ransacked British and French nurseries. One British nurseryman, John Kennedy, even had a special passport to enable him to cross with plants from one warring country to another. Josephine's gardens at Malmaison were famed for roses several years before the English garden designer Humphry Repton made his designs, among which were the very first published for a rose garden at the Earl of Bridgewater's estate at Ashridge in Hertfordshire in 1814.

The garden at Malmaison proved an enormous stimulus to large-scale hybridizing, encouraging the French nursery industry and giving rise to the famous nurseries of Descemet, Cochet and Laffay. But in 1815 war had a direct influence on the garden. The Napoleonic Wars ended. British troops overran Paris, and a whole regiment chose to bivouac in Descemet's nursery. His plants were mostly ruined, and as neither the French nor the British government would recompense him for the losses, he went bankrupt. The owner of a nearby hardware store, Jean-Pierre Vibert, had survived commercially. Interested in roses, he bought up what remained of Descemet's premises and properties, including remnants of his breeding notes and his roses. A man of great energy and acumen, he soon became one of the most influential rose breeders of the nineteenth century, fuelling the demand for rose gardens, with many of his productions being so beautiful that they are grown in gardens to this day.

With more business sense than Descemet, Vibert nursed his venture into considerable prosperity. He bred with, and offered, roses of all sorts, especially the new China roses and Tea roses. He imported the first yellow Tea, 'Parks' Yellow Tea-Scented China'. He developed the new Noisette roses. He also used traditional sorts like the Albas, Gallicas, Centifolias, Mosses, and Damasks, and so loved them that he kept breeding them even after his public had moved on to Portlands, Bourbons and the rest.

At length, in 1851, at the age of seventy-four, he sold his business to his foreman, who kept it going into the 1890s. He is supposed to have said, towards the end of his life, 'Like the rest of the world, I have thought that I adored and detested many men and many things. In reality, I have loved only Napoleon and roses.' His close family must have been chilled by this. It is perhaps fitting that his most famous climbing rose, named after a daughter, the pale 'Aimée Vibert', became a favourite flower to wind through the railings of cemetery plots. It mixes the American 'Champneys' Pink Cluster' with a double form of *R. sempervirens*.

'Champneys' Pink Cluster' shows how close the links between French and American rose fanciers had become. Brothers Louis and Philippe Noisette owned nurseries in Paris and Charleston, South Carolina, respectively. Roses moved between the two. John Champneys, a wealthy farmer in Charleston, crossed some plants he had bought from Louis: *Rosa moschata* and a China monthly. He called the best of his

The Empress Josephine, an ardent and jealous collector of roses, begonias, cape heaths and dahlias.

seedlings 'Champneys' Pink Cluster'. This was soon sent to France. Philippe himself used either Champneys' rose, or similar crosses, to produce a charming double lilac-pink climber, low on perfume, but flowering well into November. Excited, he sent plants to France, where it was marketed as 'Noisette Carnée', and became part of a whole new group of roses called the Noisettes. 'Blush Noisette' is still a marvel. American gardeners, too, were soon making their own collections. Francis Parkman assembled a collection of 1,000 different roses in a sumptuous rose garden at his summer home on the shores of Jamaica Pond, near Boston, in the 1850s. The same garden also held a vast number of new Japanese introductions.

Soon these countless sorts of new rose were exported to India, and China. In China, they caused a furore, and Chinese gardeners competed to grow 'Madame Hardy', 'Robert le Diable' and the rest. Humphry Repton, John Caie and Miss Lawrance may have been famous rose garden designers, but their fame was due entirely to the flood of new cultivars that had begun. And with the Empress Josephine as their collector and publicist, the new roses could hardly fail; the rose garden, an offshoot of the wilderness, soon became almost a synonym for the whole garden itself.

THE ROCK
GARDEN

O *n the higher alpine meadows, from the summits of the cliffs to the*
verge of the snows, is an indescribable wealth of bloom, the colour-
scheme changing from month to month as the seasons advance.
Most of the species being gregarious, absolute sheets and carpets of colour are
the result. Trollius, Anemones, Primula, Gentiana, Cremanthodium,
Cyananthus, blue and yellow, Corydalis, Meconopsis, Pedicularis, Phlomis,
Parnassia, Saxifraga, Orchis, Roscoea, Delphinium, Oxytropis, Plectranthus,
Salvia, Cerastium, Incarvillea, Morina – these are only a few of the many
genera represented, as well as Ericaceae and many peculiar species of
Rhododendron. Two of the finest, seeds of which were secured in 1913 are
the magnificent Dracocephalum isabellae *and the equally beautiful*
Anemone lancifolia . . . *Saxifragae are rampant on every hill, scree, and*
stony Meadow, brightening the dullest spots with their orange and golden
blooms. One splendid new species, a cushion plant named S. pulchra, *has*
rose-coloured petals and silvery grey foliage. Many other new species were
found on the range. Campanulaceae is well represented by several new
codonopsis and many new Adenophora. Campanula crenulata, *with its*
deep black-indigo bells is on every ledge and humus-covered boulder.

This is George Forrest (1873–1932), writing in the *Journal of the Royal*
Horticultural Society about his exploration of China, looking for plants for
a new part of the garden: the rockery. His adventures, as we will see,
were traumatic, but his books, and articles for the *Gardeners' Chronicle*,
must have launched 10,000 new rockeries per page, especially when he
wrote passages that describe the hills:

This sketch of part of the Yangtze valley, by Dr A. Barton *c.* 1895, shows the
precipitous valleys of the river system. These natural barriers have fostered an
astonishingly rich flora.

George Forrest, on horseback among potted rhododendrons and orchids on the border between China and Tibet.

But the scenery of the upper Ealwin can never be forgotten by anyone who has wondered at it in the rich sunshine which prevails after the autumn rains have given way to the first touch of winter. The great variety of rock formation, the abundant forests and vegetation, and the diversity of light effects between the summits of the ranges . . . and the abyss in which the river flows produce a vast panorama of ever-changing beauty. In the morning, the sun, as it touches the top of the Mekong divider sends wide shafts of turquoise light down the side gullies to the rivers which seem to be transformed into silver. The pines along the top of the ridges stand out as if limned by the hand of a Japanese artist. In the evening all the wide slopes of the Mekong side are flooded with red and orange lights, which defy photography and would be the despair of a Turner. The traveller whose fortune it has been to explore the great rivers of this, our north-east Indian frontier will admit that the Salwin, while it is inhospitable, difficult and barbarous, far exceeds in natural beauty all the valleys of the sister rivers, the Yang-tru, the Mekong or the Irawadi.

Of course, no gardener could do anything like that, but a yard or two of saxifrages or codonopsis, and a few pieces of stone, might at least carry the right associations.

Since the late eighteenth century, gardening has increasingly become a way of classifying plants. In this entirely plant-centred system, their presumed evolutionary relationships are ignored; only their growing conditions are considered important. This trend started with the American garden (see Chapter Three), in which plants that were assumed to like wet, peaty conditions, regardless of origin, were grouped together. As gardeners' access to an extraordinary range of lovely plants grew easier and simpler, new plant groupings emerged that demanded parts of the garden to themselves. The rockery, that still fast-evolving form of gardening, or part of the garden, is one of them.

Rockeries were, at first, pure theatre. From the middle of the eighteenth century, artificial grottoes and mock ruins became fashionable adjuncts in any garden large enough to pretend to 'landscape'. To make these whimsical and often gimcrack elements look more ancient and authentic, they were sometimes draped with ivy, or planted with plants known to like growing in rocky crevices. Wallflowers (*Erysimum cheiri*) and European saxifrages from the Alps were the most decorative plants used, until Joseph Pitton de Tournefort (see Chapter One) returned from his travels bearing lovely plants like the marjoram *Origanum tournefortii* and the violently violet *Aubrieta deltoidea*. At first rare, they were widely disseminated by the time gardeners realized how well they looked, and grew, on the new-fangled 'rockwork'.

For a long time, no gardener wanted anything the least bit reminiscent of rocky or mountainous terrain. Most eighteenth-century travellers found mountain landscapes frightening, passing through them as quickly as possible, eyes tight shut in terror. The mountains and their plants were associated with chaos: climatic, geological and social. In the popular imagination, brigands and outlaws lived here, among the peaks and ravines. Perhaps Tournefort's *Aubrieta* was the turning point. Gardeners began to wonder what other showy plants might decorate their domesticated rockwork. Some began to explore. Miller's *Gardener's Dictionary* of 1731 lists a few species now thought of as alpines: *Androsace lactea, Aster alpinus, Geranium argenteum, Gentiana acaulis* among a few other from Europe. From America, where the really rocky parts of the Rockies were as yet unexplored, he lists eastern woodlanders, now commonly found in shaded parts of rock gardens: *Sanguinaria, Trillium erectum, Uvularia*, but not much else.

In 1774, William Forsyth, Philip Miller's successor as curator of the Chelsea Physic Garden, began to assemble one of the first proper rock gardens. Unfortunately, he also set a strange precedent, probably never having looked carefully at a rocky landscape. He seemed to think that a rock garden could be made out of virtually any material remotely hard. His garden contained forty tons of assorted stone rescued from the roadside outside the Tower of London, as well as substantial quantities of flints and chalk from the nearby 'downs'. It also had some lumps of lava brought back from Iceland two years earlier by Sir Joseph Banks. This heterogeneous mix was heaped in a pile, and was rather short of plants.

In 1775, Dr John Fothergill and his friend Dr Pitcairn of Warwick Lane, London, sent the Scots gardener Thomas Blaikie (1751–1838) to Switzerland to hunt the Alps for plants. Blaikie travelled into the Jura mountains as well, sending back over four hundred parcels of plants to Chelsea. His bag included *Ranunculus glacialis, Campanula cenisia*, alpine clover (*Trifolium alpinum*), *Veronica bellidioides*, chamois grass (*Hutchinsia alpina*), *Pyrola uniflora, Androsace villosa*, ground box (*Polygala chamaebuxus*), and the enchanting alpen rose (*Rhododendron ferrugineum*). It was an immense augmentation of the mountain flora, and gardeners must have wondered quite how to integrate these new things amongst the ivies draping their mock-frightening grottoes or 'Gothick' castles.

Few gardeners had the room or means to make fake caverns and castles, but they still wanted to grow these exciting new alpines. They took up the Physic Garden's mode of rockery-making with enthusiasm. Then as now, a rockery allowed the gardener to grow large numbers of small species in a small space. It also appealed to something in human nature that likes small-scale models of something much larger and less controllable. Unfortunately, the new rock gardeners also copied Chelsea's other lead, incorporating all sorts of rubbish amongst the saxifrages, aubrietias and other new plants being illustrated in *Curtis' Botanical Magazine*. These were all immensely desirable. Between 1787 and 1804, now also under Forsyth's control, this magazine illustrated exquisite European plants such as *Cyclamen coum, Gentiana acaulis, Ranunculus gramineus, Ramonda myconi, Daphne cneorum*, and exciting Americans such as the new phloxes, especially *Phlox divaricata, P. subulata*, and *P. setacea*.

The European *Gentiana acaulis* is so intensely blue that it is not eclipsed by even the rarest Himalayan species.

Now in every rock garden, the humble aubrietia was once a rare and highly prized plant.

Gardeners had to have them, but did not know how best to show them off.

The transformation of the European rockery began in America. John Bartram had already sent over plants such as *Epigaea repens*, powerfully perfumed but difficult to grow, as well as small irises, creeping phloxes and even *Dicentra eximia*. But as the colonization of North America continued, and the continent's exploitation began, it became clear that the western lands needed to be mapped and explored, and an easy way found through the great Rocky Mountain ranges to get to the Pacific coast. Some of the old Indian tracks went through Montana, and the homelands of the bitterroot (*Lewisia*). No one then had any idea that this plant would go on to become one of the great rock garden genera, one which has fuelled many gardeners' love of alpines, and one which is still developing fast.

In 1803, President Thomas Jefferson won approval from Congress for a project that became one of North America's great adventure stories. He wanted to know if there was a route from the Atlantic to the Pacific Oceans following the Missouri and the Columbia Rivers. If the sources of the two great rivers turned out to be reasonably close to each other, then American traders would be able to compete more effectively with British fur companies and their associated traders, who were expanding southwards from Canada. He wanted to reach the western Indian tribes, to tell them that American, rather than Canadian, traders would come to buy their furs.

To lead the expedition, Jefferson selected Meriwether Lewis (1774–1809), a twenty-eight-year-old army captain, a family friend, and by now Jefferson's private secretary. Lewis was already a keen naturalist, having spent long hours as a boy tramping and hunting in the woods of Virginia. He chose a former army friend, William Clark (1770–1838), then thirty-two years old, to be co-leader of the expedition.

Lewis and Clark reached their first staging point at the junctions of the Mississippi and Missouri Rivers near St Louis in December 1803. They spent the whole of the first winter camped at the mouth of Wood River, on the Illinois side of the Mississippi, opposite the entrance to the Missouri. During that season, they recruited young woodsmen and volunteer soldiers from nearby army outposts. The mixed bag of men included ex-trappers, hopeful explorers and men who could speak Indian languages. They even found a Frenchman with a bought Indian wife who spoke several tribal languages. She proved to be of enormous worth throughout the entire period of the expedition.

The troupe broke camp on 14 May 1804. Clark wrote in his journal: 'I set out at 4 o'clock p.m. and proceeded on under a jentle brease up the Missouri.' The river journey was hard and long, and progress, by boat or along the banks, was slow and exhausting. When winter began to close in again, in early November, they were near present-day Washburn, North Dakota. They were approximately 1,510 miles from their last winter camp at Wood River. Even by the next summer, the journey was far from easy, as Lewis's journal entry for 20 July 1804 records:

For a month past the party have been troubled with boils, and occasionally with the dysentery. These boils were large tumours which broke out under the arms, on the legs, and, generally, in the parts most exposed to action, which sometimes became too painful to permit the men to work. This disorder . . . has not affected the general health of the party, which is quite as good, if not better, than that of the same number of men in any other situation.

On 30 August, Clark wrote:

A Council under an Oak Tree near where we had a flag flying on a high flagstaff . . . The Souex is a

Rhododendron ferrugineum was discovered in the Swiss Alps in 1775 by the gardener Thomas Blaikie.

The Turkish and Caucasian *Cyclamen coum* was illustrated in *Curtis' Botanical Magazine* and became an instant success.

Lewis and Clark on their expedition across America, as painted by Thomas Burnham (1818–1866).

Stout bold looking people, & well made, the greater part of them make use of Bows & arrows. Some few fusees I observe among them, notwithstanding they live by the Bow and arrow, they do not Shoot So Well as the Northern Indians the Warriers are Verry much deckerated with Paint Porcupine quils & feathers, large leagins and mockersons, all with buffalow roabs of Different Colours. The Squars wore Peticoats & a White Buffalow roabe with the black hare turned back over their necks and Shoulders.

A year later, on 21 August 1805, one member of the expedition, the interpreter and hunter George Drouilliard, was hunting along the shore of the Beaverhead River. He met a group of Shoshoni Indians. At first they were friendly, but things turned sour when one of the Shoshoni snatched his gun, and they all raced off. Drouilliard bravely gave chase, and overtook one of the tiring Indian horses. Fortunately the gun was not loaded, and instead of being shot, he managed to retrieve his weapon. In the fracas, the Indians left behind their scant belongings. Drouilliard took them back to his camp. In the haul, Lewis found 'a couple of bags wove with the fingers of the bark of the silk-grass containing each about a bushel of dryed service burries some chokecherry cakes and about a bushel of roots of three different kinds dryed and prepared for uce which were foalded in as many parchment hides of buffaloe.' One lot of roots 'were brittle, hard, of the size of a small quill, cilindric and as white as snow throughout, except some small parts of the hard black rind which they had not seperated in the preperation. This the Indians with me informed were always boiled for use. I made the experiment, found that they became perfectly soft by boiling, but had a very bitter taste, which was naucious to my pallate, and I transfered them to the Indians who had eat them heartily.' The plant was called by Indians and French trappers alike 'bitterroot.' It was to become called *Lewisia rediviva*.

Bitterroot was an important Indian winter food crop, heavy with legend. One tale described how an old Flathead Indian woman sat weeping on the bank of the In-schu-te-schu, or Red Willow River, in the shadow of the Chi-quil-quil-kane, or Red Mountains, singing a death song for her starving sons. The rising sun heard her plaint, and sent a red spirit-bird to comfort her. The bird promised that from each of her falling tears a new flower would grow, tinted with the rose of his feathers and the white of her hair, and springing from a root as bitter as her sorrow but as nourishing as her love. The prophecy came true, and her people called the plant spatlum, meaning 'bitter root'.

Later, in July 1806, Lewis collected whole plants at a place now called Bitterroot Valley and took them back to Philadelphia, where they were formally described by the botanist Frederick Pursh. The meadows where it once grew in such abundance, and which were so important to several local tribes, particularly Flatheads, Kutenais, Shoshones and Nez Perces, have now been destroyed by development.

Lewisias, which ironically became the state flower of Montana, turned out to hybridize easily. Long thought fussy, some of the new hybrids have set out from the rockery and, happily perennial in the open border, are due to colonize other parts of the garden. They have already become easy pot plants, but vigorous new plants like one called 'Little Plum' may turn out to be easy border plants too. It is a genus that has come a long way since those shrivelled roots were found in an Indian's bag.

On 23 September 1806, the tattered Lewis and Clark's Corps of Discovery arrived at last at St Louis and 'received a harty welcom from it's

The Shoshone Indians, encountered by the Lewis and Clark expedition, have a genus named after them: *Shoshonea*.

inhabitants'. The men had covered 8,000 miles of territory over a period of two years, four months, and nine days. There had been only one fatality, but there had been some terrible times. Lewis and Clark remained firm friends. Congress rewarded the officers and men of the military enterprise with extensive grants of land. The Indian woman Sacagawea, an essential ambassadress and translator for the expedition, received nothing.

However beautiful the new Americans such as lewisias, carpeting penstemons and dwarf rhododendrons were, and however arduous their collection had been, there seemed no limit to the vulgarity of the gardens in which they were planted. Wealth simply increased the awfulness of taste. Things got worse before they got, generally, better. By 1838, when General William Clark died, rockeries were beginning to look dreadful. As always, in a new and quickly developing field, all sorts of people adopted the role of 'the expert'. A writer in Sir Joseph Paxton's *Magazine of Botany* suggested, in the same year, some pretty little rockwork thus: 'the turf on which the pedestals stand is to be inclined at an angle of 45°, and the pedestals [for vases] are enclosed in small circular borders, on which may be placed fragments of rock, or shells, and by the introduction of a little soil amongst them, alpine plants may be successfully grown'. After suggesting adding a parterre and grass pyramids in the corners to hold statuary, the writer continues: 'The introduction of fountains, of chaste and unique structure, and ornamented with every variety of rock and shell, into the central compartments, with jets of water issuing from every crevice, and propelled with diverse and ever-varying degrees of force, would form most delightful and refreshing spectacles during the summer months.'

The dried root of *Lewisia rediviva* was an
important winter vegetable for local
Indian tribes. Lewis found it 'nausious'.

In the 1840s, the rockery might be composed
of broken porcelain plates, broken bricks, flints
and tattered statuary. By 1853, the *Book of the
Garden* suggested

*stones, the fused masses of brick procured from brick
kilns, or indeed, any coarse material most convenient
to be got. These are built up in the most rugged
and mis-shapen forms imaginable and afterward
covered over with Roman cement, and formed into
recesses, projections, and overhanging crags, according
to the taste of the artist. Sufficient apertures are left
for receiving soil, in which rock plants are planted.
When the whole is perfectly dry and set, it is painted
with oil paint to represent veined or stratified
granite, or any other kind of natural rockwork that
may be desired.*

It is hard to imagine how any plant at all
survived that. The most unnatural rockery was
at the Duke of Marlborough's private garden at
Blenheim Palace, Oxfordshire. Although it was
actually formed on a scar of natural rock, this
had been hewn into zig-zag paths with numerous hand-cut niches on each side to receive
plants. Most of these niches were lined with spar, a richly coloured, expensive and glittery
natural rock. The final result was a rich and sparkling effect, which can have done little to
make the plants it contained look at home. Slightly quieter in effect was the rockery at Syon
House, London, where a pile of only moderately large granite stones had been shipped
from Scotland. Assembled and planted, they were compared by most London journalists 'to
the scenery of a Highland glen'. Only Jane Loudon, the wife of John Claudius Loudon, was
brave enough to 'confess there does not appear to me the slightest resemblance. In fact, the
Syon rockwork is so overpowered by the magnificent conservatory in front . . . that it
becomes quite a secondary object . . . It consists of masses of granite, intermixed with
broken capitals planted with ornamental flowering plants, principally exotic.' However,
even she approved of some rock gardens which must have appeared equally odd in their
heyday. One she especially liked belonged to Lady Broughton, at Hoole House, Cheshire.
Mrs Loudon wrote that it

*stands quite alone, the only one of its kind. The design for this rockwork was taken from a small
model, representing the mountains of Savoy, with the valley of Chamouni . . . The plants are all
strictly alpine – the only liberty taken being the mingling of the alpine plants of hot and cold
countries, or rather of different elevations, together, and this is contrived very ingeniously, by placing*

fragments of dark stone to absorb the heat, round those that require most warmth, and fragments of white stone to reflect the heat, round those that require to be kept cool.

Graham Stuart Thomas, writing in *The Rock Garden and its Plants* (1989), says that at Hoole House, efforts were made to grow pyrolas, *Coptis trifolia* from Japan, *Calceolaria fothergillii* from Patagonia, jeffersonias, cortusas, soldanellas and so on from Europe.

That all sounds a bit better, but later in the century, the rockery of Sir Frank Crisp (1843–1919) at Friar Park, in Henley, Oxfordshire, was a model of the Matterhorn, replete with scale models of chamois goats made of tin. He took it very seriously, and when someone made fun of the whole thing, there were court cases and poison-pen letters. Another, made in 1847 under the close direction of Sir Charles Isham, at his seat of Lamport Hall, Northamptonshire, was a huge rockery wall decorated with miniature caverns designed to show off his collection of German garden gnomes. The mountain's slopes were planted with dwarf conifers. The 1850s were notable for the development of the pocket rock garden system developed by James McNab at the Royal Botanic Garden, Edinburgh. In these, small rectangular containers were made of pieces of stone, all joined together like a piece of dishevelled honeycomb. The idea was to give each contained plant its own recipe of soil. The whole thing looked horrible, and did not suit the plants either.

At last, in 1870, William Robinson (the author of *The Wild Garden*) wrote a book on alpines, *Alpine Flowers for English Gardens*, suggesting that their rockery should look like an outcrop of natural stone, with mossy rocks showing through a sward of sedums, saxifrages, pinks and so on. Unusually for Robinson, it was not a freshly minted idea. The first rock garden using a natural outcrop seems to have been made at Redleaf, at Penshurst in Kent, in 1839. The great Greek Revival house of Belsay in Northumberland had been constructed with stone from a quarry only a hundred yards away from its foundation; by the 1850s this had been turned into a splendidly romantic rock and ravine garden. In America, naturalism took a bit longer. It seems to have been General Stephen Minot Weld who made the first naturalistic rock garden, near Boston in the early 1880s. Best of all, he planted it up with a vast collection of American native plants. Back in Britain, the nursery trade slowly caught on to the new ideas, and companies like Backhouse of York, which had a thriving 'alpine' trade by the 1850s, created huge exhibits constructed with huge rocks a few decades later.

But the real impetus for change was at least partly due to a strange Englishman called Reginald Farrer (1880–1920). Farrer was born to a well-to-do family with a pleasant estate at Ingleborough, high on the limestone fells of western Yorkshire. The child had a slightly deformed palate, and as such a defect would have been outrageously mocked at the private schools of the day, his parents decided to educate him at home. He was gifted and seems to have been born with a love of flowers. When only three years old, he later wrote, he was overwhelmed when he saw his first fields of narcissus at Cap d'Antibes, where his parents had rented a house. He was soon in the south of France again, later claiming to have been thrilled at his first discovery of a lady tulip (*Tulipa clusiana*). At ten, he knew the flora of his local Ingleborough hills, and at fourteen, had made his first rock garden in an abandoned quarry on the estate. He entered Oxford University at seventeen and graduated in 1902.

He already knew a lot about gardening when, in 1902–3, he went to Japan for eight months, also managing to visit China and Korea. Entirely confident, he wrote *The Garden of Asia* in 1904. Once back in England, he tried his hand at novel-writing too, but soon realized that he could make lively copy more easily out of his gardens than out of his limited personal life. (Many associates had already noted his extreme egotism.) He became influential in the garden when he published *My Rock Garden* in 1907. It was a best-seller, catching the mood of the moment and continuously in print for the next forty years. Following books met with less success: *Alpines and Bog Plants* (1908), *In a Yorkshire Garden* (1909), *Among the Hills* (1910) and a book about the alpine plants of the Dolomites. With the rather grandiose title of *The Dolomites: King Laurin's Garden*, it appeared in 1913, just before the Dolomites became firmly out of bounds for most British gardeners because of the outbreak of hostilities in Europe. In this book, through successes and failures, he extols naturalism in

Eretrichium nanum was an alpine much lauded by Farrer, though some gardeners found it disappointing in the rockery.

planting, not so much by copying the plaster Matterhorn and the rest, but by handling rocks in as naturalistic a way as possible, and insisting that they look like natural outcrops, even in a small suburban garden of solid London clay. He seems not to have been aware of how much easier it all was among his native fells at Ingleborough. He certainly caused the end of McNab's awful 'pocket system', although he was unable to kill off what he called 'Dog's Grave' or 'Almond Pudding' kinds of rockery, still so common.

When planting his own collections, he took great trouble over plant associations. He wanted to make them look as authentic as he could, making sure too that the plants had ideal conditions for growth. In his books, he had a way of painting his plants very much larger than life, and he was sometimes accused of over-promoting plants which, once in the rock garden, failed to live up to their new owners' hopes. Sometimes the plants do indeed disappear beneath the superstructure of words. Here he is on eretrichiums:

No eye of faith is quite keen enough to gulp the whole glory of . . . those irresistible wads of silky silver nestling into the highest darkest ridges of the granites and almost hidden from view by the mass of rounded yellow-eyed little faces of a blue so pure and clear and placidly celestial that the richest Forget-me-not by their side takes on a shrill and vulgar note. The blue of Eretrichium *is absolute . . . it has a quality of bland and assured perfection impossible to describe as to imagine. And still more impossible to believe by those who have only seen the comparatively rare and squalid stars of faded turquoise which are all that* Eretrichium *usually condescends to show in cultivation – if it ever condescends to reach that pitch of ostentatiousness at all.* Eretrichium *is the typical high-alpine, only to be seen with climbing and effort; it is the motto of the Mountaineers and the crown of achievement for the walker in the Alps, who will have trudged over leagues of Flannel-flower before once he catches sight of the King of the Alps, set in blobs of sky across the face of some dark cliff or in some sunny slope of the highest ridges making blots of fallen heaven among the scant herbage of the hill.*

Reginald Farrer gardened a quarry on the family estate and insisted that alpines be grown in naturalistic surroundings.

Though many gardeners no doubt resisted the lure of the *Eretrichium*, he made it very hard for readers not to want to rush out at once in search of a *Meconopsis* or an *Androsace* of their own, perhaps from Farrer's own nursery in Yorkshire. Known as the Craven Nursery, this was where he built his first moraine, or 'scree' as he named its successors, which proved a wonderful way of growing alpines. He bored quickly, and needed greater and greater doses of horticultural and botanical beauty to keep his senses alive. The mountains of western China called.

His great Chinese trips, first with fellow plant collector William Purdom (1880–1921) and then with Euan Cox (1893 1977) lasted between 1914 and 1919. He and his companions brought back wonders such as *Allium cyaneum*, *Anemone narcissiflora* var. *villosa*, *Daphne tangutica* – surely one of the most memorable small evergreen shrubs in the garden, and overwhelming in flower (it was first found, but not brought home, by Antwerp Pratt in 1888), *Gentiana farreri*, *Semiaquilegia ecalcarata*, the marvellous shrub *Viburnum farreri* and many more. One of the most sensational alpines was *Meconopsis punicea*. He wrote

At all times and in all places the Blood Poppy calculates successfully on taking your breath away, but never does it do so more triumphantly than when you see its huge poppy flags of vermilion hovering in the sunlit patches of a copse . . . of all its race it is perhaps the most overwhelming . . . Never among all its millions could I discover the least inconstancy of colour, though needless to say I quested long and far in search of the pure albinos which must assuredly be one of the loveliest flowers on earth.

It is certainly dramatic, but in cultivation the colour of the elegantly hanging petals is a sombre rust-rose.

Euan Cox later wrote of him:

Even after the lapse of eleven years I have a vivid memory of Farrer in the hills, his stocky figure clad in khaki shorts and shirt, tieless and collarless, a faded topee on his head, old boots and stockings that gradually slipped down and clung about his ankles as the day wore on. The bustle of the early start; the constant use of the field-glasses which always hung around his neck; the discussions very one-sided owing to my ignorance about the value and relationship of the various plants; his intense satisfaction when a plant was once in the collecting tin and was found worthy; his grunt of disapproval when it was worthless . . . the Luncheon interval with its attendant cold goat rissole and slab chocolate; his enjoyment of our evening tot of rum, a necessity in the rains; and above all his indomitable energy that never spared a frame which was hardly built for long days of searching and climbing. All these I say are as fresh to me as if they had happened yesterday.

Farrer died on a 'one-man and his servants' expedition in Upper Burma. His head servant wrote to Cox that from 1 October 1920, Farrer had suffered from a cough and serious chest pain. 'On the 14th,' he went on, 'he discontinued to take his food except soda water and whisky and medicines for his benefit . . . And without giving any pain and trouble to us he breathed his last on the morning of the 19th October 1920, at about 11:30 a.m.' The servants carried his body down to the nearest out-post of Empire. His grave is marked by a memorial plaque paid for by his beloved mother.

Other collectors searching for alpine beauties in the mountains of western China and its neighbouring states had some terrible experiences that Farrer managed to avoid. The region was always turbulent and lawless, but the British invasion of Tibet, and the first Chinese attempts at its settlement, made it even more dangerous. It is worth remembering, when looking at some charming and innocent saxifrage or androsace nestling on its scree, that it probably cost some blood-spattered plant collector dear. One collector wrote, in the *Gardeners' Chronicle*, of his appalling trials:

The narrow valleys, broken by cross ridges and great spurs, are cut off from each other by difficult and dangerous passes, closed for half the year by snow. The great rivers which flow through funnel-like gorges are quite unnavigable; the upper Mekong can only be crossed by bridges consisting of a single rope composed of split bamboos, across which passengers are slung, trussed up with leather thongs like chickens ready for the spit.

Here and there in the folds of the mountains the Lamas of the yellow sect have established huge gombas, or lamaseries, and, by a combination of force and fraud, have become the real masters of the country . . . they terrorise the poverty-stricken superstitious peasantry and pay little or no regard to the nominal sovereignty of the Celestial mandarins.

In the summer of 1905, I found myself in [their territories] . . . quarters being with the hospitable and venerable chief of the Tzekou mission, Père Dubernard. He first settled at Tzekou when Napoleon III was at the height of his power, and he had never left the country since . . .

It soon became clear that Lamas meant business, and were determined to pay off old scores of jealousy against the missionaries, who had endeavoured for so many years, not without success, to deliver the people from the moral and material chains of Lamaism. Soon our friends among the Tibetans fell away from us or proved false. The mission house was indefensible, and, if defensible, had no one to defend it save two aged French priests and myself . . .

The rising moon that night saw us making our way [to safety] by a narrow and dangerous track along the right bank of the Mekong, the two Fathers on their mules, and myself and the little band of native Christians on foot; on our left roared the Mekong in furious flood; on our right rose the great Mekong-Salwin dividing range . . . in the dark we passed the lamasery of Patong.

All seemed to be going well until someone in the writer's party slipped and made a noise. A lookout on the lamasery walls noticed them and sent out a shrill signal whistle to warn the countryside of their escape. The party fled awkwardly down the steep valley, but during a desperate rest, the writer clambered up a bank to look back and see if they were still pursued. He goes on:

To the north I had a clear view of the crest of the ridge we had descended, and had not long to wait ere my expectations were realised. Suddenly, there appeared a large number of armed men running at full speed in Indian file along the path we had just traversed. I gave the alarm at once and immediately all was confusion, our followers scattering in every direction. Père Bourdonnec became completely panic-stricken . . . and made his way across the stream by a fallen tree, and, despite my attempts to stop him rushed blindly through the dense forest which clothed the southern face of the valley. However, escape in that direction I was sure would be impossible, as our delay had given the enemy time to mature their plans and close in on us. The Père had not covered a couple of hundred yards ere he was riddled with poisoned arrows and fell, the Tibetans immediately rushing up and finishing him off with their huge double-handed swords . . .

Our little band, numbering about 80, were picked off one by one, or captured, only 14 escaping. Ten wives and daughters of some of our followers committed suicide by throwing themselves into the stream to escape the slavery, and worse, which they knew awaited them if captured. Of my own 17 collectors and servants, only one escaped.

When I saw all was lost I fled east down a breakneck path, in places formed along the faces of beetling cliffs by rude brackets of wood and slippery logs. I went down towards the main rivers only to find myself, at one of the sharpest turns, suddenly confronted by a band of hostile and well-armed Tibetans, who had been stationed there to block the passage.

I fell into dense jungle, through which I rolled down a steep slope . . . tearing my clothing to ribbons, and bruising myself most horribly in the process. I then got behind a convenient boulder and made every preparation for a stand should they succeed in discovering my ruse, which I never doubted but they should.

The writer was a Scot, George Forrest (1847–1932). He hid for the next eight days and nights, trying to work his way south during the night. He had no food but a few scraps he found in his pocket. As there were dogs hunting him, he discarded his boots and waded along whatever watercourses he could find. At one point his pursuers were so close that two poisoned arrows passed through his hat. Finally, with his feet and hands swollen and torn, and half-dead with hunger and exhaustion, he no longer cared whether he lived or died. At last, he stumbled desperately into a village, determined to ransack it for food. Fortunately, he had no need to. The villagers were friendly and made arrangements to smuggle him out of the valley. Sadly, the other elderly missionary, Père Dubernard, fared far worse. He was eventually run to earth, trapped in a cave farther up the valley. Forrest wrote:

> *His captors broke both arms above and below the elbow, tied his hands behind his back, and in this condition forced him to walk back to the blackened site of Tzekou. There they fastened him to a post and subjected him to most brutal mutilation; amongst the least of his injuries being the extraction of his tongue and eyes, and the cutting off of his ears and nose. In this horrible condition he remained alive for the space of three days, in the course of which his torturers cut a joint off his fingers and toes each day. When on the point of death, he was treated in the same manner as Père Bourdonnec, portions of the bodies being distributed amongst the various lamaseries in the region.*

Forrest's terrifying ordeal deprived him of all his plant material, and he was too unwell after it to collect more. However, he had already sent home a few seed pods, among them a new species of *Meconopsis*, now called *M. speciosa*, and a tiny creeping rhododendron with large crimson flowers. It seems not to have long survived, or been given a name. His employer was a wealthy businessman, Arthur Kiplin Bulley, who was creating a nursery in Cheshire.

This was only one of the extensive journeys Forrest made through China between 1904 and 1932. The readers of the *Gardeners' Chronicle* were able to follow his adventures in issue after issue, even if some tender stomachs were churned by his stories. Yet, the more they read, the more they had to have the gorgeous plants he was describing. These really were astonishing. He was responsible for introducing some of the most desirable plants for screes and rock gardens, including many species of speckle-flowered *Nomocharis* (now mostly *Lilium*), countless species of *Primula*, the now ubiquitous but glorious *Gentiana sino-ornata*, three species of *Adenophora*, alliums, androsaces, a good handful of anemones, irises, omphalogrammas, roscoeas, saussureas and *Trollius*. Some of his most gorgeous introductions include *Primula bulleyana, P. beesiana, Rhododendron forrestii, R. radicans, Arisaema candidissimum, Roscoea cautleyoides, R. humeana, Allium beesianum* and *Codonopsis meleagris* (formerly *C. ovata*). Any or all are enough to create sheets of sumptuous colour, though perhaps less exciting if reached by a short trip over the lawn rather than by the swinging bamboo-and-rope bridges that Forrest used to cross the Mekong. Suburban gardeners seldom risked a brush with the Yellow Lamas. Few, too, had to face Forrest's luxuriantly described insect life:

> *On the other hand, the river banks at a low altitude, and where wholly sheltered from the north winds, have an almost tropical climate, and vegetable and insect life is both vigorous and troublesome. Creatures with inconveniently long legs plunge suddenly into one's soup; great caterpillars in splendid but poisonous uniforms of long and gaily coloured hairs arrive in one's blankets with the business-like air of a guest who means to stay. Ladybirds and other specimens of Coleoptera drop off the jungle down one's neck, whilst other undesirables insert themselves under one's nether garments. The light in the tent attracts a perfect army of creatures which creep, buzz, fly, crawl and sting. Scissor insects make the day hideous with their strident call, and the proximity of Lissoo coolies introduces other strangers, of which* Pulex irritans *[the flea] is by far the least noxious.*

Not all of his lovely introductions were especially keen to grow away from their native hills, a fact that brought into being the sort of gardener who enjoys this sort of challenge to his or her nurturing skills. This enthusiasm has, at base, little to do with aesthetic concerns, although some impossible-to-grow plants can indeed be lovely to look at. Groups of connoisseurs grew up, devoted to the plants of the high hills, and calling themselves alpine garden societies or rock garden clubs.

Great collectors like William Purdom or Frank Ludlow (1885–1972) and George Sherriff (1898–1967) all worked in the steep valleys of China and Tibet. Botanists from Kew and Edinburgh still go, and still find new species. We have fewer plants from other continents, even though they have immense mountain chains and mountain systems almost as rich in species as the Himalayas, and every bit as romantic. Here is Ira Gabrielson, writing in her book *Western American Alpines* (1932):

Farrer searched in vain for a white *Meconopsis punicea*, sure it would be 'one of the loveliest flowers on earth'.

The outstanding range in our territory is the Steens Mountains [in Oregon], whose summit is slightly under 10,000ft, and whose easterly face is a sheer basaltic cliff of 4,000ft. Less known, but equally picturesque is Fiart Mountain, sixty miles to the west, with its sheer face to the westward. [On the slopes are] phlox in abundant variety, Erigerons of the usual types but also including strange lithic gray-leaved shrubs which hold much garden promise, Eriogonums in bewildering profusion, penstemons, oenotheras, lewisias, linums, and many others furnish the floral display which at times for a few brief days is spectacular. . . .

Near the corner of the three states where the Snake splits this range with its gigantic canyon and where every tributary has a canyon, unnoticed only because of its proximity to its greater neighbor, is some of the most spectacular scenery to be found in the United States. Towering ridges, snow-capped peaks, mile deep canyons, and mighty precipices mingle in such wild confusion as to benumb the imagination of the beholder. . . . Entire cliffs are covered with the pale green rosettes of Lewisia columbiana; *whole slopes glow with the soft pink of* Phlox vispida. *One entire talus slope stands out vividly in my memory, blue enough to match the sky above with the flowers of* Penstemon venustus, *a tiny meadow by a lake, high in the Wallowas, glowing with the velvety blues of* Gentiana calycosa, *a hog-back ridge whose entire summit carried a soft blue tone from the nodding croziers of* Mertensia pulchella.

There remain far more plants to come into our gardens from mountainous regions than Lewis and Clark, or any rock gardener of the past, can ever have imagined.

WATER

GARDENS

ater means life. It is no wonder that from the very beginnings of gardening, and civilization itself, water has been prized. The gardens of ancient Mesopotamia were filled with its noise as it splashed into containing pools, swirled down runnels or spouted out of cooling springs. Astonishing feats of engineering brought water from the wet mountainsides to the dry gardens of the plains. Springs and wells were sacred. The place where water entered the city or local neighbourhood was a public space for meeting and for show. Wealthy communities gave their fountains grand sculptural surrounds, often depicting the gods and goddesses of water, even of the sea itself. Until relatively recently, in the gardens of the West and much of the Middle East, little changed. Water was used, not to support plants, but for its own intrinsic qualities. It was part of the display of the garden, meant to glitter, to spurt and splash, sometimes to cool. Pools, tanks, canals, runnels were all edged with stone margins or, in the north, crisply cut grass. Even in the landscape gardens of eighteenth-century England, the expensively excavated lakes were kept clear of any plants that might obscure the reflective surface, however eager the plants were to colonize.

In the East, particularly in China and Japan, gardening had taken a slightly different route. Water was just as important as it was in the West, and quite as enveloped in magic and in the spiritual, yet it was never divorced from the plants and soil of the garden in the way that characterized Western tradition. It was immensely admired. Although some gardens were based entirely on water and rocks, there were never

Ogata Korin (1650–1716) painted several screens to illustrate the *Tales of Ise*. This one, depicting nothing but deep violet Japanese irises, is one of the most beautiful.

On his arrival on the settlement of Deshima in 1690, Engelbert Kaempfer made this woodcut diagram of the island. The enclave later welcomed Carl Thunberg and Philipp von Siebold, and many Japanese plants travelled to Europe from its jetty.

fountains or the carved and scalloped water chutes known as chadars: water's formal possibilities were not a concern of Chinese and Japanese gardeners. Water was for reflection and a surface in which to borrow the sky, but also a place for fish and for plants. Two plants were especially important: the sacred lotus (*Nelumbo nucifera*) and the iris (*Iris ensata*).

In the West, attitudes to water in the garden changed slowly. The second of these beautiful plants was sent to Europe in the 1690s by Dr Engelbert Kaempfer. The first of the three major botanist-doctors working for the Dutch East India Company office out of Deshima, Japan, he was followed by Dr Carl Thunberg (see Chapter Four) and Philipp von Siebold (see Chapter Seven). It was Thunberg who named the plant, known locally as Hanashōbu, *Iris ensata*. Siebold did not realize this, and called it *I. kaempferi*. It can still be found, incorrectly, under that name. (Just to add to the confusion, some Japanese gardeners use the name *I. laevigata*. Western botanists see this as a separate species, though it may have been used in the breeding of the garden forms of *I. ensata*.)

Whatever the taxonomic status of the flower, its perfectly shaped, intense violet-blue flowers, held just above the broad green leaves, have been admired in Japan since at least the eighth century. They appear in poems found in *Manyoshu*, an anthology compiled in about 760, made up of traditional poems written between 300 and 750. While some of them use the iris as a metaphor for a beautiful woman, more prosaic ones allude to the flower's use for dyeing fabric. The eleventh-century Japanese writer Seishonagon said that all violet things, whether flowers or fabrics, were the most beautiful and that *I. ensata* was the most beautiful flower of all. The flowers also appeared in carvings and architectural decoration from the twelfth century and, gloriously formalized, in the elegant heraldic devices of Japanese nobles. Those whose badge it was decorated their clothes and armour, even their ox-drawn carriages, with the real flower. Many 'iris' clans still exist.

Japanese artists loved painting them. Towards the end of the seventeenth century, Ogata Korin painted several folding screens depicting irises. One of these, now at the Metropolitan Museum of Art, New York, also shows the eight wooden bridges from the mid-tenth century *Tales of Ise*. 'Ise' is now one of the names of a group of iris cultivars that existed when Korin was working, and which can still be grown.

Kaempfer's irises caught European gardeners' fancy. Almost anything from that mysterious country captivated the West, for since 1633, the Tokugawa shogunate had adopted a policy of national isolation that continued until the signing of the Kanagawa Treaty 221 years later in 1854. Between those years, Japan maintained contact with only three countries: China, Korea and the Netherlands. From China and Korea, little information about Japan reached Europe. Through the Netherlands, there came a trickle, from the artificial island of Deshima. However, Kaempfer was overwhelmingly inquisitive. He was also a brilliant doctor, with an amusing and warm personality. He easily made friends with the Japanese guards and the numerous translators. He helped them through illnesses, and taught them about Western medicine. Better still, he could easily drink his Japanese contacts under the table, and before they became insensible, his new friends talked about their fascinating country. He recorded everything they told him in meticulous detail. Unlike Siebold's friends, none got into trouble, even though they had sworn terrifying oaths in ink and blood not to fraternize with the Europeans. He even got some of them to bring him plants from the nearby gardens and hills, saying that he needed herbs for his medicines.

Kaempfer had had a peripatetic childhood. He was born Engelbert Kemper, the second son of Johannes Kemper, in Lemgo, Germany, on 16 September 1651. At four years old, he attended the Lateinschule (grammar school) in Lemgo, but moved at the age of six to the one at Hameln. Soon after he was at high school in Lüneburg, and from 1670 at the one in Lübeck. He studied at the University of Krakow, then at the University of Königsberg, and by 1681, he was in Sweden, studying medicine at Uppsala University. By now he was polished in the ways of the world, and began attending the court of Charles XI in Stockholm. Desperate for more travel still, he got himself appointed secretary of the Swedish legation to the Persian court in Isfahan, setting off in that capacity in 1683. According to the English translator of Kaempfer's subsequent book *Amoenitates Exoticae* ('Exotic Pleasures'), published by Sir Hans Sloane, 'After a dangerous passage over the Caspian Sea, where they were like to have been lost, through the violence of an unexpected storm, and the unskilfulness of their Pilots, (the ship having two Rudders, and consequently two Pilots, who did not understand each other's language) they got safe to the Coasts of Persia, and landed at Nisabad, where they staid for some time, living under tents after the manner of the natives.'

Kaempfer was in Isfahan for a year and a half, partly because the Sultan Süleyman II's astrologers kept the Sultan terrified of a malignant constellation and he refused to see any stranger during that time. It was only on 30 July 1684 that the stars moved into a better position. The Sultan then threw a lavish party for his court, and for the foreign ambassadors waiting to see him. There were dozens. They came from the Kings of Sweden, France, Poland and Siam, from the Tsars of Muscovy, from the Emperor of Germany, from several Arabian and Tartarian princes, even from the Pope in Rome. Dr Kaempfer attended too. The Europeans had deep motives. Although some, like the Swedes, wanted to establish trade with Persia, as well as routes through it to the East, some were trying to detach Isfahan from the influence of the Sultan of Turkey. The diplomacy was all in vain, and Süleyman was not minded to be helpful to Sweden, or willing to break with Constantinople. The Swedish embassy was recalled. Kaempfer should have gone back too. He had been offered a very lucrative post as chief doctor to a prince in Georgia, but he wanted to go further east than Georgia or north-west back to Sweden. By chance the fleet of the Dutch East India Company was sailing in the Persian Gulf, and he got himself appointed instead as chief 'Surgeon to the Fleet'. On 30 June 1688, he set sail for India via Muscat on the Horn of Arabia. After many adventures, two years later he arrived in Deshima.

The highlights of his two years in the European enclave were the annual trips to Edo (now Tokyo) to be displayed at the Imperial Court. He was there first in March 1691, and again in spring 1692. Each trip was something of a festival, for native princes, lords and vassals of the Emperor were at Edo too. The Dutch party consisted of three or four important European inhabitants of Deshima, surrounded by an escort of nearly two hundred Japanese. The Europeans travelled in palanquins (covered litters) carried by up to twelve bearers, although Kaempfer tried to travel on horseback whenever possible, so that he could see more of the surrounding countryside. The whole expedition, including twenty or thirty days in the capital, took about twelve weeks. When on a horse, Kaempfer carried on his saddle 'a very large Javan box', which he filled with 'plants, flowers, and branches of trees, which I figured and described'. He had a compass concealed inside so that he could map the journey. He wrote that his escorts 'were extremely forward to communicate to me, what uncommon plants they met with, together with their true names, characters and uses, which they diligently enquired into among the natives.' Perhaps he travelled with a large stock of alcohol too. On the journey to Edo, the Dutch were treated like performing animals, closely guarded during the day and locked in at night. On arrival, they were put through tricks. Kaempfer and his superiors were obliged to dance, sing, jump and mime. Their party tricks had to be shown not only in front of the Emperor, but also at the houses of the Edo nobility.

Kaempfer left Japan in 1692, stayed a while in Java, then set out for home aboard the *Maelstrom*, with the humble job of office clerk. He arrived in Amsterdam on 6 October 1693. He resumed his busy life, and it was not until 1712 that a Lemgo printer brought out his *Amoenitates Exoticae*. Only around a fifth of that book is devoted to plants, but it included the first descriptions and illustrations of shrubs and flowers totally new to Western gardeners: *Aucuba*, *Skimmia*, *Hydrangea*, *Chimonanthus* and *Ginkgo*, *Lilium speciosum*, *L. lanceolatum* (still often grown as *L. tigrinum*), two magnolias, various *Prunus*, azaleas and tree peonies, and nearly thirty varieties of *Camellia*. The book was a sensation, but he had a much larger work in preparation. However, now working as doctor to the Count of Lippe and his family, he was kept extremely busy, and found working on this next book very difficult.

The English translator of *Amoenitates Exoticae* wrote of Kaempfer's end:

> *The long course of his Travels, the fatigues of his profession, and some private misfortunes in his family, had very much impair'd his constitution, and in the latter part of his life he was often troubled with the Colick, of which he had two very severe attacks, one in November 1715, and another at the beginning of 1716. This last fit laid him up for three weeks, however he recover'd it so far, that he was able to attend the Count de Lippe and his Family, as their Physician, at Pyrmont, and return'd, in July, to his Country Seat at Steinhof near Lemgow in pretty good health. On the 5th of September following he was suddenly seized with fainting fits, and a vomiting of blood, which continued upon him all night reduced him very low. From that time he continued in a lingering condition, though not altogether without hopes of recovery, having gather'd strength so far, as to be able to walk about his room: But on the 24th of October, having been ever since this last attack troubled with a nausea and loss of appetite, his vomiting of blood return'd upon him with great violence, and a fever, which lasted till the second of November, on which day he died, at five in the evening, 65 years and six weeks old. He was buried in the Cathedral Church of St Nicolas at Lemgow.*

The tiger lily (now *Lilium lancifolium*), grown in the East for its edible bulbs, was brought to the West by Kaempfer.

He died with the manuscript and notes of his *History of Japan* scattered around him. They might all have been lost had not Sir Hans Sloane purchased them from Kaempfer's nephew between 1723 and 1725. Sloane got his librarian Scheuchzer to translate the work, which appeared with notes by Scheuchzer in 1727, under the grand title *The History of Japan Together with a Description of the Kingdom of Siam 1690–92 by Engelbert Kaempfer, M.D. Physician to the Dutch Embassy to the Emperor's Court and translated by J.G. Scheuchzer, F.R.S.*

Scheuchzer was a devout Christian and unfortunately some of Kaempfer's racier material outraged him. It was omitted or distorted. Fortunately, a modern translation has recently been produced. Despite the modifications made by Scheuchzer, the book was a huge success. It was translated into French and Dutch by 1729, back into German by 1756, into Russian by 1773 and into Japanese by 1782. In 1791, Sir Joseph Banks published a

When Kaempfer visited the Imperial Court at Edo, he found thirty sorts of camellia, several of which were brought to America in 1785 by André Michaux. Pictured here is a *Camellia japonica* painted by Georg Dionysius Ehret, based on Kaempfer's original illustration.

small selection of the botanical drawings made by Kaempfer as *Icones selectae plantarum quas in Japonia collegit et delineavit Engelbertus Kaempfer.*

The irises that Kaempfer had so admired did not make a lasting impact in Europe. Additional forces were needed to make the conquest and the irises were gaining strength in their native country. From the 1840s onwards, florists' societies in Japan, who were quite as abundant and enthusiastic as any in Britain, Holland or France, took up *Iris ensata*, already long moved away from its wild form when collected by Kaempfer, and vastly developed it. One famous breeder, Sho-od (or Showo) Matsudaira, produced around two hundred named varieties. Though most of these are now thought of as Edo Irises, some of the most flamboyant were bred in the Higo district. In these, the flowers' styles are so broad and colourful as to be almost indistinguishable from petals. The petals themselves are flared and overlapping. Not surprisingly, these irises created a sensation in Japan. When they reached Europe in the 1860s, they created another. Every Western gardener had to have some. And, as *I. ensata* thrives in the wet soil at the margins of ponds, every gardener, even if not yet in thrall to the water lily, had to have a pool. Many were disappointed with their performance outside in the garden. The original Higos were bred for pot culture, and were to be admired indoors, where the sumptuous petals were at no risk from rough weather. Indoors, too, the flowers changed after opening: by the second day they often nearly doubled in size. Japanese connoisseurs claimed that flowers were at their best at midnight on the second day. Some were, and are, double, even treble, and under perfect conditions can sometimes reach twelve inches across. Gardeners in the West began to collect the 'Ise' strain of *I. ensata*, more suitable for the garden, with single flowers in pink, pale blue and the ancient indigo, and with narrower and longer leaves. Modern forms also have strong and weather-resistant petals.

In western Europe, the earliest gardening reference to the water lily is in Philip Miller's *Gardener's Dictionary*. He writes, 'in some gardens I have seen plants cultivated in large troughs of water, where they flourish very well and annually produce great quantities of flowers.' While Japanese irises are hardy, few Western gardens could support the sub-tropical lotus (*Nelumbo nucifera*), an important garden plant in India and southern China. Few Western gardeners could afford to grow the astonishing *Victoria amazonica*, yet somehow the idea of water lilies, rather than lotuses, took off. European representatives of the genus *Nymphaea* have plain white flowers that even insects mostly ignore. Gardeners began to look enviously at the smaller water lilies of the tropics and sub-tropics. The southern states of America had lovely things such as *Nymphaea texensis*. Central and South America had endless exciting species. Africa had *N. zanzibarensis* or the enticing yellow-flowered *N. burtii* from Tanganyika. Australia had the wonderful *N. gigantea*, with huge flowers varying from violet blue to white or even pink. Breeders began to wonder if any of these could be crossed into hardy species, to give hybrids hardy in Europe, but with large, even perfumed, flowers. If so, without the expense of providing warm water for them, gardeners could have all the romance of the East. After all, the true water lily was an ancient garden plant, portrayed in the decoration, pottery and furniture of Egyptian pharaohs. In China, water lilies,

The secretive M. Latour-Marliac, who never revealed his breeding techniques or the species that he used.

This contemporary illustration shows the cultivation of sub-tropical water lilies at Latour-Marliac's nursery.

especially the white and perfumed *N. tetragona*, had been grown at least since the eleventh century, when Chou Tun-I wrote 'it has been fashionable to admire the peony; but my favourite is the water lily. How stainless it rises from its slimy bed. How modestly it reposes on the clear pool, an emblem of purity and truth. Symmetrically perfect, its subtle perfume is wafted far and wide; while there it rests in spotless state, something to be regarded reverently from a distance, and not to be profaned by familiar approach.'

In 1854, in a garden at Temple-sur-Lot in the Department of Lot et Garonne in western France, a gardener called Joseph Bory Latour-Marliac had an important revelation. His garden, below the ancient castle of Marliac, contained a series of warm-water springs, to which he'd never given much thought. He had recently read an article by the botanist Lemaire, who bemoaned the fact that the bright colours and large flowers of tropical nymphaeas weren't found in the hardy species. Suddenly he realized that he could use them to feed pools that would be warm enough to grow tropical water plants. Marliac's imagination was fired.

He started to assemble a collection of different species from all over the world. Almost paranoid about being copied, he refused to reveal the sources of his material. However, the plants grew in their new surroundings. He tried to cross them, and seems to have worked for several years without much happening. Suddenly, in 1879, he bred *Nymphaea* 'Marliacea Rosea'. Nothing could then stop him. Other breeders tried to copy his success, but he continued to be very vague about which species he was using, and of techniques he used for crossing them. He seems to have used the hardy *N. alba* and its Swedish variety *N. a.* var. *rubra*, crossing them into the exotic *N. odorata*, *N. mexicana*, *N. tuberosa* and *N. tetragona* (*pygmaea*). He then produced more than seventy new varieties. Many were extraordinarily beautiful, some were perfumed, and only three were commercial failures. Everyone, including the artist Monet, just had to have them. Some of the Marliac water lilies were immense sprawling plants. Others were small and neat. Suddenly, there was a point in having a pool, in whatever size of garden. There was a water lily variety that was suitable.

Other breeders, like Amos Perry in Britain, tried to repeat his crosses, but were either unable to get seed, or produced only worthless seedlings. Alas, in 1911 Latour-Marliac went to his grave taking most of his secrets with him. His garden still exists, and is devoted, of course, to showing a colossal collection of water lilies, including some of the glorious Australian *Nymphaea gigantea* group of water lilies. These have not been used much in breeding yet, although they do grow well in hot-summer regions like Texas. Great things are expected from them, generally accepted as the largest and most beautiful of all the species in the genus *Nymphaea*.

As well as a passion for the glitter and reflectivity of open water, the seventeenth- and eighteenth-century gardener also had a passion for drainage. With everyone's hatred and fear of bogs and marshes, the garden, unless it was the 'American' section of a large estate, was dried out to make it suitable for both feet and flowers. Flower borders had, at least since medieval times, been raised above the general soil level, using board or stone margins. Even in modest cottage gardens, and where possible, this was undertaken until late into the eighteenth century, and many older gardens still have the stone kerbs used for this purpose. However, once irises and water lilies made the pond an essential garden element in the nineteenth century, gardeners saw the advantage of moist, even

A bill from Latour-Marliac, totalling 106 francs 10 centimes, for water lilies for Monet's garden at Giverny.

An illustration from *The Garden* magazine, showing the sumptuous form of one of Latour-Marliac's new varieties.

soggy, ground. They discovered the huge flora that grows in precisely those conditions, and plant collectors were busily bringing them back to Europe at just the right time. Plants such as primulas, rodgersias, meconopsis, ferns, hostas, astilbes, podophyllums and ligularias all combined to make up the great 'marginal' flora.

At this time, the genus *Primula* included some ancient garden plants, from the double white primroses to the more modern laced polyanthus. All were short, no taller than about twelve inches. No gardener was prepared to imagine a primula four or five feet high. Yet, in 1925 in Nang Dzong, in the furthest reaches of the Brahmaputra River, where it descended from the Tibet plateau, a plant collector found one in huge quantities:

It was most happy in the woodland brooks, which in summer overflow and flood the thorn brakes. Here it manned the banks in thousands and, wading into the stream, held up the current. It choked up ditches and roofed the steepest mud slides with its great marsh-marigold leaves; then in July came a forest of masts, which spilled out a shower of golden drops, till the tide of scent spread and filled the woodland and flowed into the meadow to mingle with that of the 'Moonlight' primula. And all through August it kept on unfurling flowers and still more flowers, till the rains began to slacken and the brooks crept back to their beds, and the waters under the thorn brake subsided; but the seeds were not ripe till late October.

Not surprisingly after such a write-up, every gardener wanted the plant. *Primula florindae*, as it was called, was a huge success, flowering well into August, and even becoming an aggressive weed in some Scottish gardens. Few gardeners would care.

It is indeed a massive plant, the largest of all the primulas. It grows throughout south-east Tibet, and the Tsangpo Basin from Tsari to the Pachakshiri, often among drifts of the fine *Primula alpicola*. The species cross cheerfully, and will also include *P. sikkimensis* in the relationship. The progeny often contains plants with splendid chestnut to orange flowers. All are strongly perfumed, and alone make a marginal garden an object of desire.

The collector was Frank Kingdon-Ward (1885–1958). He named *Primula florindae* after his first wife, Florinda. It was, like her, large, stately and with a taste for show. They did not have an easy relationship; he was not an easy man. Born in 1885, the son of a professor of botany at Cambridge University, Kingdon-Ward might have been expected to hate plants. In fact, he loved them, but did hate anything approaching a settled, comfortable or conventional life. He left Cambridgeshire for Shanghai as soon as he could, and after a brief spell teaching, headed off into the wilds.

He became a garden-oriented travel writer, eventually publishing hundreds of articles and twenty-five books about his remarkable journeys. When he was unable to live by the pen, he financed his travels by collecting for seed firms and syndicates of gardeners. But he seems not to have needed much money; like many explorer-collectors, he was a loner, and like many modern ones, liked travelling light. He got by on a number of trips taking little sustenance but milk and living off the land. Sometimes he travelled with a companion. He made the *Primula florindae* trip through Tibet and Nepal with Lord Cawdor, a Scottish aristocrat with a handsome Scottish castle. Cawdor's own journals suggest that he found

Frank's company a trial by silence. Kingdon-Ward wrote at times chillingly of the Earl. Many found Kingdon-Ward austere, even bitter, and on his travels he was often consumed with intense loneliness that sometimes turned into bouts of suicidal despair.

His real love was the great river valleys of China, Tibet and Burma. On one of his first trips he described the upper Yangtze:

Frank Kingdon-Ward in Assam, Burma, c. 1949.

> *For two entire days the trail over the mountains led through a gorge of exquisite beauty, the cliffs, covered with pine and bamboo, rising abruptly two or three thousand feet above the ice-choked stream, making a grand play of colours in the winter sunshine. At one time alongside the frothing torrent, at another giving precarious foothold amongst the bush-clad precipices which yet towered far above, the trail wheeled sharply round bend after bend as it followed the sinuous curves of the river, affording endless views of matchless beauty . . . a tiny white temple nestling amongst the dark pines which clothed a tongue of land; a glowing ochre scarp, several hundred feet high, crowned by waves of feathery bamboo.*

He loved living in those countries too, whether watching a band of brigands winding through the passes or experiencing the excitement of shooting 200 miles of rapids halfway down the Yangtze River:

> *On 7th September we reached Kweichow-fu on the borders of Szechwan and Hupei, and saw before us the cliffs of Bellows Gorge towering to the sky, and the dark slit into which the river plunged. Suddenly the sun was hidden behind the mountain peaks, a blast of cool air whistled out of the ragged rent in front of us, and we sped between vast cliffs rising over three thousand feet on either hand; we seemed to be speeding to some frightful destruction in the bowels of the earth. There were no rapids now. The confined water boiled and writhed around us; huge whirls sprang into existence everywhere with the crash of the avalanche, and we were at the mercy of the river, broadside on, stem first, flying round and round, while the lon-pan stood at the tiller yelling at the four oarsmen who stood on the forward deck, rowing like men demented to keep the boat's head straight on.*

The brigands were less frightening, and were traditional figures in the landscape. Agriculture couldn't support the population, so brigandage became a seasonal occupation. Fighting, too, among the local tribes, or between tribesmen and Chinese, had been going on since ancient times. The western provinces, remote and ethnically complex, had seldom been under more than nominal control by Peking. Kingdon-Ward kept out of the brigands' way as much as possible, but could not help noticing that

> they formed nonetheless a striking picture, winding in single file up the narrow ravine, rather more than two hundred of them. There were Lissus and Minchias, sturdy little tribesmen with muscular chests and swarthy complexions, often ferocious of aspect, carrying rifles, most of them muzzle-loaders; men with extraordinary-looking guns of abbreviated length and immense calibre, after the pattern of a blunderbuss; others carrying scarlet banners and long trumpets; and half a dozen men, including my friend Captain Li, riding ponies. Occasionally the trumpeters put the long trumpets to their lips and throwing back their heads, made the welkin ring; and on they hurried, banners fluttering; till they wound out of sight on the narrow gorge.

On another occasion, described in one of his best books, *In The Land of the Blue Poppy* (1913), he writes of an impromptu entertainment he was given when, while lying comfortably in a mountain hut, writing up his diary for the day,

> in stalked three Tibetans, all of them over six feet high. Their coarse gowns were tied above their knees, the right shoulder thrust jauntily out exposing the deep muscular chest, and they were bootless. One of them carried a fiddle, consisting of a piece of snakeskin stretched over a bamboo tube with strings of yak hair, upon which he scraped vigorously with a yak-hair bow. There was little enough room, but my visitors soon lined up, stuck out their tongues at me in greeting, and began to dance, to and fro, up and down, twirling round, swaying rhythmically to the squeaky notes of the violin (there were only two notes on which to ring the changes), and singing in high-pitched raucous voices. . . . I can still picture the scene in that dim little smoke-blackened room, the rain lashing down outside, and the roar of the river below us, while I lay back on my bed enjoying it hugely, all cares forgotten. Those great giants of men looked strangely weird in the flickering light of the blazing torches.

Ironically, while collecting plants that altered European gardening for ever, he came across evidence of the universality of plant collecting, and the way in which plants cheerfully disseminate themselves across the globe. He and Lord Cawdor stopped off at Napo Dzong on the banks of the Gyamda River in south-eastern Tibet, staying in the local governor's house. It was splendidly set up, and even had glass in the windows. He writes: 'The paved yard was a regular flower-show, gay with Hollyhocks, Asters, Sunflowers, Dahlias, Pansies, Geraniums, Roses, Poppies, Brompton Stocks, Tropaeolums and other favourites. Clearly the dzong-pen [the local governor] was a man of taste, and advanced thinker, and a traveller. He had been to Calcutta and had brought back with him a tin of Sutton's Seed; hence the Mammoth Show.' The contents of the tin, designed to appeal to homesick Europeans, would have been intensely exotic for a Tibetan garden. Later in the same journey Kingdon-Ward received a letter from the Tibetan government asking him to send them some of the seeds he collected, 'as the Dalai Lama is very fond of flowers, and at his private residence on the outskirts of Lhasa grows a great many, which he tends with loving care'.

During his long collecting career, he found glorious plants such as the incomparable yellow-flowered *Rhododendron wardii* and *R. macabeanum*. He found gentians too, as well as cotoneasters, berberis and *Prunus*. He found splendid bulbs such as the exquisite lily *Lilium mackliniae*, named after his second wife Jean Macklin, whom he married, and loved, when he was sixty-five years old. But perhaps the most astonishing discovery was yet another good 'marginal': the glorious blue poppy (*Meconopsis betonicifolia*). It had first been seen by the Abbé Delavay (see Chapter Five), then by the military explorer F. M. Bailey and then by George Forrest (see Chapter Eight), but it had not been successfully introduced. Kingdon-Ward's huge seed collection, from its base in the village of Tumbatse in Nepal, established it safely in cultivation. Back in Britain it was a sensation. There were mass plantings of it in Hyde Park in London, and at Ibrox Park, Glasgow, constantly surrounded by admiring crowds. At the 1927 Chelsea Flower Show, seedlings were sold at a guinea apiece. A few years later it had become so widespread that packets of seed were advertised at a shilling.

Good marginal plantings were adding plants apace. The gorgeously textured foliage of the rodgersias were a huge addition. The six species, all emanating from the Himalayas, China, Japan and Korea, are named after Commodore Rodgers of the United States Navy, who discovered *Rodgersia podophylla* in Hakodate, Japan, in 1855. He sent material back to America, and Asa Gray described it in 1857. The two Chinese species, *R. aesculifolia* and *R. pinnata* are now common garden plants. The first was described by A. Batalin from specimens collected by Potanin in Gansu and Sichuan in 1885, and by Augustine Henry from Hubei in 1887 and Sichuan in 1889. Writing of it in the *Gardeners' Chronicle* in 1902, Henry said: 'It is a plant of the mountains of Central China, occurring in shady places, numerous plants growing together. . . . The rhizome is used as a drug.' Henry must have sent some to the Veitch nursery, for they had it in commercial quantities by 1911. The other species was also introduced by Augustine Henry, who sent seed to Kew in 1898, the plants raised from it flowering in 1902.

Henry, who also added other marginal genera to the fringes of our pools, was a fascinating man. Unusually for this book, he almost totally avoided the destiny of so many plant collectors, seeming never to have been completely consumed by the collecting mania that destroyed so many others. Indeed, halfway through his life, he changed career, and turned his back on the plants of China and the Yangtse gorges for ever. However, he was an exceedingly successful plant collector, who began collecting on the banks of the rapids down which Frank Kingdon-Ward plunged with such excitement. The rapids were far more than just a visually breathtaking if dangerous impediment to the traveller. They were of considerable economic importance to the Chinese state. The lands around the upper part of the river produced rich crops of drug plants and food crops which were all consumed in the lands around the river's lower stretches. The rapids acted as a customs barrier, as the boats that risked them were either unloaded, or at least much slowed down, during their passage downriver. This gave customs officials a chance to inspect and tax the cargoes. By the 1880s, the Chinese government had set up a customs service staffed by Europeans, believing that native Chinese officials were too easily corrupted. The Imperial Chinese Maritime Customs Service recruited the young Augustine Henry.

Augustine Henry, painted by Celia
Harrison in 1929.

Though he was born in Dundee, Scotland in 1857, Henry's parents moved immediately to Ireland, where he was brought up and educated. With a master's degree from Queen's College, Belfast, and a smattering of Chinese, the young man soon had enough medical training to land a post as an Assistant Medical Officer in China. First based at Shanghai, in 1882 he was soon posted to the town of Ichang, in Hubei Province – with its treaty port of Shashi, 1,000 miles from Shanghai up the great river – where he was recruited by the Customs Service. His customs duties took up only a few hours a day and, almost as a hobby, he began to look first at the drug plants that passed through his hands, then at the more general flora around Ichang. In search of advice, he wrote to the Director of the Royal Botanic Gardens at Kew, Joseph Dalton Hooker, and later to his successor, Hooker's son-in-law, William Thiselton-Dyer. He received very encouraging letters, the first of which enclosed a leaflet of routine collecting instructions. To this day, Kew still gets hundreds of similar letters from would-be botanists, and until recently, used to send out leaflets and advice without expecting much in return. A few months later, in November 1885, Henry sent them his first collections. Quite unprepared, the botanists at Kew were stunned to receive a thousand perfect herbarium specimens, among which they found ten new genera.

William Thiselton-Dyer was so enthusiastic that he immediately wrote to Sir Robert Hart, the Inspector General of Chinese Customs, to request that Henry be given leave from the service in order to collect more widely in the mountains west of Ichang. Once that was granted, Kew financed the next of Henry's botanical expeditions. The mountains of Hubei Province turned out to be even richer than expected. Henry found many new conifers, ten new maples, many roses and viburnums, new lilies, rhododendrons, prunuses, pyruses and loniceras. He began to accumulate plants named after him. *Lilium henryi* was one, soon followed by *Clematis henryi*, *Parthenocissus henryana*, *Rhododendron augustinii* and the evergreen climber *Lonicera henryi*.

On one trip back to Europe he married. At first, his new wife, Caroline, seemed to acclimatize well to the unfamiliar conditions at Ichang, but then fell ill. The year 1893 was terrible for them both. Henry's letters to Thiselton-Dyer contain worried passages about her health. In May she was desperately unwell. In June the weather was dry and she seemed better. By July it was clear that she had to have a better climate. Henry arranged for her to go to Denver in Colorado, accompanied by his favourite sister, Mary, who had arrived in Ichang for the purpose. The two women set out on the huge journey in January 1894.

Meanwhile, in America, something was afoot that would affect Henry's life. Charles Sprague Sargent was trying to involve London's Veitch nursery in a joint venture with his own organization, the Arnold Arboretum of Harvard. He wanted James Herbert Veitch, with whom he had already travelled in Japan, to go on an intensive collecting trip to central and eastern China. Veitch's owner and James Herbert's uncle, Sir Harry Veitch, was not happy. In a letter to Sargent, dated 10 January 1893, he played the Victorian autocrat, and refused to allow his nephew and heir to remain away from the family business for so long. Sargent was gainsaid, but was still hearing stories from London about the marvels emerging from the region of the upper Yangtze.

By 1894, Augustine Henry was getting alarmed. The Japanese were at war with China. It seemed a good time to get out. He dreamed of getting some sort of job in Colorado, where his wife seemed to be recovering. He knew that his reputation as a botanist was spreading, so in May he wrote hopefully to Sargent at Boston, Massachusetts, hinting that he needed a job, and offering to sell Sargent his own marvellous herbarium. Sargent wanted the material, but Henry was only of use to him in China. Sargent wrote back encouragingly, but was vague. Henry thought he would take a gamble and go to America anyway. As he was packing up his books and collections, a telegram arrived from his sister Mary. His wife had died. It was a colossal blow. It took him several years to come to terms with it. He wrote to a friend: 'I think I might have saved her had I fought more strenuously, if I had taken the decision to leave China sooner.'

Time passed. Henry remained in China and had several other postings from the Chinese Customs Service. By 1898, Sargent was still searching for a man to collect there for the Arnold Arboretum. Finally, after many attempts to lure Henry into his grasp, he asked Henry, point blank, if he would collect for him alone. Henry gave Sargent all sorts of advice about what needed doing. He suggested the routes that a collector should travel. He even offered to help anyone that Sargent appointed. But he was tired; he wanted to get back home. He refused.

In October 1899, shortly before leaving China for the last time, Augustine Henry welcomed a visitor in the remote village of Szemao (now Simao) in Yünnan Province. At this meeting, Henry handed on the collector's mantle, and also the collector's destiny. In 1900, Henry sailed to Britain, and never returned to China. He became interested in forestry, and helped to establish a forestry school at Cambridge University. Later he became Professor of Forestry at the College of Science in the University of Dublin, and led a campaign for the reforestation of Ireland's green land. Back in China, the 'new boy' was Ernest Henry Wilson who, more interested than Augustine Henry in getting living plants back to Europe, has had more impact on our gardens and how they look than any other collector.

E. H. Wilson was born in 1876, in a modest cottage in the picturesque village of Chipping Campden in Gloucestershire. Apprenticed to a nursery in nearby Solihull, he found his vocation instantly. He fell in love with plants. By 1897 he was working at Kew Gardens and seemed determined to become an academic botanist. He allowed himself to be diverted from this aim by going to work for Veitch's nursery. The lure was the offer of a well-financed collecting trip to China. He set off westwards, sailing from Liverpool on 11 April 1899, on board the *Pavonia*, arriving in New England on 23 April. The Arnold Arboretum was his first stop. Sargent was interested but, as yet, made no move. Wilson went on across the United States, and sailed for China from San Francisco on 6 May. Augustine Henry was now in Yünnan, 1,000 miles inland from Hong Kong. Wilson went to see him to get his advice. It took him four months to reach him. He spoke no Chinese, and found travelling very difficult. However, once he began to learn Chinese, he discovered that he could very easily develop a rapport with the native people he met.

Wilson's route to Szemao required that he travel southwards from Hong Kong to Tonking in French Indochina. He got aboard a small steamer that took him up the Red River to Laokai (Lao Cai), a jungle town on the Chinese frontier. From there he got a small native boat to Manhao, then assembled a caravan of mules and sedan chairs to reach Szemao. In later trips to China, he usually bought his own boats to make travel easier and more comfortable, even if, as it turned out, it was no less hazardous.

After two trips for the Veitch nursery, which brought many wonders into the garden, Sargent could wait no longer. During the winter of 1905–6 Sargent meant to investigate the temperate flora of Peru and Chile. After only a few months there, he changed his itinerary, and determined to return to Boston via England in order to meet Wilson face to face. Wilson was guarded, and Sargent had to return to Boston empty-handed. Sargent wrote to him on 28 June 1906, urging that he give 'serious thought to the proposition for another journey to China and that you will come to see your way clear to doing this. I am more than ever convinced of the importance of further botanical investigation in western China and of the fact that you are the only man to undertake this work with the prospect of carrying it out successfully. I think that the financial part of it can be managed here if you are willing to undertake the work.' Wilson signed on the dotted line later that year. Sargent had signed up one of the greatest plant collectors of all time.

By now, Wilson was married, although he usually left his wife behind with friends in Britain when he was in China. She complained bitterly, but accepted that she could not go with him. In spite of ocean liners, the first motorcars and other civilized advances, collecting in remote places was still dangerous. Wilson seems to have had, like a cat, nine lives. He recounted the following events from one of his trips in his book *Plant Hunting* (1927):

I noticed my dog suddenly cease wagging his tail, cringe, and rush onward, and a small piece of rock hit the path and rebounded into the river some 300 feet below us. I shouted a order and the bearers put down the chair. The two front bearers ran forward and I followed suit. . . . A large boulder crashed into the body of the chair, and down to the river it was hurled. I ran instinctively, ducked as something whisked over my head and my sun hat blew off. Again I ran; a few yards more and I would be under the lea of some hard rocks. Then feeling as if a hot wire passed through my legs, I was bowled over, tried to jump up, found my right leg was useless, so crawled forward to the shelter of the cliff, where the two scared chair-bearers were huddled. . . . The pigskin puttee on my right leg was cut slantingly as if with a knife and forced round my leg; the toe cap of my boot was torn off and with it the nail of my big toe; the right leg was broken in two places below the knee. . . .

E. H. Wilson at an inn at the Tumen-Yalu divide in Korea in August 1917, on his way to his historic meeting with Augustine Henry at Szemao in China.

With the legs of my camera tripod I improvised splints, and while these were being bandaged to my legs the mule-caravan [that we had] passed in the morning loomed into view. The road was too narrow for them to turn back and they dared not stand still until I could be moved forwards since we knew not when the rock slide would recommence. There was only one thing to do. I lay across the road and file of mules stepped over my body. Then it was that I realized the size of the mule's hoof. There were near fifty . . . of them and each stepped clearly over me as if accustomed to such obstacles. Nevertheless, I breathed freely when the last was over!

As this trip, the last he made to China, had resulted in the collection of *Lilium regale*, he henceforth referred to his 'lily leg' when the pain of the wounds sometimes returned.

His collecting trips had many such moments, yet his ninth life was spent not in China, but in Boston. By this time, Sargent was dead, and the humble boy from Chipping Campden was director of the august Arnold Arboretum. In spite of his success in America, the comfortable collecting trips that he now took with his wife to Japan and Korea and the success of his many books, he still dreamed of retiring to the enchanting valleys of his native Gloucestershire. By 1930 his plans were fairly advanced, and he and his wife decided to drive across the city to see their newly married daughter. They were killed in a car accident.

Wilson's plants covered the entire spectrum of gardening. Even on his last Asian trip to look at the little-explored flora of the Korean peninsula, he found lovely things such as the Korean forsythia (*Forsythia ovata* 'Nakai'). He found that at the Diamond Mountains, a beautiful part of Korea, where waterfalls crash noisily from misty cliffs and the slopes are thick with maples, birches, and oaks.

Today, even a modest water garden will show the gardener's debt to E. H. Wilson. You can plant one with the jagged and handsome foliage of his rodgersias, spires of his ligularia flowers decked out with butterflies, his irises, his primulas and more. Add in his lilies, and set the pool against a background of some of his own favourites from among his discoveries: maples like the paperbark (*Acer griseum*), its trunk wrapped in fluttering sheets of translucent mahogany-coloured bark, or his hardy variant of the silk tree (*Albizia julibrissin*), or the amazing handkerchief tree (*Davidia involucrata*), or the tea crab apple (*Malus hupehensis*), with its drifts of scented spring flowers and clusters of golden apples in autumn. Underplant them with thickets of the rosy dipelta (*Dipelta floribunda*), or the beauty bush (*Kolkwitzia amabilis*), or the sumptuously coloured Korean stewartia. Whole gardens can be built using only Wilson's plants and many of these will have a place in our gardens for as long as we make them. Something like three thousand species used him as a way of colonizing the furthest continents.

For his 1907 expedition, E.H.Wilson bought a houseboat in Shanghai. He called it the *Harvard* and took it as far up the Yangtze River as he could. Here, it is moored at Ichang.

COUNTER-REVOLUTION

T he first great wave of new plant introductions in the sixteenth century was exciting for gardeners who wanted the best and the most beautiful novelties in their gardens, but it had its casualties too. Old garden plants, often inhabitants of the garden for many centuries, seemed dull in comparison. They were thrown out. Even as long ago as the end of the seventeenth century, John Parkinson bemoaned what he thought was the loss of a few old familiars in the garden. In the 1750s, Philip Miller wrote that he knew of at least eighteen lost variants of lily. He hoped that 'when they are once fix'd in a Garden, they are not very subject to decay . . . therefore from such places there may be Hopes of retrieving those flowers again.' What he meant by 'such places' were old gardens in the distant countryside where they might be safe from fashionable taste.

The wave of plants introduced in the nineteenth and early twentieth centuries was far larger, and far more turbulent, creating, as we have seen, entirely new sorts of gardens and whole new markets for plants. It caused equally huge casualties among older garden plants. The sense of loss felt by Parkinson and Miller became, in the nineteenth century, a flood of sentimental nostalgia. This affected all but the most hardened plant collectors. Even the deeply unsentimental William Robinson wrote, in *The Wild Garden*, that 'some are looking back with regret to the old mixed-border gardens; others are endeavouring to soften the harshness of the bedding system by the introduction of fine-leaved plants, but all are agreed that a great mistake has been made in destroying all our sweet old border flowers.' One anonymous writer in

The overwhelming rate at which new garden plants were arriving created a nostalgia for ancient garden flowers and for old-fashioned cottage gardens in general. *The Flower Garden* was painted by Abbot Fuller Graves, *c.* 1900.

A show of new fruit varieties from Ellwanger & Barry's Mount Hope Nursery. George
Ellwanger was equally interested in flowers discovered in abandoned farmstead gardens.

the *Gardeners' Chronicle* wanted once more the gardens of 'quiet country villages where sweet-
scented jasmine and Woodbine, purple Clematis and monthly Roses fight longingly for a
place beside the rustic porch; while the little plots in front of white thatch-roofed cottages
afforded a variety of bright blossoms for the nosegay of the past', apparently oblivious of
the fact that the purple *Clematis* x *jackmanii* had only been in cultivation for about twenty
years. Soon, a whole section of the gardening public was transfixed by the supposed
simplicity and ease of old country gardens. New flower-arranging 'stars' such as Mrs
Oliphant and Miss Hope collected and publicized old-fashioned flowers. Writers and
gardeners such as Miss Willmott, Mrs Ewing and Miss Jekyll studied the already vanishing
ways of the countryside while raiding cottagers' gardens for nice and preferably long-
forgotten plants.

Even the forward-looking United States proved not to be immune to the worship of a
'golden age' of gardening, a time before exotics had burst in through the garden gate.
Nurseryman, banker and writer George Ellwanger brought out a book called *The Gardens
Story* in 1896. Designed especially for the new American market, it complained: 'The prim
modern garden, too, almost always lacks a pleasing feature of the ancient garden when
rightly carried out; it has so few spots to lounge in. There is a dearth of garden-seats, niches,
and benches, and vine-draped arbours and cloistered summerhouses. And where has the
old sun-dial disappeared, that used to count the time so leisurely and shadow the passing

hours?' He goes on to proclaim how much he misses the old farmstead gardens that once grew all sorts of lovely sweet-smelling things that could no longer be found, or would no longer grow 'in our gardens today'. Ellwanger's old-fashioned flora included snowdrops (*Galanthus*), daffodils (*Narcissus*), imperials (*Fritillaria*), muscari, larkspurs (*Consolida* and *Delphinium*), campanulas, bachelor's buttons (*Tanacetum parthenium*), monkshood (*Aconitum*), double white poppies (*Papaver* species), sweet clover (*Melilotus indicus*), snow pink (*Dianthus plumarius*), white phloxes, dicentras, sweet williams (*Dianthus*), tall yellow tulips, sword grass and ribbon grass, tradescantias, sweet peas, valerians, madonna lilies (*Lilium candidum*), white and purple stocks (*Matthiola*), lily of the valley, briar rose, white day lily (he probably meant hosta), tiger lilies, dahlias, hollyhocks (*Althaea*), sunflowers (*Helianthus*) and all the European herbs. It was very much the same flora that the first American garden designer A. J. Downing had been recommending as recently as 1849.

Ellwanger was an interesting and influential man. He was born on 2 December 1816, at Gross-Heppach, in Wurtemberg, then an independent principality, now part of Germany. A biographical article in the *Rochester and Post Express* in 1895 records that Ellwanger's father had some vineyards, but that the Napoleonic Wars and a long run of bad seasons had kept the family poor. The young George dreamed of living in America, and to that end, joined a florist and nursery business in Stuttgart where he could become better trained than he could be in his home town. By 1835, he had learned the trade, and set off across the Atlantic. After sixty-two relatively easy days, he 'saw Staten Island in the full glory of its June foliage'. He had relatives already established at Tiffin, Ohio, and went to join them. He also had to learn English. Finally he settled in Rochester in New York state, prospered, and in 1839 began business for himself. The region was expanding fast, and he realized the new settlers would need fruit trees. Soon fascinated by them, he started a collection. He bought out the establishment of Reynolds & Bateham and purchased eight acres of land on Mount Hope Avenue, Rochester.

In 1840 he went into partnership with Patrick Barry, a young Irishman who edited a newspaper called *The Genessee Farmer*. Later, in 1852, Barry also took over A. J. Downing's *The Gardening Magazine*, when Downing drowned when the paddle steamer *Henry Clay* sank, having caught fire on the River Hudson. The Mount Hope Nursery became one of the largest nurseries in the United States. Ellwanger and Barry worked hard. At first, they lived in the sheds behind the glasshouses, but when those burnt down in August 1841, they took to the road, peddling their undamaged plants through western cities and villages in order to raise funds with which to rebuild and expand. Their importance, though, lies in their passion for collecting. Most new settlers bought their fruit and vegetable stock from drifting peddlers whose cheap seeds and plants were often useless, even if they grew. Ellwanger and Barry ordered named saplings from Boston and New York, often of the stocks originally brought in by the first European settlers. Gripped with enthusiasm, Ellwanger went back to Europe in December 1844 to find even more stock. Journeying through England, France and Germany, all countries then busily breeding new fruit varieties, he bought on a huge scale. The diligences and stagecoaches in which he travelled must have looked strange, topped off with bunches of young peach and apple trees, bundles of vine canes and

The young Gertrude Jekyll brought her artist's
training to the use of colour in flower borders.
Her books were hugely influential.

raspberries, and hampers of strawberry plants. Once back in New York state, he sold on some of the material, and used the rest to breed varieties that suited their new conditions. The site of his labours still exists at Mount Hope Avenue and, still with its fruit trees, is open to the public.

Ellwanger also began to sell flowers associated with the new nostalgia. He found a big market, for the passion for old flowers and old fruit coalesced into a whole new movement in gardening, and a new sort of garden was born: the cottage garden. In them, sentimental owners strolled along grassy paths between borders of supposedly old-fashioned flowers, past sundials and dovecotes, new cut topiary and trim hedges. To find cottage garden flowers, amateurs from all walks of life, though mostly middle class, set off into their own countryside and peered hopefully over the garden gates of tumbledown cottages or urban shacks. Some advertised in the garden press for old sorts of carnation or auricula. In Britain in the 1880s, the energetic Mrs Ewing founded the Parkinson Society for those who wanted to grow plants introduced by John Parkinson, or those plants about which they could feel suitably sentimental, or which reflected their lack of interest in bedding plants and the very latest highly bred delphinium.

Nowadays it is hard to realize that even at that time parts of the English home counties were remote and undisturbed, the natives speaking impenetrable dialects, having distinctive modes of dress and living in conditions that looked extremely primitive from the perspective of London suburbanites. However horticulturally interesting their quest, conditions were not quite as dangerous as they were in Amazonia or Yünnan, and so explorers of British gardens of the past could not write gory or dramatic tales of their adventures. The movement did not really produce famous collectors, although it did spawn minor characters such as the wealthy Reverend Henry Harpur Crewe, rector of Drayton Beauchamp in Buckinghamshire. Most active in the mid-century, he found some lovely things, including a double-flowered form of the wild golden yellow wallflower (*Erysimum cheiri*). The plant he found, now widely grown, may have been the same plant admired by Parkinson, although it may equally be a double form thrown up by a wild population in more recent times. He also found a hybrid leopard's bane (*Doronicum* x *excelsum*) that bears his name.

The great garden designer Gertrude Jekyll (1843–1932) became a noted collector too. It is a pity that the images usually associated with her – of a plump, grumpy-looking old woman wearing run-down and misshapen old boots – are at such odds with her handsome and energetic youth. She was both talented and adventurous. She travelled around the Mediterranean, painting, studying local crafts and looking at local plants. No mountain or desert blunted her determination. She described her practices as follows: 'As the collection increased I began to compare and discriminate, and of various kinds of one plant to throw out the worse and retain the better and to train myself to see what

Part of Gertude Jekyll's own garden at Munstead Wood, Surrey, where she used the full palette provided by the latest flowers.

made a good garden plant.' She was confident enough of her taste to send specimens to the Royal Botanic Gardens at Kew in order to improve their chances of conservation. When she became famous, notably through her connection with the society architect Sir Edwin Lutyens, she even exported her style of design to America. It did not always go down well. She was asked to provide designs for the garden of the Glebe House in Woodbury, Connecticut. By 1926, what was a pretty but modest eighteenth-century farmhouse had become a museum. Its trustees wanted a garden that would, more or less, echo a garden of the right sort of period. Gertrude Jekyll gave it an astonishing 600 feet of classic English-style herbaceous border, a planted stone terrace and an intimate rose 'allée'. Too much in the 'grand manner', it was rejected. The plans were rediscovered in the late 1970s, and Jekyll's present fame has ensured that it has now been completed according to the original plans.

However much romanticized, or even inflated, the cottage garden has been, it is still a popular garden ideal. Discovering and preserving old garden plants have become widespread and important aims. In Britain, the National Council for the Conservation of Plants and Gardens was set up in 1982. It now looks after many hundreds of National Collections, publishes an annual directory of those collections' holdings and has around 10,000 members. In North America, the Garden Conservancy preserves notable gardens and is responsible for the North American Plant Preservation Council which concentrates on plant preservation.

Some gardeners, though, have a more radical agenda still. Why stop with garden plants of the nineteenth, or even the sixteenth, century when much of the country's original native flora is at such risk of disappearance? Many gardeners now want gardens that look like idealized native meadows, or prairies, or even rainforest. The movement is, of course, most important in regions where the flora is extremely rich, not already well explored and at risk

Roberto Burle Marx's own garden at Barra de Guaratiba, outside Rio de Janeiro,
packed with architectural fragments and plants native to Brazil's Atlantic and
Amazonian jungles.

from the pressure of an expanding human population. Brazil, in spite of all the collectors
in this book, not to mention the hundreds who have been left out and the many botanists
still collecting there, is a perfect example. Gradually, the Brazilian government has come to
realize the extent of its native flora, and the asset that it represents. That it has needed the
pleas and advice of botanists and naturalists is clear, but the Brazilian flora has also needed
a collector-publicist. In Roberto Burle Marx, it found it.

He was born on 4 August 1909, into a wealthy Brazilian business family, with a house on
a grand boulevard in São Paulo. When Roberto was four years old, the family moved to Rio
de Janeiro, where his father was closer to the political centre, and his mother, who was an
accomplished opera singer, would feel more at home in its sophisticated circles. Roberto,
who had poor eyesight, was kept out of formal education. However, he was insatiably
curious about the world, could sing and, in spite of his eyesight, wanted to be a painter. He
studied art at the Escole de Belas Arte in Rio, but Europe was the centre of innovation at
that time. In 1928 he began studying in Germany. It was there that he had his personal
revelation. He became interested in plant form and started looking at the tropical plants at
the Dahlem Botanical Gardens. He was overwhelmed to discover that many of the most
beautiful grew close to the family home in Rio. His direction was set: after his return to

Brazil in 1930, he surrounded his own new home there with gardens packed with thousands of rare species from Brazilian forests and swamps, especially those of his great loves – orchids, palms, water lilies and bromeliads.

He was already a well-connected artist, designer and plantsman, and landscape design was a natural synthesis of his talents; he was soon landing exciting and important commissions. He helped to open the eyes of other Brazilians by using only Brazilian plants in his schemes. He had plenty to choose from. With nearly 55,000 native species, Brazil is now known to be the country with the richest flora on the planet. Humboldt and Bonpland were right to be overwhelmed. Burle Marx's collection and his passion for collecting grew so fast that he bought an old estate in Barra de Guaratiba in 1949. With several hundred acres, part steep hillside, part mangrove swamp, it had an old house with marvellous views, a tiny sixteenth-century chapel and masses of potential. Marx set about turning the estate into garden, plant nursery and nature reserve. The plantings covered the major ecological regions of Brazil, from its rainforests

Burle Marx's use of native Brazilian plants spurred other landscape designers to re-examine their own country's flora.

to the strange watery Pantanal. He gave the garden structure by building walls made out of carved stonework salvaged from Rio's eighteenth- and nineteenth-century buildings which were being demolished. He built fountains, pools and water chutes. All were draped with orchids, bromeliads and clambering philodendrons. There were banks of bougainvillea native to Rio de Janeiro, collected by Philibert Commerson and Jeanne Baret back in 1767 (see Chapter Six). There were banana plantations as well as carefully preserved fragments of the state of Rio de Janeiro's fast-disappearing 'Atlantic forest'.

Hugely influential as an artist and architect, and with an exceptionally expansive personality, Marx was a major and, more importantly, local advocate for the Brazilian flora. He constantly entertained Brazil's rich and influential élite at his lovely house, its courtyards flamboyantly decorated with Brazil's most extraordinary plants. He tried to show everyone, amid the lavish hospitality, how marvellous the flowers of the country were, how much they were endangered, and how much they were worth preserving. Sometimes his expeditions to collect them seemed merely extensions of the partying, and with a shout of 'Come, all my beautiful children, my beautiful crazies!' he would set off with a throng of clients and friends, loaded with cameras, insect repellent and broad-brimmed hats, into the tropical forests. If Brazil now begins to lead the way in the preservation of the vast diversity of the

South American flora, the movement owes a great debt to this plump, ebullient man commemorated in the names of dozens of plants, from begonias such as the crinkly-leafed *Begonia burle-marxii* to astonishing pieces of botanical engineering such as *Heliconia burle-marxii*. Currently, about 7 per cent of the Amazon region is 'preserved' as much as that is possible, and the 'indigenous areas' add another 24 per cent. Regions further south, but almost as rich in species, are in a less good state, with less than 1 per cent under official protection. That there is anything at all is largely because of him. In 1985, he gave his estate to the National Institute for Cultural Heritage, who now open it to the public. He died on 4 June 1994.

This thoroughgoing approach to old or historic varieties of plants interested people far beyond his own neighbourhood. By the early twentieth century, the United States Department of Agriculture (USDA) was beginning to think of trying large-scale breeding programmes on almost any plant that could be of commercial use to American farmers. Most of the fruit species brought to America by the European settlers, and which were now commercially important, had not first originated in Europe. They had been domesticated further east, in Turkey, Armenia, Northern India and China. USDA wanted to explore the very old variants of crops still existing in those countries to see if they had characteristics, perhaps disease resistance, or tolerance of cold, that would be useful crossed into new varieties for the American grower. But first they wanted a sure-fire winner: a medicinal plant. A tree whose crushed seeds yielded 'chaulmoogra oil' was one of their most important projects. According to local legend, chaulmoogra oil had been revealed in a dream to an ancient king of Siam as a cure for his leprosy. It had certainly been used against the disease in Southeast Asia for more than a thousand years. The tree from which it comes, *Hydnocarpus kurzii* (now sometimes put in the genus *Taraktogenos*), is rare. It is also poisonous, and its oil, when swallowed, made patients seriously sick. Some American doctors tried to inject it, but it caused terrible ulcers. The oil was not available in sufficient quantities to see if it could be refined in any way. Seed was required. USDA needed a collector who was a tough traveller, who knew enough botany to recognize the tree when he saw it and who also spoke Chinese. They cannot have been expecting anyone very remarkable. The man they got was Joseph Rock.

Let us meet him, probably as he would have most liked, riding with his retinue through the hills of China. He is preceded by a group of unruly, half-destitute soldiers, some of their guns held together with wire. Then come a dozen or so Nakhi coolies, themselves and their pack animals heavily laden. Much of the baggage consists of Rock's personal belongings. He cannot travel without all the materials for a smart Viennese dinner: tablecloths of linen damask, napkins, silver cutlery, elegant glassware and books, so that his cook can make proper Austrian meals. He is obsessed with his personal hygiene, and so needs a folding bath made by Abercrombie & Fitch. He also travels with a large wardrobe filled with suits and expensive shirts so that he will never lose status when visiting even the most insignificant of chieftains. He is reputed to travel with a dinner service of purest gold, making him a natural target for the sort of people of whom he is most frightened.

The expression on his face gives nothing away. Inside, he is terrified of the bandits rumoured to be following him in the hope of rich pickings. He has quarrelled with the soldiers and now cannot trust their loyalty. He suspects the coolies are carrying opium, even though he carefully sniffs at each man first thing in the morning to check that they have not been smoking it. He broods on what he sees as a snub by the hostess at a Boston dinner party six months ago. He has written in his diary: 'Personality cannot be developed in solitude. . . . It must be surrounded by other living beings to make itself felt. What we often call personality is the power to perceive the weakness in others in a twinkling of an eye and thus dominate by sheer arrogance and self-forwardness like a rooster charging a council of hens among a few grains of wheat, scattering them, and then picking up leisurely the rest. The hens look on with cowed heads.'

In the roar of the river far below, he hears his father's voice intoning the last rites. However, Joseph Rock's father was not a priest, but a humble pastry cook working in the kitchens of Count Potocki's winter palace in Vienna. He was a terrifying, anger-filled, religious maniac who had constructed a tiny altar in his drab apartment, and got his children to play the role of his priestly acolytes. Joseph's mother had died in 1890 when he was six. With the body lying in state, his father insisted on him placing flowers in her chilly hands. Two weeks later, Joseph's only other source of comfort, his grandmother, died too.

Joseph first ran away from home when he was eight. He was hoping to reach his mother's relatives in Hungary, with whom he had been happy. He got no further than the outskirts of Vienna before he was robbed of his few pennies and the food he had taken from his father's larder. He played truant from school in order to visit his mother's grave, or to wander, fascinated, among the exotic fairground performers of the Prater. He was often to be found in the company of fire-eaters, jugglers, sword swallowers and storytellers. He discovered that he had a talent for tongues and started to learn Arabic and Chinese. His pockets were full of scraps of card with Chinese characters printed on them. He began to dream of running away to Peking and Lhasa. When he was at school, he so wrapped himself in ideas of grandeur and mystery that his fellow pupils called him 'the Count'.

In 1901, he begged his father to let him join the Austrian navy. His father had determined he should be a real priest, and swore that it was the seminary or death. So Joseph ran away from home for ever in 1902. Taking menial jobs as a tourist guide or as a seaman, he travelled around Europe and North Africa. He only went back to Vienna when his father died, and he lived briefly with his sister Lena. Soon, Rock left for England, but in its damp climate discovered that he had tuberculosis. Panicking when he began to cough blood, he rushed back to Lena. Vienna was worse than London, and he headed south to Italy, then to Tunis, and wound up on the island of Malta. Dreaming of warmer climates still, he recovered enough to work his way to the Orient. Finally, almost by chance, he drifted to the shores of Hawaii. He became interested in its plants, began teaching others about them, and remained on the island between 1908 and 1919. Having drifted and dreamed for so long, his destiny was being forged. He saw the place for a botanist-explorer advertised by USDA's Office of Foreign Seed and Plant Introduction. He got the job.

On 11 February 1922, Rock finally entered his dreamland, and reached the far western border of China. He had with him two medical missionaries, six carriers, two guides and a cook. One of the missionaries was Dr Ernest Muir, a Scot, who believed that the oil from

Joseph Rock at the Nyorophu Island
Shrine in China.

the chaulmoogra tree offered real hope to
lepers. The expedition's stores, including Rock's
bath, were carried by fifteen horses. The party
inched into the mountains from Siam for three
months. Passing from one tribal region to
another, often being chased by bandits, it
reached a Chinese outpost in remotest Yünnan.
Rock wrote:

*The moon rose shortly before our arrival . . . and the
sun was just setting, and the hills in the distance were
purple. The sky was slightly hazy, and the full moon
gently riding on the pale lilac haze, herself a pale
silver disc, with the land masses clearly showing. . . .
A much-faded Chinese flag was implanted almost in
the center of the road. To the left of it was a bamboo
wooden shanty where the Chinese official, a small
dirty fellow with a kindly smile, gave us a rather nice
reception. Several Chinese were sitting about dressed
in blue . . . and entered into a lively conversation.*

They passed over the border, and were shown the way on to Chieng Law. He found the
chaulmoogra tree, and he sent back large quantities of seed. Some of it was sent to the
University of Hawaii, where twenty-seven acres of it were planted at Waiahole, Oahu, and
where the oil's active compounds were first extracted. Sadly, they were found to be too toxic
to use, and probably ineffective anyway. Sulphonamides and their derivatives also appeared
from pharmaceutical laboratories at much the same time, so whether chaulmoogra oil was
of any real use was never finally tested. Nevertheless, the trip made Rock famous. He was
commissioned by the editor of the *National Geographic Magazine*, Gilbert H. Grosvenor, to
write about the Southeast Asian chaulmoogra oil plant as a possible cure for leprosy. He did,
and took the photographs for the article too. It was such a success that he went on to do a
further nine articles for the magazine, with romantic titles such as 'Experiences of a Lone
Geographer: An American Explorer Makes his Way through Brigand-Infested Central
China'. They made exciting reading. On his trips back to America, he was lionized, but that
made him only more difficult and paranoid still. He retreated.

From 1922 to 1949 he lived almost continuously on the road in China. The natives knew
him as 'Hef', and thought him a man of quick and violent temper. He became so stocky
that he commissioned local carpenters to build special chairs and a desk to accommodate
his size. He collected some 60,000 plant specimens for American institutions, mostly the
Smithsonian. He shot 1,600 bird specimens to give to American ornithologists. Fascinated
by the ancient culture of his Nakhi bearers, he became an anthropologist. He collected
hundreds of ancient hieroglyphic manuscripts, sometimes donating them to American

libraries, sometimes selling them to private collectors. Many of these he had translated by local wise men who understood the ancient language. He wrote about them too, notably in books such as *The Ancient Na-Khi Kingdom of Southwest China* (1947), and the grandly titled *Lamas, Princes, and Brigands: Joseph Rock's Photographs of the Tibetan Borderlands of China*. He died in Hawaii in 1962. His many splendid photographs are in the archives of the Royal Botanic Garden, Edinburgh.

USDA financed only his first trip. On his return, he was poached by another influential, and rather more prestigious, American organization, the Arnold Arboretum of Harvard. USDA was not pleased. It had become more and more intent on copying the English Henry VIII, sending collectors abroad to discover new varieties of good things to eat. It therefore needed another collector to explore China. It found Frank Meyer.

Frank Meyer, 'tired but satisfied' after a successful day's collecting in Shanshi, China, on 26 February 1908.

Meyer's story goes like an arrow for, unlike Rock, he knew he was a gardener and plant collector even when he was still almost a child. Born Frans Meier, on 29 November 1875 in a small house in the docklands of Amsterdam, he was a bright child, but poverty gave him little prospect. At fourteen, he became a jobbing helper, and later a gardener, at the Amsterdam Botanical Garden. Its director, Hugo de Vries, recognized the boy's enthusiasm and intelligence, and began to train him to be his laboratory assistant, teaching him French and English as well as botany. Frans was restless and wanted more still. He began to explore Holland. With almost no money, he often walked the fifty miles to the dunes, sleeping outdoors all night. He made a herbarium, studied more languages, mathematics, science and drawing. He kept studying botany. He left home to live in a boarding house in Amsterdam. He went to concerts, became interested in Buddhism and theosophy, and read Schopenhauer. He became fascinated by the idea of an ultimate and irrational will, and he learned from his acquaintances that he was not the only man in the world who suffered from depression. For a while, when he was twenty-three, he joined a Utopian colony founded by the Dutch poet Frederick van Eden, and based on the ideas of Thoreau. The colony, called Walden, operated on the principle that all would share in the work and in the fruits of their toil. He did not stay long: it was too restricting.

He wanted to set off on his travels, to get away from the pearl-grey skies of Holland and see the lemon and orange orchards that were so vivid in his dreams of Italy and blue-shadowed sunshine. To do this, he simply bought a map and a compass and started walking south, paying no attention to roads or to the useful tracks of others. In one alpine pass, he nearly lost his life in a blizzard. Descending into the foothills in Italy, he startled a farmer who asked where he had come from. 'Across the mountains,' replied Meyer. 'Impossible,' the farmer objected, 'there are no roads.' There weren't.

Meyer left Europe for good after working at some commercial nurseries in England. At last, he had enough money to get to America. On 12 October 1901, he left Southampton on the SS *Philadelphia*. He wrote to friends in Amsterdam: 'I am pessimistic by nature . . . and have not found a road which leads to relaxation. I withdraw from humanity and try to find relaxation with plants. I live now in expectation of what will come.'

He found work readily in nurseries and botanic gardens, where his skills were always of use. A tireless wanderer, he hiked for hundreds of miles through Mexico. Then, wanting to see the World Fair in St Louis, he made his way there on foot and found a job at the Missouri Botanical Garden. He was fascinated by the World Fair. His boss, Dr William Trelease, had invited de Vries over from the Amsterdam Botanical Garden to give some lectures, and was astonished when de Vries and his best propagator, now calling himself 'Frank Meyer', turned out to be old friends. Things were setting fair. Suddenly the miracle happened: the dream of his youth came true. On 10 March 1905, a telegram from Adrian J. Pieters of USDA arrived. Meyer was offered the chance to go searching for the cultivated plants of China. He telegraphed back immediately: 'Great thanks for your offer. Accept it. Will be ready any time but would like to stay here a few weeks yet.' He telegraphed his mother: 'I have big news.' But he must have found it hard to believe, for he added that 'the offer is a beautiful one even if it does not go through'.

It did, and he ended up making four great trips to Asia, collecting immense quantities of plant material, travelling very simply and cheaply, worrying as much about filing his expenses from places where the currencies varied constantly in both nationality and value, as about bandits and the sheer physical dangers of plant collecting. He bought gifts for his friends, who were drawn mostly from the places where he worked. When travelling he wrote them letters. He often expressed loneliness and depression, even a curious sense of incompleteness. 'Loneliness hangs always around the man who leaves his own race and moves among an alien population,' he acknowledged, and tried hard to believe Ibsen's statement that the strongest man is he who stands alone. However, he also often wrote of the thrill of finding new plants, and the beauty of the places where he found them. He even sent his recommendations for his superior's new garden back in America. He had heard that David Fairchild and his wife had ordered over a hundred flowering cherries from Suzuki's nursery in Rokohama, Japan. Meyer thought that sounded lovely, and replied:

If you plant cherries as a spring delight, do not fail to plant Japanese maples for fall effects. Have you a brook? If so, plant Iris kaempferi. *There are dreams of beauty among them. Do you love weeping trees? The weeping pagoda tree is delightful. Plant also a few clumps of the Chinese tree peony and have some big Chinese porcelain vessels in which you can plant lotus. Have also a few clumps of magnolias. They are so noble in the early spring. Have some white-barked birches, the most elegant of all northern trees. If you can get a specimen of the* Davidia involucrata *sent to England by [E. H.] Wilson, do try it.*

The garden was called In the Woods, and on his trips back to America, when he worked on his collections, it would become a much-loved place. America had become 'home'. He didn't visit Holland again.

In 1918, he was back in China. Laden with material, though suffering from some unspecified ailment of his innards, he dreamed of returning to a settled life. He wrote that he expected to take a steamer down the Yangtze, possibly stopping at Kiukiang (Jiujiang) to inspect tung oil plantations. A week later Meyer told his family that he was not really enjoying looking at the Yangtze Valley in June. It was too hot. He had become less able to tolerate being uncomfortable. Sleep was difficult. His appetite was not good. He was worried about China's political instability, about the teeming insects, about the diseases that surrounded him. He was tired out. He wanted to visit his family in Holland. He was worried for them, for it seemed, from China, as if the First World War was still raging. He commented, bitterly, that travelling might seem a pleasure to someone who stayed at home; however, a traveller longed to have a home and a garden, and never to have to move on.

He stopped off at the town of Hankow and, complaining of 'stomach trouble accompanied by vomiting', stayed at a comfortable hotel for Europeans. It was noisy. Western naval officers kept insisting that he come to have a drink with them. Intestinal infections often make the sufferer desperate for a darkened room and silence. He and his servant-guide moved to a cheaper 'native' hotel where he wouldn't be bothered, and after a few days he seemed better. His servant, Yao-feng Ting, thought that he looked thinner even than when they left Ichang.

On Friday 31 May, Meyer and Yao-feng boarded a Japanese riverboat, the *Feng Yang Maru*, under a Captain Inwood. It was to take them down the Yangtze to Shanghai. Practically all foreigners except missionaries travelled first-class. Meyer, modest as usual, or perhaps still thinking of the Hankow Hotel, chose the cheaper Chinese variation of first-class accommodation. The next day, he was still not feeling well enough to visit the tung oil plantations as he had planned. Worse, a British insurance man, Islay Drysdale, boarded the steamer at Kiukiang. For some reason, he too wanted to use the Chinese first-class, and so had to share Meyer's cabin. They seem to have spent most of the day talking as the boat sped downstream through the surging currents. Drysdale left the riverboat at Anking at 4 p.m. Soon after, Captain Inwood looked in to see how Meyer was. He replied that he was well except for a headache. That evening he ate a full Chinese dinner. Yao-feng Ting served tea in his master's cabin. Meyer was better.

About 11.20 p.m., Meyer left his cabin and wandered up on deck. He was seen by the deck steward. It was a clear night. The *Feng Yang Maru* was passing the light-boat off Barker Island. The river swirled past. Forty minutes later the cabin boy reported to Captain Inwood that he could not find Mr Meyer. Inwood started a search. The boat wasn't large. Frank Meyer was not on board. The officers searched along the guards and rails. Meyer's disappearance had left no trace.

There we leave him, on that June night; the lights of the *Feng Yang Maru*, and the pulse of its engine, vanish into the darkness. Meyer's body, arms akimbo, is tumbling over and

The elegant Shuen Tan He covered bridge spanning a mountain river in western China,
photographed by Joseph Rock. There was commonly a fee for passage.

over in the rough embrace of the river. He will drift ashore four days later and be found by
a local fisherman. There will be enquiries. Islay Drysdale will be interviewed. Chinese
passengers will be suspected. Nothing will be discovered, and no explanation found.

In his cabin trunks seeds were discovered that are still influencing our lives, and which
are finding their way into the breeding programmes of a huge diversity of garden plants.
His materials can be found in the tough *Zoysia* grasses that make green the lawns and
fairways of California, Oklahoma and Texas, in drought- and wind- resistant elms, in
disease-resistant chestnuts, in mildew-resistant spinaches. Among other material that he sent
back to America are sumptuous seedless persimmons only now finding their way into
commerce, hawthorns with fruits as big as crab apples, fast-growing Chinese cabbages,
splendid decoratives such as the tough yellow rose (*Rosa xanthina*), and the tiny and delicious
lilac (*Syringa meyeri* var. *palibiniana*) so long cultivated in Chinese gardens that it has no known
wild relatives.

There was also an unusually hardy lemon, one that would go on to make a fine backyard
plant in all the warm states of the United States, and to make huge commercial plantations
for juicing fruits in Florida, Texas, South Africa, and New Zealand. Even in northern
Europe, as far north as remote parts of Scotland, it would become a popular garden-centre
citrus, its fragrant flowers standing out in brilliant white amongst the glossy leaves and
young green fruit: Meyer's lemon (*Citrus meyeri*).

Today, of course, plant collecting is very different. Much more of the planet is opened
up. Collectors can arrive on site by helicopter or jeep. They can transmit pictures of plants

growing live in the remotest places of the globe to experts in London, Paris, Edinburgh, Boston, Vienna with libraries and herbaria to hand. A plant can be determined as 'new' almost instantaneously, and a market for it created soon after. However, there are also new barriers between a plant in the wild and the distant gardeners who might grow it. The Convention on Biological Diversity, signed during the Rio Earth Summit held in Rio de Janeiro, Brazil, in June 1992, is a legally binding agreement for the conservation and sustainable use of biodiversity. It came into force on 29 December 1993, with the aim of protecting a country's botanical assets so that it can get some financial return if its plants turn out to be desired by gardeners, or to contain a pharmacological bounty. A new species cannot get into commerce without the agreement of the country in which it was found. However, the Convention is almost impossible to police, and is not retrospective. After the great age of plant collecting that finished in the mid-twentieth century, it seems to bolt the treasury door long after much of the treasure is freely available.

Meyer's lemon, probably an ancient cultivar, is now grown worldwide.

Yet contemporary plant collectors, in areas such as Bhutan or the Cerrado regions of South America, say that huge numbers of species still await discovery and liberation. However many expeditions there have been up the waters of the Yangtze, or the Amazon, or over the crunching gravel of the Karoo Desert, there are still seasons that have not been covered, still inlets or valleys not yet traversed. So many species have arrived in the garden that the genetic potential of the mix has hardly been tapped. At any moment, a new plant discovery, or the development of a group of plants by an unknown gardener or nurseryman, may have the potential to transform our gardens all over again. Gardeners will see.

Meanwhile, there is a colossal flora available to every gardener who wants to explore it. If you garden, let your collector's instinct loose. Let plants in all their fantastical diversity pour themselves into your garden. Diversity is everything. Plant breeders and hybridists can increase it. Gardeners can preserve it. So don't dead-head: let seed pods form. Sow what you get; each seed in the packet, or at the bottom of the crumpled and dusty envelope. You might find nothing new or more beautiful than the plants you already have. On the other hand, you might create a wonder, something that starts us all off in a new direction. And even if you don't, at least sow each seed. Each seedling, however small, is a part, as we all are, of the glory and abundance of the world.

CHRONOLOGY

1519	Cortez invades Mexico
1547	Pierre Belon collects plants in Crete and Turkey
1574	Leonhardt Rauwolff collects medicinal and economic plants in Alepp
1597	John Gerard publishes his *Herball*
1598	The first Dutch expedition sets sail for Japan
1637	Tradescant the Younger's first trip to North America
1673	Founding of the Chelsea Physic Garden for the Apothecaries' Society
1678	John Banister arrives in Virginia
1680	The first heated glasshouses are built at Leiden Botanic Garden
1687	Hans Sloane sails to Jamaica, and starts collecting
1700	Tournefort and Aubriet set sail for the Orient from Marseilles
1712	Mark Catesby arrives in North America
1731	Philip Miller publishes the first edition of the *Gardener's Dictionary*
1753	Linnaeus publishes *Species Plantarum*
1767	Philibert Commerson discovers *Bougainvillea* near Rio de Janeiro
1770	Joseph Banks aboard the *Endeavour* sails into Botany Bay
1772	Masson and Thunberg both arrive at Cape Town
1775	Thomas Blaikie is sent hunting for alpine plants in Switzerland
1777	Joseph Dombey sails for South America with Ruiz and Pavon
1785	André Michaux arrives in North America
1799	Humboldt and Bonpland arrive in Venezuela
1803	Meriwether Lewis and William Clark reach their first staging post in Illinois
1808	Thomas Nuttall begins work in Philadelphia
1825	David Douglas arrives at the mouth of the Columbia River
1826	Philipp von Siebold arrives in Japan
1838	Charles Fremont begins mapping in the western United States
1840	William Lobb sails to Rio de Janeiro to collect tropical plants
1843	Robert Fortune starts collecting in China and Japan
1848	Joseph Dalton Hooker starts collecting in Sikkim
1862	Abbé David reaches Peking
1879	Joseph Bory Latour-Marliac produces his first new water lilies
1894	Amos Perry starts a nursery specializing in herbaceous plants
1899	E. H. Wilson meets Augustine Henry in Yünnan
1902	Reginald Farrer travels to Japan and begins writing about gardens
1905	Frank Meyer is appointed plant collector in China by USDA
1905	George Forrest is almost killed fleeing from Tibetan lamas
1908	Gertrude Jekyll publishes *Colour Schemes for the Flower Garden*
1909	Frank Kingdon-Ward starts collecting in China
1922	Joseph Rock crosses the borders of China for the first time
1930	Burle Marx returns to Brazil, fascinated by its native flora

SELECT BIBLIOGRAPHY

Allan, M., *The Tradescants, Their Plants, Gardens, and Museum, 1570–1662*, 1964

Bothing, D., *Humboldt and the Cosmos*, 1973

Bretschneider, E., *History of European Botanical Discoveries in China*, 1898

Brett-James, N., *The Life of Peter Collinson*, 1925

Briggs, R., *'Chinese' Wilson: a Life of Ernest H. Wilson*, 1993

Catesby, M., *The Natural History of Carolina, Florida and the Bahama Islands*, 2 vols, 1731–43

Coats, A, M., *Garden Shrubs and their Histories*, 1963

—, *The Plant Hunters*, 1970

Cowan, J. M., *The Journeys and Plant Introductions of George Forrest*, 1954

Cox, E. B. M., *Farrer's Last Journey*, 1926

Cunningham, I. S., *Frank N. Meyer: Plant Hunter in Asia*, 1984

Davies, J., *Douglas of the Forests: the North American Journals of David Douglas*, 1980

Ewan, J. and N., *John Banister and his History 1678–1692*, 1970

Fisher, J., *The Origins of Garden Plants*, 1982

Fortunc, R., *Three Years' Wanderings in the Northern Provinces of China*, 1847

Fox, R. H., *Dr. John Fothergill and his Friends*, 1919

Fremont, J. C., ed. Nevins, A., *Narratives of Exploration and Adventure*, 1956

Gilmore, J., *British Botanists*, 1946

Graustein, J. F., *Thomas Nuttall, Naturalist*, 1967

Harper, F., *The Travels of William Bartram*, 1958

Kaempfer, E., trans. Scheuzer, *History of Japan*, 1728

Keswick, Maggie, *The Chinese Garden: History, Art and Architecture*, 1988

Kingdon-Ward, F., *The Land of the Blue Poppy*, 1913

—, *The Romance of Plant Hunting*, 1924

Lancaster, R., *Travels in China*, 1989

Lauener, A., *The Introduction of Chinese Plants to Europe*, 1996

Lemmon, K., *The Golden Age of Plant Hunters*, 1968

Lyte, C., *Frank Kingdon-Ward*, 1989

Miller, P., *Gardener's Dictionary*, 8th ed., 1768

Mitchell, A. and House, S., *David Douglas: Explorer and Botanist*, 1999

Oliver, S. P., ed. G. F. Scott Elliott, *The Life of Philibert Commerson*, 1909

Savage, J. R. W. and André, S., *François Michaux*, 1986

Sponberg, S. A., *A Reunion of Trees*, 1990

Sutton, S. B., *Charles Sprague Sargent and the Arnold Arboretum*, 1970

—, *In China's Border Provinces: the Turbulent Career of Joseph Rock*, 1974

Tournefort, J. P. de, trans. Ozell, J. A., *Voyage into the Levant*, 1718

Welsh, S. L., *John Charles Fremont: Botanical Explorer*, 1998

Whittle, T., *The Plant Hunters*, 1970

Wilson, E. H., *A Naturalist in Western China, with Vasculum, Camera and Gun*, 2 vols, 1913

I have consulted many regional floras, monographs and 'plant group' books, which have proved too numerous to list. I have also read many web pages. My considerable thanks are due to the owners of the most useful ones, but it has not been possible to list such a fluid resource.

INDEX

PHOTOGRAPHIC ACKNOWLEDGMENTS

The Publishers have made every effort to contact holders of copyright works. Any copyright holders we have been unable to reach are invited to contact the Publishers so that a full acknowledgment may be given in subsequent editions. For permission to reproduce the images on the following pages and for supplying photographs, the Publishers thank those listed below.

AKG, London: 9, 26–7, 28, 76, 94, 103, 119, 121, 127, 130, 142, 170
AKG, London/VISIOARS: 151
Photographic Archives of the Arnold Arboretum: 144, 185, 187, 199
The Art Archive: 39, 45 (Natural History Museum, London), 66–7 (Dagli Orti), 149 (Dagli Orti), 154, 173 (Museo Tosio Martinengo Brescia/Daglia Orti),
The Art Archive/Eileen Tweedy: 37, 59, 81, 115, 118
Bridgeman Art Library: 5 (British Museum, London), 13 (British Museum, London), 16 (The Stapleton Collection), 18 (Fitzwilliam Museum, University of Cambridge), 25 (Natural History Museum, London), 29 (Ashmolean Museum, Oxford), 42–3, 64, 89 (New York Historical Society, New York), 112 (Natural History Museum, London), 128–9 (The Stapleton Collection), 152–3 (Royal Geographical Society, London), 158, 159 (New York Historical Society, New York), 188–9 (David Findlay Jr. Fine Art NYC)
By permission of the British Library: 21 (CdeB, iv & v 10.tab.29)
©**Chatsworth Photo Library**: 106–7, 146
©**The Right Hon. The Earl of Derby**: 51
Historic Hudson Valley, Tarrytown, New York: 138, 139
Courtesy of Hunt Institute for Botanical Documentation, Carnegie Mellon University, Pittsburgh, PA: 55, 91, 110
©**The Jekyll Estate**: 192
Museum of Garden History: 36, 73
Courtesy of the Board of Trustees, National Museums and Galleries on Merseyside: 90
Nezu Institute of Fine Arts, Tokyo: 168–9
Haruyoshi Ono, Landscape Architect, Rio de Janeiro, Brazil: 194, 195
Private Collection: 58, 82–3, 101, 136, 156, 157, 193
Read's Nursery, Hales Hall, Norfolk: 203
Royal Botanic Gardens, Edinburgh: 198, 202 (Rock photo archive © National Geographic Society, Washington, DC)
Royal Horticultural Society, Lindley Library: 2, 10–11, 15, 22, 30, 31, 34, 41, 46, 48, 49, 60, 69, 84, 85, 86, 96, 98, 100, 117, 124, 135, 140, 143, 160, 162, 163, 167, 174, 179, 182
©**Stapeley Water Gardens Ltd., UK**: 176–7
University of Rochester Library, Rochester, NY: 190

PUBLISHER'S ACKNOWLEDGMENTS

Commissioning editor Frances Lincoln
Project editor Michael Brunström
Picture editor Sue Gladstone
Designer Becky Clarke

Editorial assistance Anne Askwith,
  and Serena Dilnot
Index Margot Levy
Production Kim Oliver